# The **New** Mutual Fund Investment Advisor

### Richard C. Dorf

Probus Publishing Company
Chicago, Illinois 60606

©Richard C. Dorf, 1988

ALL RIGHTS RESERVED.   No part of this publication may be reproduced, stored in a retrieval system, or transmitted, in any form or by any means, electronic, mechanical, photocopying, recording, or otherwise, without the prior written permission of the publisher and the copyright holder.

This publication is designed to provide accurate and authoritative information in regard to the subject matter covered. It is sold with the understanding that the publisher is not engaged in rendering legal, accounting or other professional service. If legal advice or other expert assistance is required, the services of a competent professional person should be sought.

FROM A DECLARATION OF PRINCIPLES JOINTLY ADOPTED BY A COMMITTEE OF THE AMERICAN BAR ASSOCIATION AND A COMMITTEE OF PUBLISHERS.

**Library of Congress Cataloging in Publication Data Available.**

ISBN 0-917253-19-1

Printed in the United States of America

1  2  3  4  5  6  7  8  9  0

# Preface to the Paperback Edition

It is an understatement to say that the investment climate, in the relatively short time since this book was first published in hardcover, has changed dramatically.

Investors have witnessed the single largest stock market decline in the history of Wall Street. Increased volatility in the financial markets increases risks dramatically. The frightening speed at which new economic information is made available, as well as the interaction and interdependence of international financial markets, demand that investors, now more than ever, keep a watchful eye on their investments. So it comes as no surprise that investors increasingly depend on a sound mutual fund strategy as a deterrent to uncertainty, complexity and high risk.

Mutual funds provide diversification, professional money management and a strategy to fit every investment philosophy. At the same time, they offer flexibility—investors can easily adapt as the investment and economic climate changes. Mutual funds, now more than ever, are reasonable alternatives to other investment choices!

A successful mutual fund investor requires skill, insight and most of all diligence. No investor can afford to be passive: to buy and hold for the long term is at best risky. Mutual fund investors must be active, understanding the risks as well as the rewards of their investment choices. Investors must monitor not only fund results, but also sales loads, management fees and other costs associated with mutual funds.

This, of course, is exactly what *The New Mutual Fund Investment Advisor: A Guide for the Serious Investor* is all about. The concepts in this book, both fundamental and advanced, will equip mutual fund investors with the knowledge and skill necessary to survive and even prosper in these uncertain times.

Onward to successful investing!

*Richard C. Dorf*
*January, 1988*

# Contents

**Chapter 1**  **The Mutual Fund Advantage**  1
Introduction  1
The Theory of Efficient Markets, the Individual
    Investor , and the Mutual Fund Advantage  2
Why the Intelligent Investor Selects Mutual Funds  7

**Chapter 2**  **An Overview of the Mutual Funds Industry**  11
The Origins and Growth of the Mutual Funds
    Industry  15
Load versus No-Load Funds  16
The Benefits and Costs of Owning a Mutual
    Fund  20

**Chapter 3**  **Choosing a Mutual Fund**  25
The Prospectus and Annual Report  25
Fund Services  32
Monitoring Mutual Fund Fees and Management
    Changes  33
How to Purchase a Fund  37
Discount Broker Mutual Fund Account  39

**Chapter 4**  **Classifications and Characteristics of Funds**  41
Classifying Funds by Objective and Risk  41
Growth Funds  46

v

Aggressive Growth Funds   48
Growth and Income Funds   50
Income and Bond Funds   52
Money Market Funds   55
Specialty Funds   58
Gold Funds   64
International Funds   67

**Chapter 5**   **Fund Performance**   **71**
Introduction   71
Modern Portfolio Theory and Fund Investing   72
Performance Calculations   73
Calculating Risk   79
The Risk Adjusted Return   86

**Chapter 6**   **Selecting a Portfolio of Funds**   **93**
Advantages of Building a Portfolio of Funds   93
Adjusting the Fund Portfolio to Meet Your Personal Objectives   95
Time Horizon   98
An Efficient Portfolio of Funds   99
How to Use Past Performance to Select Funds   105
Does Fund Size Affect Performance?   106
The Two Fund Portfolio: A Viable Alternative   108
A Fund of Funds   109

**Chapter 7**   **Market Timing**   **111**
Timing Mutual Fund Purchases and Redemptions   111
Timing the Business Cycle   118
Moving Averages   123
Business and Economic Indicators   133
The Cash Flow Indicator   144
Cost Averaging Timing Methods   146
Timing Services versus a Buy and Hold Strategy   151
Appendix: Exponential Moving Average Calculation   156

**Chapter 8**   **Monitoring Mutual Fund Performance**   **157**
Charting Fund Performance   163
Portfolio Records   167

## Contents

**Chapter 9**  **Tax Considerations**  169
Taxes and Distributions  169
Taxes upon Redemption of Shares  176
Four Methods of Calculating Capital Gains  177
Tax Strategies: Keeping Your Tax Liability Low and Avoiding Unnecessary Taxation  180
Tax Managed Funds  182
Tax-Free Bond Funds  183
The Possible Effects of the Proposed Tax Reform Act of 1986  185

**Chapter 10**  **Retirement Plans**  187
Investing for Retirement  187
Individual Retirement Accounts  188
Managing Your IRA Funds  191
The Keogh Retirement Plan  192
SEP, 401 and 403 Plans  193
Choosing a Portfolio of Mutual Funds for a Retirement Plan  195

**Chapter 11**  **Withdrawal Plans**  199
Withdrawals from IRAs and Keogh Plans  201
Dollar Cost Averaging Withdrawals  202

**Chapter 12**  **Estate Planning**  205
Mutual Funds and Estate Planning  205
Taking Title of Mutual Funds  206
Mutual Funds in Trusts  209
Gifts to Minors  210

**Chapter 13**  **Strategies for Investing in Mutual Funds**  213
Challenges of the Economy  213
The Stock and Bond Markets  217
Market Cycles  220
Strategies for Mutual Fund Investors  220
Advisory Services for the Mutual Fund Investor  224

**Appendix A**  Glossary  229

**Appendix B**  References  235

**Appendix C–1**  Magazines and Newspapers  237

**Appendix C–2  Mutual Fund Advisory Letters and Information
          Sources     239**

**Appendix C–3  Computer Services and Programs     243**

**Appendix C–4  Mutual Fund Selection, Timing and Advisor
          Services     245**

**Appendix D  Addresses of Selected Funds     249**

**Index    251**

# Chapter 1

# The Mutual Fund Advantage

## INTRODUCTION

*Mutual funds* are investment companies that issue and sell redeemable securities that represent an undivided interest in the assets held by the fund. They are operated by companies that manage fund investments in a broad number of areas with a wide degree of return and risk, including stocks, bonds and government securities.

Mutual funds are convenient and flexible investment alternatives. They offer desirable levels of liquidity and can be a highly efficient—and often inexpensive—way to receive the benefits of portfolio diversification and professional money management. There are, in fact, several exceptionally good reasons for investing in mutual funds, each of which will be more or less significant depending on individual investor goals and preferences.

The mutual fund industry has grown to include an ever wider range of funds to suit an equally wide range of investment objectives. In 1985, mutual funds hit new sales levels, attracting more than $46 billion in investments in the first half alone—more than in all of 1984, which had been a record year! Load, low-load and no-load mutual funds encompass a broad array of investment instruments and investment strategies, and, along with the growth of fund families, offer individual investors nearly limitless opportunities to create wealth without ever venturing outside the mutual fund marketplace.

While such a broad range of choices offers us more opportunities than ever, it also means that we must become wiser mutual fund shoppers. This requires a solid grounding in the fundamentals of mutual fund investing. Of even greater import is the fact that the mutual fund marketplace avails the knowledgeable and sophisticated investor with a unique opportunity to earn handsome returns.

One can, of course, choose less sophisticated approaches to fund investing than my statements may imply. Favoring convenience and lower, yet acceptable, rates of return is a legitimate, and for many, an intelligent investment strategy. However, the material presented in this book is designed to benefit those investors who seek to maximize their returns by taking an active approach to fund investing.

## THE THEORY OF EFFICIENT MARKETS, THE INDIVIDUAL INVESTOR, AND THE MUTUAL FUND ADVANTAGE

In 1979, common stocks, according to the S&P 500 index, had an 18 percent return and in 1980, returned 32 percent. What would you have predicted the return to be in 1981? Would you have predicted the return to be a loss of 5 percent? And could you have imagined that in the following year (1982) the S&P 500 index would show a gain of 21 percent?

Attempting to explain market behavior is a major preoccupation of market theorists. Does past market activity have a calculable bearing on future market activity? How does information about the economy, individual companies, and world events affect the market? Is there a way to beat the market consistently? These are the principal questions with which market theorists concern themselves.

One outcome of such theoretical probing is the widely used—if not wholly accepted—theory of efficient markets.

According to this theory, stock price behavior for any given stock has a statistical quality similar to that of a series drawn from a table of random numbers—hence the term *random walk*. This aspect of the theory of efficient markets holds that period-to-period price changes of a stock are statistically independent, or very nearly so. In other words, the price of a stock in one period has no relation to its price in any other period. If this hypothesis holds, a stock's price will move randomly.

Also, according to this theory, a perfectly efficient market is one in which every stock's price equals its investment value at all times [Sharpe, 1985]. This assumes that most investors have instant, equal and simultaneous access to current information about the future, and that all market participants are equally good at predicting the outcome expected to result from this information and act to adjust their portfolios accordingly. Thus, as all investors act on their information, market prices adjust instantly to reflect their actual values. It follows, therefore, that no stock price can be "improperly" priced for very long.

If an investor in an efficient market systematically earns a return in excess of the current market return, then, according to the efficient market theory, we must conclude that he either possesses information not presently available to other investors or is simply lucky. Luck, however, is inherently random and cannot, therefore, produce consistent results.

In order to be a successful investor according to the theory of efficient markets one would have to possess all information regarding all securities in all markets and continually follow all economic news and world events. What is more, one would also have to act immediately after having received all of this information.

At this point, it is important to put the theory of efficient markets into proper perspective. As a theory, it is not an exacting reflection of reality, a mirror, as it were, detailing vividly what, why, and how things happen in the market. Rather it is an hypothesis about what would (perhaps should) happen if all the interplaying forces that drive the market were to respond in an utterly rational, and, as we have described, near instantaneous manner. It goes without saying, even our most perfectly engineered machines have difficulty in filling this order.

Notwithstanding our imperfect reality, the theory of efficient markets nevertheless provides a very useful model for capturing the dynamic relationships of price activity, investor response and the impact of information on the market.

The efficient market theory also can provide conceptual depth to our intuitive sense of market dynamics. For example, we know that institutional investors, investment management firms and the like, are in a far superior position than the individual investor when it comes to following world and economic news and acting on that news accordingly and promptly. What is more, the extended use of market diversification by large institutional investors (pension funds, banks, *et al.*) who hold substantial positions in numerous companies—including such bellwether firms as IBM, AT&T, etc.—has made the market more efficient than it has ever been before.

So where does the individual investor fit in this scheme? As we have stated, proponents of the theory of efficient markets allege that the only possible way an investor can outperform the market *while assuming a level of risk equivalent to that of the market* is precisely by being in possession of and acting on information not generally available to others. Otherwise the only way an investor can obtain rates of return better than the market is by assuming levels of risk greater than the market's. Following our efficient markets hypothesis, we know that the past history of stock price movements and trading volumes contain no information that will enable the investor to do consistently better than simply using a buy-and-hold strategy in managing a portfolio.

In light of the theory of efficient markets, what then should your approach, as an individual investor, be? Assuming that this theory is generally true, analyzing publicly available data such as income statements and other investment fundamentals will probably not lead to bargains in the stock market. Nor is it likely that you will have access to inside information. So how do you construct a portfolio that will provide acceptable returns without incurring unacceptable risk?

One very good answer to this question is to use mutual funds. On a risk-adjusted basis—a concept that we will define in detail—few investment vehicles can provide as acceptable returns for the individual investor. If we consider the three commonly used measures of investment risk—*standard deviation*, *alpha* and the *beta* coefficient—our point will become all the more salient.

Standard deviation is the measure of variance of an investment's actual returns from its expected returns. It uses the variability of an investment's return as a measure of risk. Investors, therefore often seek securities that maximize average returns over time while minimizing the standard deviation. The S&P 500 market index, for instance, earned 7.5 percent from 1971 through 1980, with a relatively high standard deviation of 13.5 percent. The index' high standard deviation suggests that the S&P 500 was less profitable and far more risky than one would have expected.

The *beta* coefficient and *alpha* measure what are referred to as an investment's systematic and unsystematic risk factors, respectively. Systematic risk represents an investment's market risk. That is, if the entire stock market moves up or down, a stock within that market is expected to change in value as well. The *beta* coefficient is used to determine an investment's volatility relative to the volatility of the market as a whole.

Unsystematic risk, measured by *alpha*, indicates an investment's changes in value that are associated with its individual business or financial risk and not with market movement. For an individual stock, for example, it may represent the effects of the company's labor problems or the impact on its business of a competitor's launch of a successful new product.

If an investment's systematic risk is equal to the market it will have a *beta* equal to 1.00. An investment that has a *beta* of 1.20 is said to have returns that are twenty percent more volatile (or riskier) than the market's. If an investment's *alpha* is positive, it means that the stock performs better than the market, given its *beta*. For instance, if an investment has an *alpha* of zero and a beta of 1.00, it is performing exactly the same as the market.

There appears to be a direct correlation between return and risk; that is, the higher the reward, the higher the risk. Therefore, investors should seek to maintain risk levels that are proportional to their returns. Bearing excessive risk, moreover, does not ensure excessive returns. Not all securities with the same levels of risk have the same degrees of return.

Since unsystematic risk is associated with an individual company or industry, it can be diversified away in a large portfolio—a strategy often followed by large institutional investors, but truly difficult for most individual investors except through mutual funds.

Portfolio diversification plays an important role in *alpha* risk reduction, and will under certain circumstances stabilize a portfolio's *beta* coefficient. A diversified portfolio might include stocks and/or bonds from a telephone company, an oil company, a bank, a gold mining firm, and a manufacturing company. The impact of particular events on the returns and growth of any one of these firms may not apply to the other firms in the portfolio and therefore, the risk within the portfolio, as measured by *alpha*, is reduced due to its diversification.

As Figure 1-1 illustrates and several studies have indicated, 10 to 15 securities in a portfolio will reduce the major extent of unsystematic risk. *Since mutual funds typically hold more that 15 securities, they, of course, provide excellent diversification opportunities*.

Although the *beta* coefficient gives an investor a good indication of the systematic risk associated with a particular security, it should not be relied on solely when selecting a particular security because it can and does change over time.

However, unlike *beta* coefficients for individual securities, the *beta* coefficient for a portfolio composed of ten or more securities is fairly stable over time. Changes in the individual *beta* coefficients tend to average out; while one stock's *beta* coefficient increases, another declines. A portfolio's historical *beta* coefficients, then, can be used to forecast it's future *beta* coefficient, and this projection will be more accurate than similar forecasts of an individual security's *beta* coefficient.

The concepts of standard deviation, the *beta* coefficient and *alpha* are extremely important in selecting and purchasing mutual funds and are referred to frequently throughout the remainder of this book, as well as in most other literature about mutual funds. They are covered again in greater detail in Chapter 5.

## WHY THE INTELLIGENT INVESTOR SELECTS MUTUAL FUNDS

There are about 1,300 mutual funds in existence today with total assets exceeding $400 billion. There are funds for al-

**FIGURE 1-1**
**The Reduction of Risk Due to Portfolio Diversification**

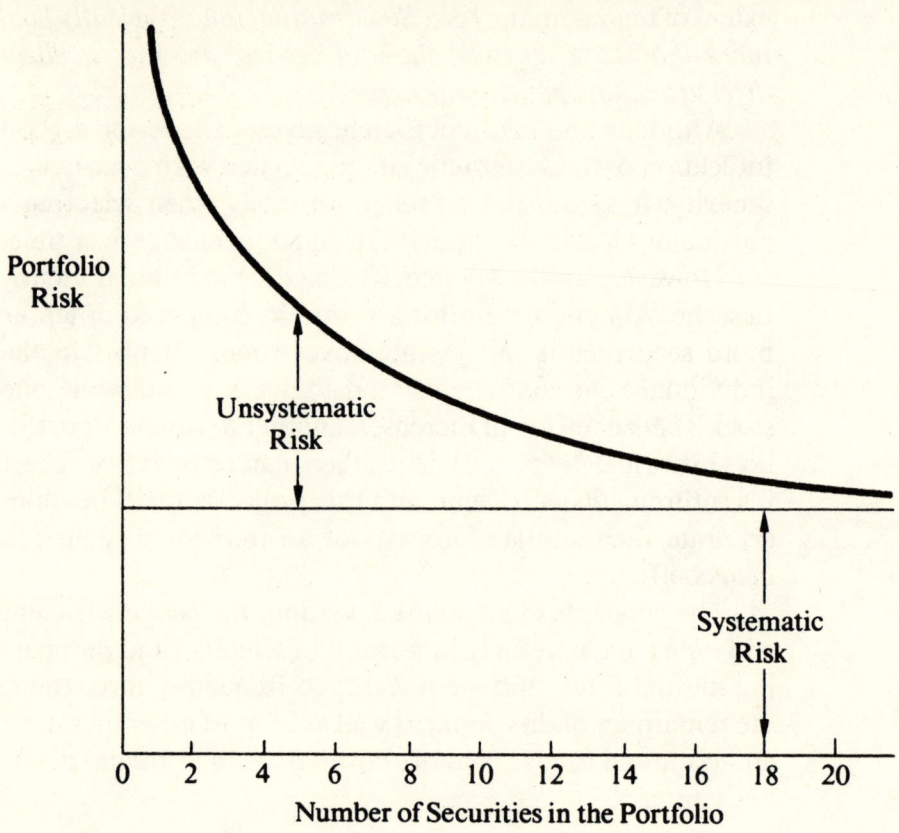

most every investment objective possible, including aggressive growth, growth, growth and income, income, bond, municipal bond and money market. This has lead to a dazzling array of funds from which to choose. Through mutual funds you can invest in mortgages, foreign securities, high yielding "junk" bonds, municipal bonds, convertible bonds and the speculative stocks of new firms.

In the chapters to follow we will explore the implications of what was only suggested in these introductory pages. We will revisit frequently the issues of risk and reward and diversification, and we will see how to apply the tools of investment evaluation to the pursuit of individual investment objectives. We will also discuss tax treatment, retirement plans and other issues relevant to mutual fund investing.

# Chapter 2

# An Overview of the Mutual Funds Industry

Successfully managing a portfolio of securities requires dedicated interest, timely and accurate information and specialized knowledge. Most investors are able to obtain these necessary requisites only by engaging the services of a professionally *managed investment company,* that is, a financial institution that is engaged solely in the business of investing in securities.

While other companies, such as banks and insurance companies, also invest in securities, the investment company's sole business and purpose is to invest in a pool of financial assets and pass the returns directly on to their shareholders. Thus, income to investment company shareholders is directly related to the income prospects of the investment company's portfolio of investments. Furthermore, the prices of investment company shares are directly related to the market value of the securities in the company's investment portfolio.

Investment companies set clearly defined investment objectives for the combined funds of a large number of investors with similar objectives. They invest judiciously to seek those common objectives, and thus enable investors to share all income and expenses, as well as portfolio profits and losses.

Investment companies are regulated by the Investment Company Act of 1940, which, among other things, requires investment companies to disclose their investment activities, to redeem shares held by investors on demand, and to issue periodic financial reports to investor-shareholders.

The universe of various investment companies is shown in Figure 2–1. A *unit investment trust* is a form of investment company organized as a trust to issue redeemable securities, each of which represent an undivided interest in a unit of the specified securities. The unit, or pool, of assets is fixed at the outset, so there is no further management of the portfolio required after the initial selection of securities is made. Trust participants usually hold their certificates to maturity.

*Management companies* on the other hand, actively engage in the management of a pool of assets on behalf of its shareholders. They can be either open-end or closed-end companies. A *closed-end* management company has a fixed number of shares outstanding and does not issue or redeem shares upon demand. Most closed-end company shares are listed and sold on a stock exchange, where their prices are determined by investor demand in a manner similar to other publicly traded firms.

*Open-end investment companies*, more commonly referred to as *mutual funds*, continuously offer new shares to investors and guarantee to redeem their shares at net asset value (NAV) per share at any time. (A fund's per-share NAV is determined by dividing the fund's total asset value at any given time by the number of shares it has outstanding at that time.) The concept of mutuality stems from the fact that there is only one class of owner who proportionally shares the gains or losses of the fund with all the other owners. The three principal types of mutual funds are: (1) common stock funds; (2) bond funds; and (3) money market funds.

**FIGURE 2-1**
**The Universe of Investment Companies**

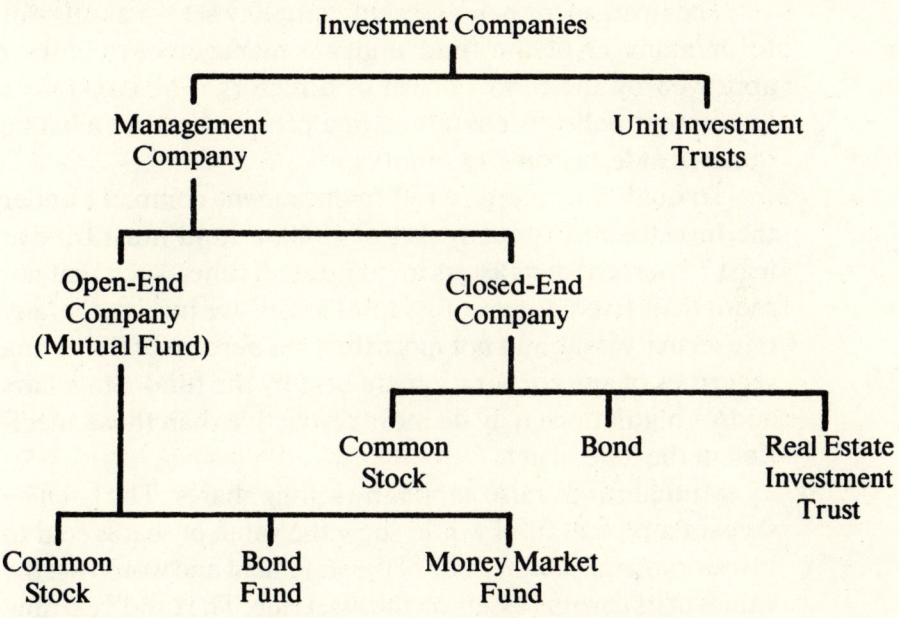

*Mutual funds* are corporations chartered by the states to conduct business as investment companies. They are registered with the Securities and Exchange Commission and with each state in which they intend to do business. The business affairs of the funds are carried out by it's board of directors and officers. The funds actually are owned by its shareholders who elect board members and approve operating policies, such as changes in the fund's objectives, the hiring or firing of investment advisors, and the establishment of the advisor's compensation.

The investment management company serves as advisor to or manager of the fund under a management contract approved by the fund's board of directors. The company's investment policy is contained in a prospectus that must be updated at least every 14 months.

To qualify as a registered management company under the Investment Company Act of 1940, a fund must have at least 75 percent of its assets invested at all times, such that not more than five percent of its total assets are invested in any one security issue and not more than ten percent of the voting securities of any corporation are held by the fund. State laws and/or regulations may be more restrictive than those specified in the federal act.

Mutual funds raise capital by selling shares. The balance sheet of a typical fund would show the value of shares sold to investors on the liability side of the statement and would list the values of its earning assets on the asset side. The fund's earning assets are the securities it purchases that produce income from two sources: dividends or interest, and capital gains. Mutual funds generally do not incur debt, although the charters of some funds permit them to borrow money for investment purposes. The cash obtained from selling shares to the public is invested directly in income-producing securities.

Investment companies are not taxed on income from interest, dividends or capital gains since these are "passed through" to shareholders through periodic distributions.

Mutual fund income and capital gains are taxed only at the level of the individual shareholder. By purchasing the shares of a regulated investment company, investors retain their own tax position and do not suffer double taxation on both the investment company's income and then on the distribution of that income, or what is left of it, when they receive it in the form of a distribution. The fund is a conduit through which investment income flows directly to its shareholders from the securities held in the portfolio. The shareholder's investment income and capital gains distributions received from the fund are treated exactly as if he had bought and sold securities without the fund serving as intermediary.

## THE ORIGINS AND GROWTH OF THE MUTUAL FUNDS INDUSTRY

Closed-end investment companies originated in Belgium and Britain in the mid-1800's. The open-end type of investment company started in the U.S. in 1924 when Massachusetts Investor Trust established the first mutual fund. Investor interest and confidence grew rapidly after the Investment Company Act of 1940, which provided a regulated format for operating mutual funds.

Mutual funds have never held over eight percent of the market value of all listed shares of the New York Stock Exchange. However, they began to experience rapid growth in the 1970's as money market and bond funds grew in size and number. While total assets were $448 million in 1940, they grew to $138 billion in 1980, as shown in Table 2–1.

In 1973, over 93 percent of total fund assets were in common stock funds, with the remainder in bond funds. Money market mutual funds, first introduced in 1970, grew tremendously, and by 1983 reached $200 billion in assets. An incredible record. Annual fund sales for the 1975–84 period

TABLE 2-1
**Mutual Fund Assets and Number of Funds**

| Year | Assets (Millions) | Number of Funds |
|---|---|---|
| 1940 | $448 | 68 |
| 1950 | $2,530 | 98 |
| 1960 | $17,383 | 161 |
| 1970 | $50,654 | 361 |
| 1980 | $138,333 | 564 |
| 1984 | $308,700 | 1,100 |

are summarized on Figures 2-2 and 2-3. By 1983, money market funds accounted for more than 55 percent of total assets held in open-end funds while common stock funds declined to only about 26 percent of the total.

There were 361 total funds in 1970. However, by 1983 there were 1,026 funds—653 stock, bond and income funds and 373 money market and short-term municipal bond funds. By mid-1985, the number of mutual funds had grown to 1,345 (1,054 regular funds and 291 money market funds).

Clearly, the mutual fund industry is exploding. If one includes the $240 billion of money market and short-term funds held as of April 1985, a total of $404 billion was under management in mutual funds. Mutual fund sales grew to an all-time monthly high of $9.5 billion in April 1985.

## LOAD VERSUS NO-LOAD FUNDS

A fund's load charge is the sales commission an investor pays when buying a share in the fund. *Load* funds charge a commission when shares are purchased and no-load funds do not.

**FIGURE 2-2**
**Annual Sales of Mutual Funds for 1975–1984***

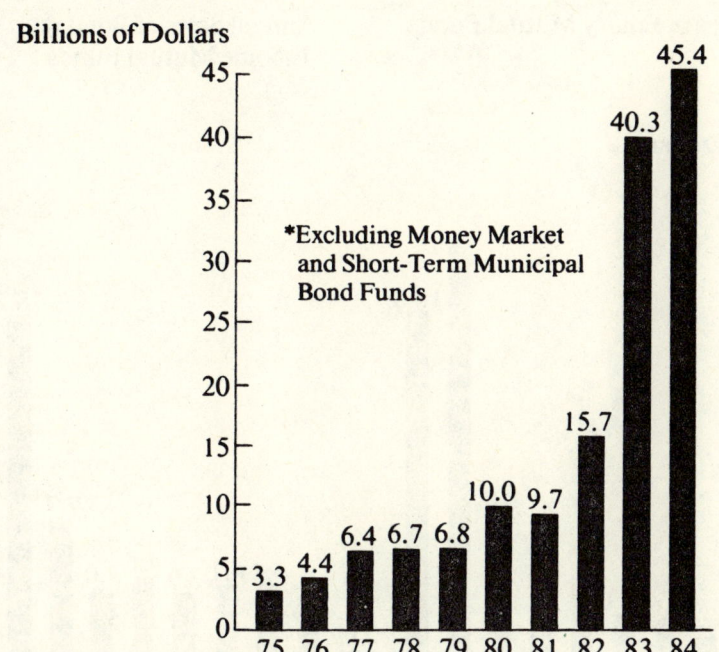

Source: Investment Company Institute

**FIGURE 2-3**
**Annual Sales of Equity Mutual Funds and Bond and Income Funds for 1975–1984**

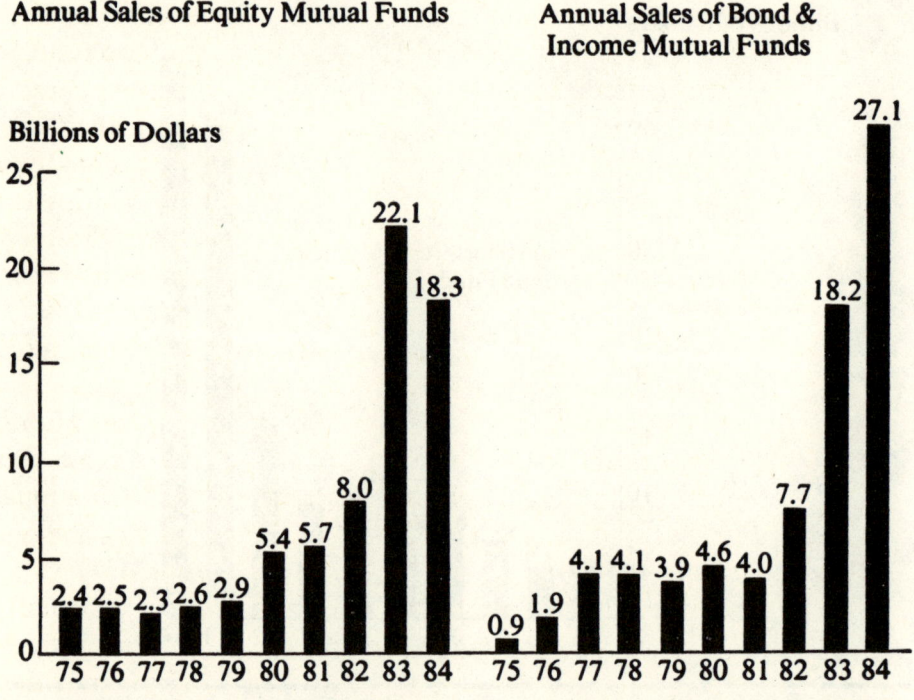

Source: Investment Company Institute

That, and the method in which the shares are purchased, are the primary differences between the two. Load charges typically range from 4 to 8.5 percent of the fund's share price at time of purchase. Most load funds offer a quantity discount. For example, a fund may charge 8.5 percent for a purchase under $10,000 and reduce the charge in steps down to 4 percent for purchases over $100,000. In 1984, less than one-half of all funds were load.

One generally can determine whether a fund is a load or no-load fund by comparing its offer price to its net asset value in the newspaper's mutual fund listings. When the two values are listed and they are different, you know it's a load fund. In contrast, the use of the letters "N.L." in the offer price column indicates that it is a no-load fund and, as a result, the shares are bought and sold at the net asset value. Occasionally, a no-load fund will have a small back-end load amounting to a 1 to 2 percent commission of the value of shares redeemed. There has been a number of no-load funds, or *low-load* funds, that charge a sales commission of 1 to 2 percent.

Although most load funds charge their sales commissions up front when the investor makes a purchase, there is a growing trend on the part of some brokerage sponsored funds to disguise the load charge in the form of redemption fees (which could be as high as 5 percent) and hidden annual distribution fees that run from 1 to 1.5 percent of average assets.

In comparing load and no-load funds, investors usually consider only the up-front sales charge. They do not examine the prospectus to compare yearly management fees and other fees. Both factors must be assessed when determining the true cost of fund shares. For example, if a load fund has a 5 percent sales charge and an annual management fee of 0.5 percent, compared to a yearly management fee of 1.0 percent for a no-load fund, assuming that the performance of both are the same, if the shares of both were redeemed in ten years, they will have earned the same net return. And, in fact, if they are held beyond the tenth year, the load fund will actually start yielding a higher net return upon redemption.

Some important advantages of buying load funds may include:

1. Ability to purchase and redeem shares through broker/dealer on a specific day.
2. Review of individual investment objectives with broker to select appropriate fund.
3. Continuing contact with broker to review changing conditions and investment needs.

Many people use their stock brokers or financial planners to purchase load funds because they value their advice. While it may be reasonable to purchase a load fund, I believe it is unreasonable to purchase a fund that reinvests dividends with a sales charge. If you find it necessary to select a load fund, make sure that it is one that reinvests your dividends at the net asset value without assessing additional sales charges.

## THE BENEFITS AND COSTS OF OWNING A MUTUAL FUND

As we discussed earlier, one of the most important benefits of purchasing a mutual fund is *diversification*. Diversification, we know, is beneficial because it reduces portfolio risk by spreading one's holdings to include a variety of industries and companies.

Another important benefit is *professional management*, which can relieve the investor from the extensive effort required to track various stocks and stay informed of changes in economic and investment conditions. The fund manager makes fund investment decisions based on his analysis of large amounts of information about companies, industries and the economy.

The investment *selection* process is more manageable than individual stocks or bonds since one only has to choose an investment from the universe of about 500 available mutual funds (non-money market funds). By contrast, the stock and bond market investor is faced with selecting his investment from thousands of securities.

Mutual funds also are relatively *easy to buy and sell*. In many cases it can be done through the mail or with a simple phone call.

*Transaction costs* can be lower for mutual funds, especially for no-load funds. Individual investors buying stocks and bonds on their own, particularly those purchased in odd lots, must pay higher commission rates than mutual funds pay for the purchase of securities. And, these transaction cost savings are passed on to fund investors. After an initial purchase in a fund, investors may purchase additional shares in small amounts—as little as $250 and even less.

Mutual funds are a very *liquid* investment, since the shares are readily redeemable at the option of the shareholder. No-load funds are redeemable directly from the mutual fund by mail and some funds offer a telephone service. In addition, many funds offer checkwriting services that permit immediate liquidity.

Another benefit of a mutual fund investment is the *reduction of paperwork*. If you have held 20 or 30 different common stocks or bonds, you know that keeping track of cash dividend payments, stock splits, interest payments, purchase and sale prices, and brokerage commissions and fees is a time-consuming chore. With a mutual fund investment, the number of dividend and interest checks is reduced. Each mutual fund shareholder is sent a report once a year indicating the returns earned and transactions made during the year. The mutual fund also holds the investor's securities and provides periodic reports of individual holdings. These services can be especially advantageous at tax reporting time.

Mutual funds also offer *flexibility* through their many

services and types of available accounts. These include a range of options that make investing convenient. Among these are lump-sum accounts, automatic reinvestment accounts, accumulation accounts, withdrawal accounts, exchange privileges, and other options that permit an investor to tailor a mutual fund investment program to his or her particular needs.

One important factor in the rapid growth of mutual funds has been the increasing popularity of *mutual fund families*. Fund families generally consist of two or more stock and/or bond funds and a money market fund under one management company, where exchange privileges between the funds are offered. Fund families accounted for over 70 percent of total no-load fund assets in 1983.

The *costs* of ownership of mutual funds can be significant and may include (1) a purchase or load cost, (2) portfolio transaction costs, (3) management and other fees, (4) and uncontrollable tax consequences. Mutual fund fees are discussed in more detail in Chapter 3 and the tax consequences in Chapter 9.

Total fees for mutual funds as a function of fund size are shown in Figure 2–4. These include both investment advisory or management fees and non-advisory fees. As the chart indicates, it's not until an equity fund's assets reach $250 million or more that their costs become competitive with money-market and municipal bond funds.

Of course, the ultimate factor in determining the suitability of investing in mutual funds is their performance as compared to other investment alternatives available. This issue is discussed in depth throughout the book. However, one indication of fund performance compared to the S&P 500 and the record of bank trust departments is shown in Table 2–2.

## FIGURE 2–4
**Advisory and Non-advisory Fees as a Percentage of Total Net Assets by Size of Fund in Assets**

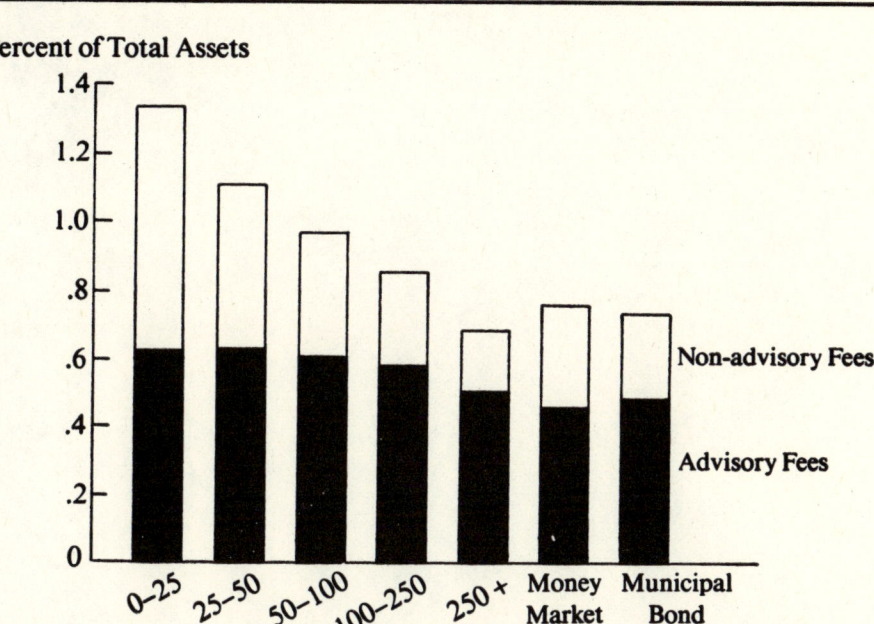

### TABLE 2–2
**Annual Rate of Return (%) for Periods Ending October 31**

| Year | 1979 | 1980 | 1981 | 1982 | 1985 |
|---|---|---|---|---|---|
| Bank Trust Departments | 15.1 | 31.0 | 2.4 | 15.7 | 23.1 |
| Mutual Funds | 20.2 | 35.1 | 0.9 | 15.8 | 22.5 |
| S&P 500 | 15.1 | 31.7 | 0.4 | 16.1 | 27.8 |

*Source:* Hamilton, Johnston & Co.

# Chapter 3

# Choosing a Mutual Fund

## THE PROSPECTUS AND ANNUAL REPORT

The process of selecting and acquiring mutual fund shares begins with the fund's *prospectus*. All mutual funds are required to provide prospective investors with a prospectus, which is a formal description of the mutual fund, including its investment objectives and policies, the services it offers, any investment restrictions it has imposed, the names of its directors and officers, its purchase and redemption requirements and its financial status.

In addition to the prospectus, the prospective investor should request the fund's latest annual report and what is called the "Form B" prospectus. Since 1984, the Securities and Exchange Commission has permitted funds to issue a simplified, or shortened, version of the prospectus, but nevertheless requires that omitted information be included in a "Statement of Additional Information", or Form B prospectus, that is available on request from the fund. It provides supplementary information such as details of fees and a listing of investments held in the fund's portfolio.

The prospectus provides a myriad of per-share financial and portfolio information for the most recent ten fiscal years. Data relating to investment income, operating expenses, dividends, realized and unrealized gains or losses on securities, and net asset values, are displayed. Also, portfolio turnover and the ratios of expenses and net investment income to average net assets are provided.

When inspecting a fund's prospectus you should take particular note of:

1. The statement of the fund's investment objectives and strategy.
2. The details concerning all sales and redemption charges.
3. The disclosure of any investment restrictions the fund must adhere to.
4. The various services offered by the fund.
5. Management and non-advisory fees.
6. The financial statements.

The cover page of a sample prospectus for the Windsor fund is shown in Figure 3-1.

The selection of a mutual fund should be made by matching your investment needs with the objectives, performance, and services of candidate funds. A key step is thus the identification and recording of your investment objectives and needs. The factors that you should consider include expected return, the level of risk you feel you can reasonably tolerate, your needs for liquidity, the level of services you require, the time horizon of your investment, and the level of investment performance you are seeking. These are outlined in Table 3-1. Completing the table should enable you to match your objectives to the best fund for your purposes. Many of these factors are discussed in greater depth in later chapters, but you should be able to select a fund, or at least drastically

## FIGURE 3-1
### The Cover Page of the Prospectus for the Windsor Fund

# Windsor
## FUND
Vanguard Financial Center/Valley Forge/Pennsylvania 19482

**PROSPECTUS— February 28, 1983**

| Investor Information Center<br>800-523-7025<br>800-362-0530 (In Pennsylvania) | Client Services Center<br>800-523-7910<br>800-362-7688 (In Pennsylvania) |
|---|---|

### INVESTMENT OBJECTIVE AND POLICIES

**WINDSOR FUND** is a no-load mutual fund which seeks long-term growth of capital and income by investing primarily in common stocks. The Fund's secondary objective is to endeavor to provide current income. Of course, the achievement of these objectives cannot be assured.

Windsor Fund's stocks are selected principally on the basis of fundamental investment value. Key to the valuation process is the relationship of a company's underlying earning power and dividend payout to the market price of its stock. The Fund's holdings are usually characterized by relatively low price-earnings ratios and meaningful income yields and, at the time of purchase, are often deemed to be overlooked or undervalued in the marketplace. In this sense, the Fund's strategy can be characterized as "contrarian" in nature.

### TO OPEN AN ACCOUNT

To open an account in Windsor Fund, complete the Account Registration Form on page 23 of this Prospectus. If you need assistance in completing the Form, please call the Investor Information Center telephone number shown above. There is no sales commission. The minimum initial investment is $500; the minimum for subsequent investments is $50.

*Investors should read and retain this prospectus for future reference.*

---

**THESE SECURITIES HAVE NOT BEEN APPROVED OR DISAPPROVED BY THE SECURITIES AND EXCHANGE COMMISSION NOR HAS THE COMMISSION PASSED UPON THE ACCURACY OR ADEQUACY OF THIS PROSPECTUS. ANY REPRESENTATION TO THE CONTRARY IS A CRIMINAL OFFENSE.**

---

54 Years of Service to Investors . . . Over $5 Billion of Assets

**TABLE 3-1**
**Selection Factors**

1. Size of Initial Investment _____

2. Investment Period
   Long Term _____      Intermediate Term _____      Short Term _____
   (More than 5 years)  (3–5 years)                  (6–24 months)

3. Liquidity Required
   Highly Liquid _____              Moderately Liquid _____

4. Tax Exempt
   Yes _____                        No _____

5. Risk Accommodated
   Low Risk _____      Medium _____      High Risk _____

6. Services Required
   Telephone Redemption _____       Checkwriting _____

7. Performance (Annual Return Expected)
   High _____              Intermediate _____           Moderate _____
   (More than the         (Equal to the S&P 500,        (8 to 10% annually)
   S&P 500, 15–18%        or approximately 12%
   annually, or           annually)
   higher)

8. Investment Objective
   Type of fund:       growth—common stock      _____
                       growth and income        _____
                       income—bond              _____
                       income—tax free          _____

narrow your choices, on the basis of the table at this point.

Let us consider the financial information provided in the 1984 prospectus for New Horizons fund shown in Figure 3-2. We can see that for the ten years shown, the portfolio turnover rate grew from 13 percent in 1974 to 45 percent in 1983 and that the expense ratio consistently ranged between .53 percent to .65 percent. The income ratio (the ratio of Net Investment Income to Average Net Assets) reached a maximum of 2.2 percent in 1980. (Note: This reflects New Horizon's classification as a growth fund with emphasis on capital appreciation and not on current income. The classification of funds is discussed in Chapter 4.)

New Horizon's performance is measured by calculating its return for the year from the distributions it made and the increase in its net asset value (NAV) or share price for the year. *The Net Asset Value* (NAV) is determined by dividing the net assets by the number of shares outstanding at any given time. The return for one year is calculated from:

$$\frac{\text{Annual return}}{\text{in percent}} = \frac{\text{Ending NAV} + \text{distributions} - \text{initial NAV}}{\text{initial NAV}} \times 100 \qquad (3\text{-}1)$$

Then the 1983 return for New Horizon is:

$$\text{Return} = \frac{(\$17.90 + \$.96 - \$15.90)}{\$15.90} \times 100 = 18.6\% \qquad (3\text{-}2)$$

Funds usually provide performance records in annual reports that go back several years, some even go back to the start of the fund. For example, the annual rate of return for Windsor fund for the five-year period ending Oct. 31, 1984, assuming the reinvestment of all income dividends and capital gains distribution, was 22.3 percent (as shown in Figure 3-3). The fund's annual rate of return since its inception in 1958 was 12.2 percent, which was almost 40 percent better than the S&P 500's 8.8 percent annual return for the same period. If an investor placed $10,000 in Windsor on October 23, 1958 and reinvested all distributions, the value of this

## FIGURE 3-2
## The Condensed Financial Information for the New Horizons Fund from the May 1984 Prospectus

**PER SHARE INCOME AND CAPITAL CHANGES**
**(For a share outstanding throughout the year)**

The per share income and capital changes for the years ended December 31, 1974 through 1983 included in the following statement have been examined by Wooden & Benson, independent accountants, whose reports thereon were unqualified.

| | Year Ended December 31, | | | | | | | | | |
|---|---|---|---|---|---|---|---|---|---|---|
| | 1983 | 1982 | 1981 | 1980 | 1979 | 1978 | 1977 | 1976 | 1975 | 1974 |
| Net Asset Value, Beginning of Period | $15.90 | $16.06 | $19.53 | $13.01 | $9.75 | $8.17 | $7.32 | $6.66 | $4.86 | $8.02 |
| Investment Activities | | | | | | | | | | |
| Income | .28 | .26 | .44 | .40 | .29 | .22 | .14 | .11 | .11 | .13 |
| Expenses | (.12) | (.07) | (.09) | (.08) | (.06) | (.06) | (.04) | (.04) | (.04) | (.04) |
| Net Investment Income | .16 | .19 | .35 | .32 | .23 | .16 | .10 | .07 | .07 | .09 |
| Net Realized and Unrealized Gain (Loss) on Investments | 2.80 | 2.62 | (1.82) | 6.80 | 3.19 | 1.52 | .82 | .66 | (1.82) | (3.17) |
| **Total From Investment Activities** | 2.96 | 2.81 | (1.47) | 7.12 | 3.42 | 1.68 | .92 | .73 | 1.89 | (3.08) |
| Distributions | | | | | | | | | | |
| Net Investment Income | (.20) | (.35) | (.32) | (.23) | (.16) | (.10) | (.07) | (.07) | (.09) | (.05) |
| Realized Net Gain | (.76)* | (2.62)* | (1.68)* | (.37)* | — | — | — | — | — | (.03) |
| **Total Distributions** | (.96) | (2.97) | (2.00) | (.60) | (.16) | (.10) | (.07) | (.07) | (.09) | (.08) |
| Net Asset Value, End of Period | $17.90 | $15.90 | $16.06 | $19.53 | $13.01 | $9.75 | $8.17 | $7.32 | $6.66 | $4.86 |
| Ratio of Expenses to Average Net Assets | 0.61% | 0.56% | 0.53% | 0.54% | 0.60% | 0.59% | 0.60% | 0.62% | 0.65% | 0.64% |
| Ratio of Net Investment Income to Average Net Assets | 0.83% | 1.64% | 2.11% | 2.20% | 2.18% | 1.68% | 1.41% | 0.99% | 1.22% | 1.47% |
| Portfolio Turnover Rate | 45.2% | 35.9% | 34.7% | 32.7% | 25.3% | 28.9% | 14.8% | 19.7% | 25.8% | 12.9% |
| Shares Outstanding at End of Period (in thousands) | 75,706 | 75,393 | 54,543 | 49,697 | 46,506 | 45,309 | 48,178 | 48,326 | 49,376 | 41,857 |

* Distribution from security gains includes $.03, $.01, $.02, and $.01 in 1980, 1981, 1982, and 1983, respectively, of realized taxable gains attributable to the unrealized appreciation of securities at the date they were acquired from the Edie Special Growth Fund, Inc.

## FIGURE 3-3
## The Performance of Windsor Fund Compared with the S&P 500

This chart shows the lifetime record of a $10,000 investment in Windsor Fund, from its inception on October 23, 1958, to October 31, 1984, along with the performance of the S&P 500 Index over the same period. Clearly, the Fund's consistently-applied "contrarian" policy oriented towards stocks representing "good value" has proven successful over the long-term.

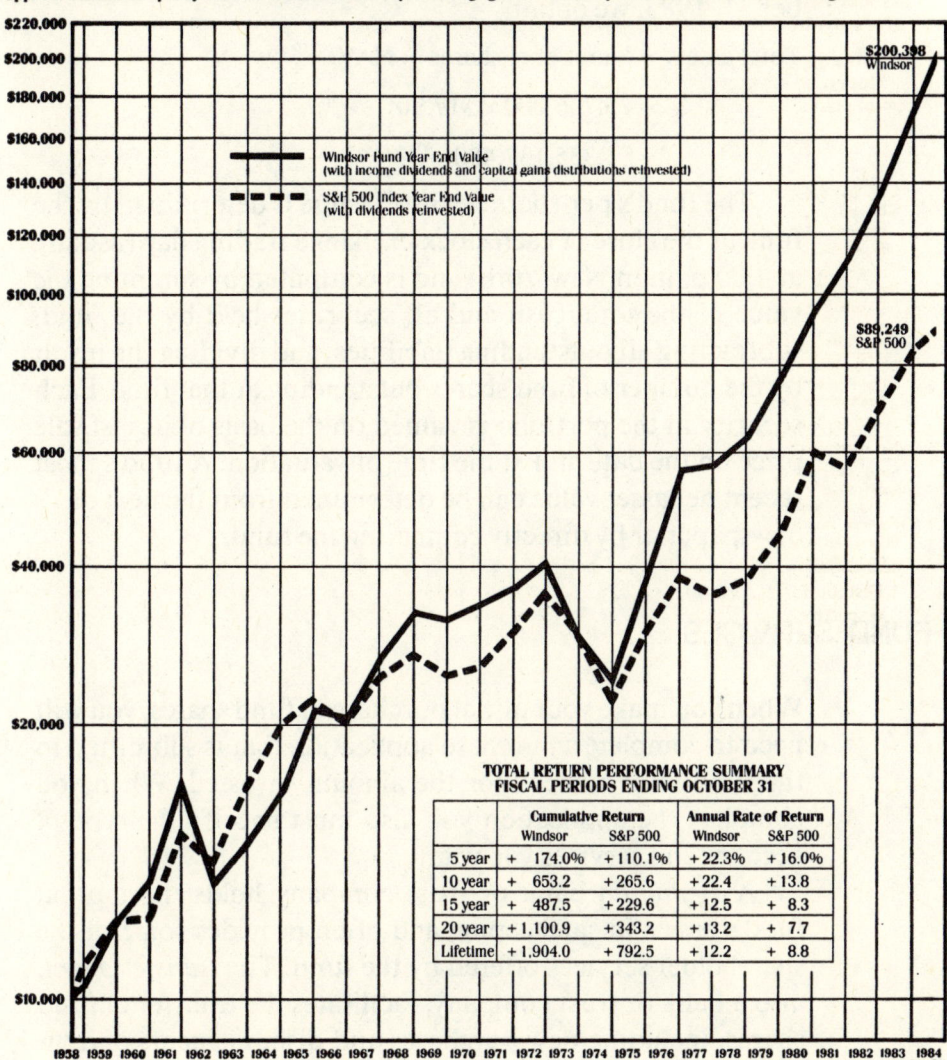

**TOTAL RETURN PERFORMANCE SUMMARY**
**FISCAL PERIODS ENDING OCTOBER 31**

|  | Cumulative Return | | Annual Rate of Return | |
| --- | --- | --- | --- | --- |
|  | Windsor | S&P 500 | Windsor | S&P 500 |
| 5 year | + 174.0% | + 110.1% | + 22.3% | + 16.0% |
| 10 year | + 653.2 | + 265.6 | + 22.4 | + 13.8 |
| 15 year | + 487.5 | + 229.6 | + 12.5 | + 8.3 |
| 20 year | + 1,100.9 | + 343.2 | + 13.2 | + 7.7 |
| Lifetime | + 1,904.0 | + 792.5 | + 12.2 | + 8.8 |

investment would have been $200,398 as of October 31, 1984.

To determine the total assets held by the fund, simply multiply the number of shares outstanding by the net asset value. To determine New Horizon's total assets as of December 31, 1983, we obtain

Total assets = Number of shares × NAV

= 75,706,000 × $17.90

= $1,355,137,400

The fund's per-share net asset value is determined by the fund at the close of each stock exchange trading day (usually at 4:00 p.m. in New York) and is computed by summing the value of the total cash and all securities held by the fund, subtracting all outstanding liabilities, and dividing the result by the number of fund shares outstanding at that time. Each security in the portfolio is valued on the basis of its last sale price on the date and at the time of valuation. A fund's most recent net asset value can be determined from the next day's newspaper or by directly contacting the fund.

## FUND SERVICES

When you make your initial purchase of fund shares, you will need to complete a purchase application that is submitted to the fund with a check for the amount invested. When you complete the application you also must specify the type of account and services you want.

A *custodian* bank or trust company holds the mutual fund's assets in safekeeping and often provides some of the shareholder services offered by the fund. The *transfer agent*, also a bank or trust company, facilitates the transfer of fund shares, including new purchases and disbursements of dividends, and maintains shareholder records. Often a single bank serves as both custodian and transfer agent.

Most funds offer an attractive array of services. The initial purchase of shares is readily accomplished by submitting an application. Another form is used to systematically add to your investments in the fund. Many funds provide for automatic periodic deductions from your checking account into the fund. Another service is a telephone redemption request to wire transfer funds directly into your checking account.

Investors also have several options regarding the distribution of dividends and capital gains. Most investors elect to have all distributions reinvested. Some reinvest only capital gains distributions, but have monthly dividends sent to them or to their banks.

With the recent development and rising popularity of *mutual fund families,* many investment companies have begun to offer several funds, each with its own distinct investment objective. One company's family of funds might include a growth stock fund, an income fund, a municipal bond fund, and a money market fund. This family of funds generally would also permit investors to exchange or switch their shares between funds by telephone order.

The amount of mutual fund assets currently under management by the largest families is impressive. Fidelity Investments, the largest no-load fund family, has over $10 billion under management in 26 funds, excluding money market funds. Including money market funds, Fidelity has $27 billion in assets. The next largest family, the Vanguard Group, has over $7 billion in 26 funds, also exclusive of money market funds. Both Dreyfus and T. Rowe Price, two other large family funds, exceed $3 billion in fund assets.

## MONITORING MUTUAL FUND FEES AND MANAGEMENT CHANGES

Mutual fund investors should be willing to pay for reasonable costs of management and administration. However, keep in mind that fund fees and costs directly reduce the return on your investment in the fund. It pays, therefore, to review closely all the costs of a fund and to keep up with changes. *And they do change*. For example, as we discussed earlier, some no-load funds have instituted low-load charges and some funds recently have instituted a fee for exchanging between funds within a family. Also, look for hidden charges, such as redemption charges or "12b–1 fees".

One significant cost of owning a mutual fund is the advisory or *management fee*, which is the compensation paid to the professional managers who administer the fund's portfolio. These fees generally equal 0.50 to 0.75 percent of the average dollar amount of assets under management (although small funds sometimes have assessments as high as 1 percent). Unlike load charges, which are one-time costs, management fees are assessed annually and are paid regardless of the portfolio's performance. There also are the *administrative* or non-advisory costs of operating the fund, such as costs for engaging the services of transfer agents, custodians, legal and auditing services, and printing and postage, which also are assessed annually.

A number of load funds, including many sponsored by brokerage firms, have eliminated or reduced their front-end sales charge to compete with no-load funds but impose a *redemption fee* when money is removed before a specified period of time. Typically, the charge is about 4 to 5 percent during the first year and diminishes gradually over a five-year period. Some funds limit redemption fees to a percentage of the principal amount of the investment; others base it on the entire net asset value at the time of redemption, which would include accumulated earnings. The declining back-end or redemption fee is more acceptable, of course, to an investor who has a low need for liquidity and who plans to hold the fund for the long term.

Another, often overlooked, fee is the *distribution expense* permitted under the *12b–1 rule* of the Securities and Exchange Commission. Distribution expenses cover such items as dealer and salesman commissions on new sales of fund shares, advertising expenses and direct marketing costs to attract new investors. A fund may choose not to assess front-end or redemption loads, but still must pay commissions to salespeople who bring in new investors. They recover these costs by charging an annual distribution fee against the fund's assets. This fee can range from .25 percent to 1 percent, but for many funds, is difficult to determine from the prospectus whether it is being charged at all. Investors should try to avoid paying this fee, but if that is not possible, try to avoid a distribution fee that exceeds 0.5 percent annually.

Table 3-2 shows how fund fees can add up. For the load fund example shown, the total annual expense is 3.15 percent, which would be an excessively high expense percentage.

Reviewing the fees shown in Figure 3-4 for New Horizon fund, we find a total annual fee of 1.26 percent. This fund did not have a front-end or back-end load nor a 12b-1 distribution fee. In general, this fee structure is reasonable and should be acceptable to most investors.

**TABLE 3-2**
**Total Investment Expenses (Annual Estimated)**

|  | Example (Holding Period = 4 Years) | Your Fund (Holding Period = x Years) |
|---|---|---|
| Front-end sales charge/hold. per. | .50%* |  |
| Management fee | .75 |  |
| Expenses | .65 |  |
| 12b-1 distribution fee | .25 |  |
| Back-end redemption fee/hold. per. | 1.00* |  |
| Total | 3.15% |  |

*Divide the front-end sale charge percent and back-end redemption fee by the holding period (hold. per.).

## FIGURE 3-4
**The Section Displaying the Fees for New Horizons Fund from the May 1, 1984 Prospectus**

### MANAGEMENT OF THE FUND

Directors

The management of the Fund's business and affairs are the responsibility of the Fund's Board of Directors.

Investment Adviser and Distributor

The Fund is advised and managed by T. Rowe Price Associates, Inc., which was incorporated in Maryland in 1947 as successor to the investment counseling firm founded by Mr. T. Rowe Price in 1937. Price Associates serves as an investment adviser to a variety of individual and institutional investors, including other mutual funds. On December 31, 1983, Price Associates was supervising more than $16 billion of assets. Price Associates, subject to the authority of the Fund's Board of Directors, is responsible for the overall management of the Fund's business affairs. The Fund pays Price Associates a monthly advisory fee at the annual rate of: .65% of the first $500 million of the average daily net assets, and .50% of such assets in excess of $500 million.

The Fund is distributed by T. Rowe Price Marketing, Inc., a wholly-owned subsidiary of Price Associates, which also acts as distributor for the other T. Rowe Price Funds.

Expenses

The Fund bears all expenses of its operations other than those incurred by Price Associates under its Investment Advisory Agreement with Price Associates. In particular, the Fund pays: investment advisory fees; shareholder servicing fees and expenses; custodian fees and expenses; legal and auditing fees; expenses of preparing prospectuses and shareholder reports; registration fees and expenses; proxy and annual meeting expenses; and directors' fees and expenses. In 1983, the ratio of operating expenses to average net assets of the Fund was .61%.

Transfer and Dividend Disbursing Agent

State Street Bank and Trust Company serves the Fund as transfer agent and dividend disbursing agent. The Bank's main office is at 225 Franklin Street, Boston, Massachusetts 02107. All mutual fund transfer, dividend disbursing, and shareholder service activities are performed by the Bank's agent, Boston Financial Data Services, Inc., at 2 Heritage Drive, Quincy, Massachusetts 02171.

In general, you should think twice about investing in a fund that has a total expense ratio of more than 2 percent. In addition, you should avoid funds that report portfolio turnover ratios of more than 100 percent a year. If a fund has a turnover ratio in excess of this, the transaction costs (which are not reported as part of its fee structure) from the brokerage commissions it is paying on its excessive market trades, could erode your returns.

When selecting a fund, try to analyze both the stability of the fund's performance as well as its management. The Nicholas fund, for example, whose performance is portrayed in Figure 3–5, has maintained a relatively stable, strong 14 percent annual return over the last ten years. This, in large part, is due to the stability of management over that period.

When fund management changes, past performance becomes a less reliable measure of future performance. Unfortunately, it is difficult to determine when management changes, since these events usually are not mentioned in the prospectus. A call to the fund or a review of the last five annual reports are probably the only expedient and reliable ways to determine if the fund's manager has changed.

## HOW TO PURCHASE A FUND

Once you have selected a fund, you can purchase your shares directly from the fund by mail if it is a no-load fund or from the salesperson or broker in the case of a load fund. Often no-load funds can be purchased by telephone using a toll-free 800 number. Usually, however, you will choose to complete and submit the application form provided with the prospectus.

Mutual fund purchases are normally made in total dollar amounts and not by a specific number of shares. Following your initial purchase, within a short time, you will receive

## FIGURE 3-5
**The Performance of Nicholas Fund over the Period September 1974 to February 1985. (The vertical scale is logarithmic.)**

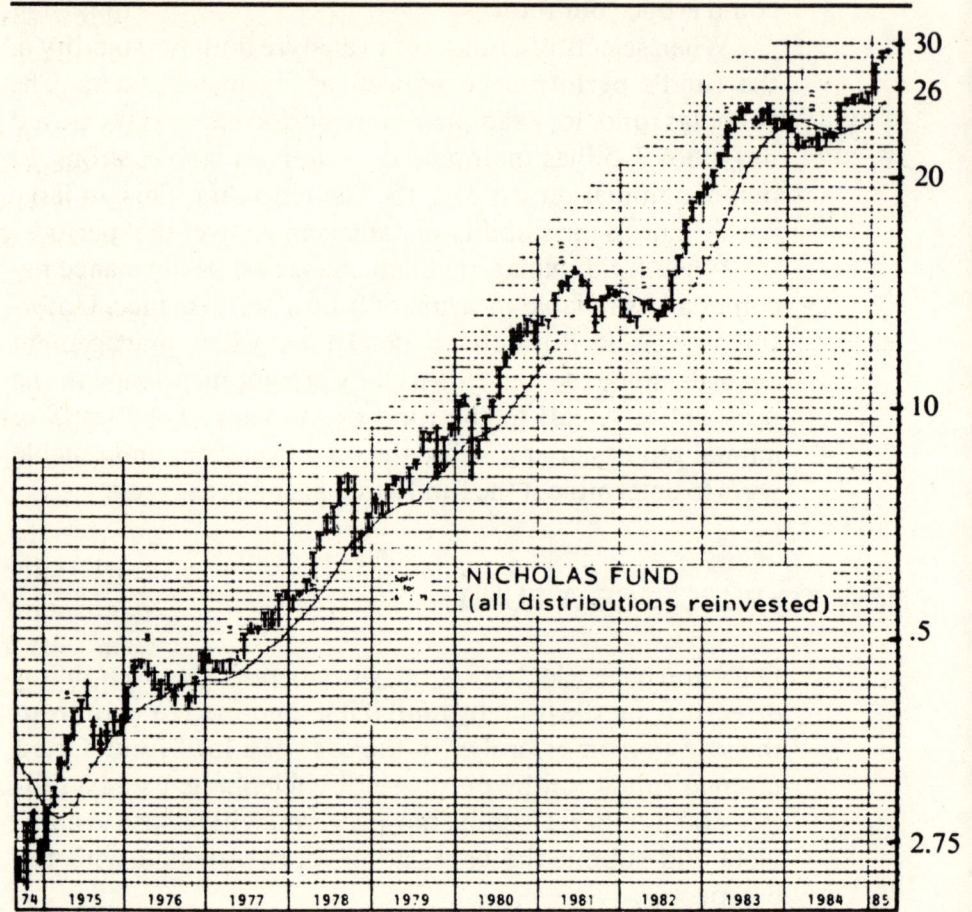

either a certificate representing the number of shares you purchased or a statement of the shares held on deposit for you. As a convenience to shareholders, most mutual funds arrange for the maintenance of "open accounts" for which no share certificates are issued unless the investor specifically requests it. Once your account is established, additional purchases may be made simply by sending a check directly to the fund's custodian, who also adds to your account all additional shares purchased through the reinvestment of capital gains distributions or dividends.

Unless otherwise indicated on the application form, a new investor is assumed to elect automatic reinvestment of dividends and capital gain distributions. This election is wise for most investors with the exception of retired persons or others who require fund income for everyday living expenses.

There are six ways to register mutual fund shares. *Individual ownership* provides for sole ownership in the owner's name. *Joint tenancy with right of survivorship* creates joint ownership that remains with the surviving owner. *Joint tenancy in common* also provides for two owners, but the ownership is placed in the estate of a deceased owner for deposition according to his or her will. Shares also may be registered to a person serving as *trustee*, *custodian*, or *guardian* on behalf of the owner of the shares. A popular account is a parent acting as custodian for a minor child under the Uniform Gift to Minors Act. The ways of registering mutual fund shares are discussed in greater detail in Chapter 12.

## DISCOUNT BROKER MUTUAL FUND ACCOUNT

Several discount securities brokers offer mutual fund accounts. The largest, Charles Schwab and Co., Inc., offers a trading service for over 200 no-load and low-load funds using a regular Schwab account. Another discount broker offering this service is C. D. Anderson.

Funds you currently own that are offered by Schwab can be deposited in your account. If you have a margin account, you can then borrow against your mutual fund shares or buy additional fund shares on margin. Mutual fund shares in your account can be sold with just one phone call. This makes your mutual fund holdings as liquid as stocks. All fund transactions appear on your monthly account statement.

The Schwab sales fee is $12 plus 0.8 percent of the principal amount for each transaction of $3,000 or less. The fee percentage rate declines for larger transactions.

The advantages of services like this are: 1) added liquidity; 2) the ability to obtain margin; and 3) the ability to switch between funds immediately upon order. The primary disadvantage, of course, is the additional sales fee charged by the discount broker.

# Chapter 4

# Classifications and Characteristics of Funds

## CLASSIFYING FUNDS BY OBJECTIVE AND RISK

Mutual funds generally are classified as income funds, growth funds, or a combination of both income and growth.

A *growth fund* has as its primary objective the growth of capital from investments in common stocks and securities convertible into common stocks. The primary objective of an *income fund* is the generation of current income from investments in bonds and other securities with high yields. These two basic categories have many subcategory classifications with more narrowly focused objectives and investment policies as shown in Figure 4–1. Fund policies are not static, however. At times, changes occur, reflecting the effects of the fund's increasing size or management's decision to alter the policy to best fit the fund's emerging characteristics.

Growth funds invest in firms that are believed to offer good prospects for price appreciation. The kinds of securities

FIGURE 4-1
**Fund Classification**

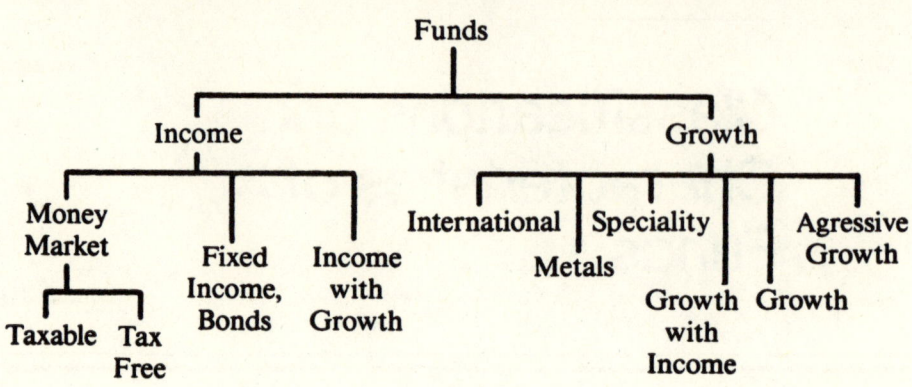

selected and portfolio management strategies pursued determine the type of growth fund. For example, on the theory that individual investors cannot beat the market's overall return, there are funds, called index funds, that are composed entirely of the stocks that comprise the S&P 500.

*Aggressive growth funds* strive for maximum capital gains, they use aggressive trading strategies, including leverage, i.e., buying on margin, and the selection of smaller high-potential growth stocks. Such funds can appreciate rapidly during bull markets, performing several times better than market averages. However, they also tend to decline more rapidly during declining markets.

By contrast *income funds* hold bonds and stocks with high-yielding coupons and dividends in order to generate cash flow. A fixed income or bond fund strives to maintain a fixed, stable yield with low volatility of fund share price.

With the high yields of U.S. government securities and other short-term money instruments that were available in

## TABLE 4-1
**Categories and Objectives of Funds.**

| Type of Fund | Money Market | Fixed Income | Income | Growth & Income | Growth | Aggressive Growth |
|---|---|---|---|---|---|---|
| Risk of share price volatility | Lowest | Low | Moderate | Moderate | High | Highest |
| Primary objective | Liquidity | Yield | Income | Growth | Long term capital gains | Maximum capital gains |
| Secondary objective | Preservation of capital | Stability of yield | Growth | Income | — | — |

the mid-1970's, *money market* funds grew rapidly. These funds hold short-term certificates of deposit, commercial paper, government securities and other short-term debt securities.

The basic categories of funds with general descriptions of their objectives and risk levels is shown in Table 4-1. Money markets have a low risk of share price volatility because the average maturity of the securities they hold is only about 40 days. Since income funds hold longer maturing bonds as well as stocks with changing yields, they offer moderate risk of share price change. The highest volatility risk is associated with growth stocks, since their prices will vary widely with changes in company earnings and the nation's economy.

Investors generally change their risk sensitivity and expected return profiles over the cycle of their lives as shown in Figure 4-2. As we begin our working careers, we can (perhaps should) seek higher returns and assume a higher level of risk because of the security of expected future income that would allow us to recover lost capital. At this stage, we would want to concentrate our investments in growth funds. However, as we approach retirement age, we become more concerned with preservation of capital than with attaining the best

## FIGURE 4–2
**Risk Accepted and Need for Current Income for an Investor Over a Working Lifetime**

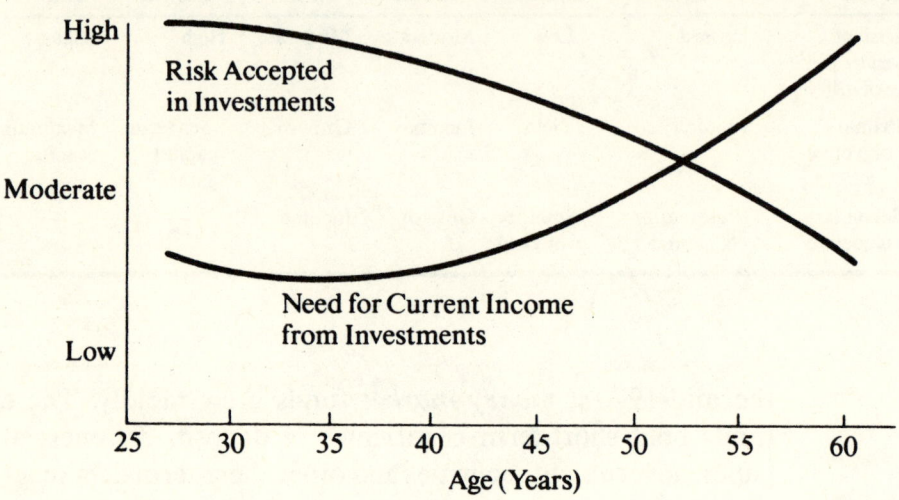

return possible. At this point, we would emphasize money market and income funds.

A breakdown of mutual fund assets by classification for 1983 is shown in Table 4–2.

Table 4–3 shows actual return performance, *beta* coefficients and risk adjusted performance for each classification for the five-year period ending in 1983. (Note: risk adjusted performance is determined by dividing the annual return by the *beta* coefficient for each classification. A more detailed discussion of risk adjusted return is provided in Chapter 5.)

It is no surprise that while the actual return was the greatest for aggressive funds, they also had the highest associated risk. On a risk adjusted basis, all the other classifications outperformed the aggressive growth funds.

## TABLE 4–2
**Mutual Fund Assets**
**December 31, 1983**

| Classification | Assets ($ Billions) | Percentage of Total |
|---|---|---|
| Aggressive growth | 18.7 | 6.4 |
| Growth | 25.9 | 8.8 |
| Growth and income | 32.4 | 11.1 |
| Income | 8.8 | 3.0 |
| Fixed income (bond) | 27.8 | 9.5 |
| Money market | 162.5 | 55.5 |
| Short term municipal bond | 16.8 | 5.7 |
| | 292.9 | 100.0 |

## TABLE 4–3
**Total Performance for the Five-Year Period 1978–83 by Fund Category.**

| | 5-Year Return (%) | Annual Return (%) | Risk (Beta) | Annual Return/Risk |
|---|---|---|---|---|
| Aggressive growth | 187.0 | 23.0 | 1.50 | 15.3 |
| Growth | 137.8 | 18.9 | 1.10 | 17.2 |
| Growth and income | 113.5 | 16.4 | 0.80 | 20.5 |
| Income | 101.9 | 15.1 | 0.60 | 25.2 |
| Fixed income | 53.9 | 9.0 | 0.50 | 18.0 |
| Money market | 79.6 | 12.4 | 0.30 | 41.3 |
| S&P 500 with dividends reinvested | 122.4 | 17.3 | 1.00 | 17.3 |

*Source: Handbook for No-load Investors,* 1984

## GROWTH FUNDS

In this section we will examine *growth funds*. These funds generally seek capital appreciation with an annual portfolio turnover rate of less than 100 percent, while holding middle-of-the-road investments. They do not hold speculative stocks nor do they employ aggressive trading techniques, such as buying on margin or short selling (that is, borrowing stock in the hope of buying it back at a cheaper price later on). Typically, their holdings include companies such as Exxon, IBM, AT & T and General Motors. They seek relatively safe long-term growth.

One typical growth fund is the 20th Century Select Investors Fund, the performance of which is shown on Figure 4–3. The volatility of the fund can be discerned by noting the variation of its net asset value for the 1979–85 period shown. Select Investors' return was 20 percent over the five-year period 1980–1984. The fund has a management fee of about 1 percent and, in 1983, had an expense ratio of 1 percent and a portfolio turnover ratio of 57 percent. As of October 31, 1984, Select Investors had $833 million in assets and its *beta* was 1.09.

Another example of a growth fund is the Nicholas Fund, which had $215 million in assets as of December 31, 1984. Its annual return for the five-year period ending in 1983 was 25.4 percent and its *beta* was 0.86, providing investors an excellent return for the risk involved.

Let us consider one of the first growth funds: T. Rowe Price Growth Fund which was founded in 1950. It grew 62.3 percent over the five years ending December 31, 1983 for an annual growth rate of 10.2 percent. It's *beta* was 1.03 and its asset size was $966 million on December 31, 1984. Because of its size and the nature of its portfolio, this fund's *beta* performance was very close to the market's.

In general, growth funds tend to outperform the S&P 500 during ascending markets and nearly match the S&P 500

# CLASSIFICATIONS AND CHARACTERISTICS OF FUNDS

**FIGURE 4–3**
**The Performance of 20th Century Select Investors Fund for the Period May 1979 to March 1985**

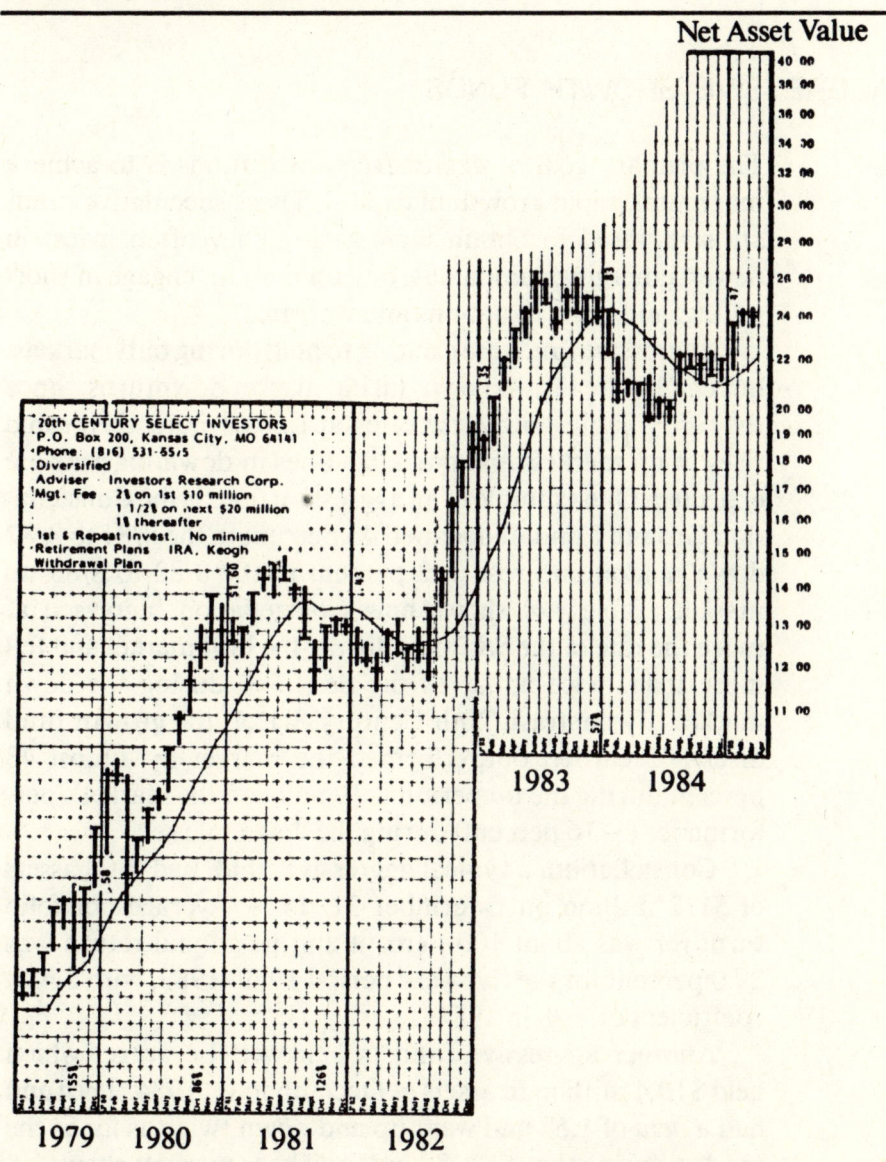

Source: Growth Fund Guide

during declining markets. Over the long-term, therefore, growth funds can be expected to return a relatively steady 14 percent annually.

## AGGRESSIVE GROWTH FUNDS

The primary goal of *aggressive growth* funds is to achieve maximum, rapid growth of capital. These speculative funds are structured to obtain large gains. They often invest in newer, emerging companies, buy on margin, engage in short selling, and trade in options and warrants.

Aggressive funds are exciting to hold during bull markets, but can be dreadful to own during market downturns. Since they are volatile, with *betas* often at 1.50 or more, their rapid rises in up markets and quick declines in down markets are expected. One example of an aggressive fund is the Constellation Growth Fund. It declined 43 percent in the 8/81 to 8/82 down market and rose 152 percent in the 8/82 to 8/83 up market. Table 4-4 shows how Constellation increased at twice the rate of the S&P 500 during the bull market and fell more than twice as far as the S&P 500 during the down market. By contrast, 20th Century Select, the growth fund discussed earlier, outperformed the market by almost 43 percent during the up period and matched the market's performance ( − 16 percent) during the down market.

Constellation, a typical aggressive fund, had total assets of $112 million on December 31, 1984. Average portfolio turnover was about 100 percent and its annual return was 29.0 percent for the five-year period 1979–1983, with a *beta* coefficient of 1.78 in 1984.

Another aggressive fund is Hartwell Leverage, which held $10.4 million in assets at December 31, 1984. The fund had a *beta* of 1.67 and went up and down twice as far as the market during the 1981–83 bull and bear markets shown on

TABLE 4-4
**Performance in Up and Down Markets.**

| Fund Type | Fund Name | Bull Up Market (%) 8/14/82–8/13/83 | Bear Down Market (%) 8/14/81–8/13/82 | Beta |
|---|---|---|---|---|
| Aggressive growth | Constellation | 151.7 | −42.8 | 1.78 |
| Aggressive growth | Hartwell Leverage | 130.8 | −34.0 | 1.67 |
| Aggressive growth | Explorer | 106.6 | −17.5 | 1.15 |
| Growth | 20th Century Select | 105.5 | −16.0 | 1.09 |
| Growth | Nicholas | 76.6 | −8.5 | 0.86 |
| Growth and income | Windsor | 61.8 | −10.2 | 0.82 |
| Income and growth | Lindner | 49.1 | 7.7 | 0.48 |
| S&P 500 with dividends reinvested | | 62.9 | −16.6 | 1.00 |

Table 4-4. Its annual return was 30.0 percent during the five-year period 1979-1983.

Aggressive funds generally do not perform well during "sideways" markets where the S&P 500 stays relatively constant or fluctuates narrowly about a constant level. During 1984's sideways market when the S&P 500 grew by 6 percent, Constellation was down 15.3 percent while Hartwell Leverage was down 31.9 percent.

Some aggressive funds invest heavily in smaller, emerging or high technology firms. While these firms have the ability to grow rapidly, they also can fail rapidly. An example of a fund that invests in emerging smaller firms is the Explorer fund which has 87 percent of its portfolio in small firms. It outperformed the market in the 1982-1983 up market and was able to just match the markets decline in the 1981-1982 down market. (See Table 4-4.) However, Explorer declined 19.5 percent during 1984's sideways market, when the market increased 6 percent.

Some analysts believe that there is a tendency of the common stocks of small firms to earn greater rates of return on a risk-adjusted basis than those of large firms. In other words, according to this theory, the returns generated by well-diversified portfolios of small-firm common stocks should be greater than what can be *explained by the additional non-diversifiable risk inherent in such portfolios*. Theory aside, these stocks are obviously appealing to aggressive growth fund managers.

Aggressive funds are good for investors who can accommodate their extreme volatility and who can hold them for the long-term. This, of course, means riding out market down turns.

## GROWTH AND INCOME FUNDS

The objective of *growth and income* funds is to provide both income and long-term growth of capital from investments in high-yielding common and preferred stocks. Growth and income fund portfolios include seasoned, well-established firms that pay relatively high cash dividends. The goal is to provide long-term growth without excessive volatility in share price. Their portfolios usually include a significant portion of public utility common stocks and convertible preferred stocks.

During the eleven-year period 1974–1984, growth and income funds returned 12.5 percent a year compared to 11.0 percent for growth funds and 14.4 percent for aggressive growth funds.

Another form of growth and income fund, often called a *balanced fund*, combines both common stocks and bonds in a single portfolio to yield capital appreciation as well as income. These funds also are referred to as *total return funds*.

The performance of several growth and income funds is shown in Table 4–5. One of these, Evergreen Total Return fund, purchases convertible bonds and preferred stocks in addition to common stocks. For the five years ending December 1983, the fund had an annual return of 21.0 percent.

TABLE 4–5
**Growth and Income Funds.**

|  | 1984 Yield (%) | Return (%) 1983 | Return (%) 1984 | Beta |
|---|---|---|---|---|
| T. Rowe Price Growth & Income (GI) | 6.6 | 32.4 | 2.1 | 0.80 |
| Fidelity Equity Income (B) | 6.4 | 29.1 | 10.6 | 0.82 |
| Evergreen Total Return (B) | 1.5 | 29.0 | 11.9 | 0.85 |
| Lindner (IG) | 5.9 | 24.4 | 12.9 | 0.48 |

GI = Growth and Income; B = Balanced; IG = Income with Growth.

Fidelity Equity Income fund had a yield of 6.4 percent at the end of 1983 and had an annual return of 24.9 percent over the five-year period 1979-1983. Fidelity Equity Income holds convertible bonds and dividend yielding stocks.

## INCOME AND BOND FUNDS

*Income funds* seek high current income from investments in bonds and other high-yielding securities. *Bond funds* invest primarily in bonds and stress high income. The only distinction between income funds and bond funds is that bond funds restrict their investments to bonds only, while income funds include other securities as well.

Bond funds traditionally are held by investors who require high current yields and low risk. *Corporate bond funds* have portfolios consisting primarily of bonds issued by corporations. *Municipal bond funds* invest in a broad range of tax-exempt bonds issued by states, cities and other local governments. The interest paid on these bonds is passed through to shareholders free of federal tax. The fund's primary objective is current tax-free income.

Investors in bond funds or income funds holding bonds are subject to interest rate risk caused by interest rate changes. Consider an example of a bond with a current yield of 10 percent with ten years to maturity. If interest rates rise by 40 percent, the percentage change in the bond price would be $-21$ percent so as to produce the same yield as a new bond over the ten year period. If interest rates fell by 40 percent, the bond's value would increase by 29 percent. It is interest rate fluctuations that cause bond fund prices to rise and fall. Generally, we can approximate the change in the bond price from a change in interest rates by the equation:

$$\Delta P = \frac{-M \times \Delta I \times CY}{150} \qquad (4\text{-}1)$$

where $\Delta P$ = percentage change in the bond price, M = years to maturity, $\Delta I$ = percentage change in interest rates (up or down) and CY = current yield in percent.

Thus, if a bond maturing in ten years that currently yields 10 percent experiences a market interest rate drop of 40 percent, we have

$$\Delta P = \frac{-5 \times -40 \times 10}{150} \quad (4\text{--}2)$$

$$= +13\%$$

Consider the T. Rowe Price New Income Bond Fund with an average portfolio maturity of five years. The fund yielded 11 percent in dividends for 1984 and its net asset value changed only 0.7 percent over the year. It shows that the relatively short maturity of its portfolio protects this fund from interest rate changes.

The Vanguard High Yield Fund had a current yield of 14.4 percent during 1984 and an average portfolio maturity of 15 years. This fund experienced a volatility in its net asset value of – 6 percent in 1984.

Bond funds can invest in (1) corporate bonds, (2) government issued bonds, and (3) "junk bonds," that is, the high-yielding, high-risk bonds issued by some companies. Table 4–6 gives the five-year average return for the three categories of bond funds for the five years ending in 1984.

With the advent of relatively high real (inflation adjusted) interest rates after 1982, bond and income funds have become attractive. *As long as inflation stays at or below 5 percent and the real interest rate of a longer term bond exceeds 6 percent, these funds will attract a sizable share of the investor's dollar.*

Municipal bond funds—there are over 40 municipal bond funds currently available—are popular with individual investors. Since these fund yields are free from federal taxes, their average yields of 7 to 10 percent a year are very attractive.

If you are in the 34 percent federal tax bracket, a 9 percent yield on a tax free fund is equivalent to a 13.6 percent taxable yield. The performance of several municipal bond funds is given in Table 4–7 and a more detailed discussion of the tax consequences of investing in mutual funds is in Chapter 9.

**TABLE 4–6**
**Average Returns for Bond Funds for the Five-Year Period Ending December 1984.**

|  | Five-Year Return (%) | Annual Return (%) |
|---|---|---|
| U.S. government bond funds | 68.6 | 11.0 |
| Corporate bond funds |  |  |
|   A rated | 72.5 | 11.5 |
| High yield junk bond funds | 78.9 | 12.3 |

*Source: Fortune,* April 29, 1985, pg. 337

**TABLE 4–7**
**Long Term Municipal Bond Funds.**

|  | % Change in NAV 1983 | 1984 | April 1985 Yield (%) |
|---|---|---|---|
| Fidelity High Yield | 12.3 | 9.3 | 9.3 |
| T. Rowe Price Tax Free | 7.0 | 6.9 | 7.9 |
| Scudder Managed Municipals | 9.3 | 9.5 | 8.8 |
| Vanguard High Yield | 10.1 | 9.1 | 9.6 |

Many investors in income tax brackets high enough to find tax-free investments attractive also are opting for added safety. Although they didn't exist a few years ago low-risk, short-term municipal bond funds are the third largest of all mutual fund categories, and at the time of this writing have reached $34 billion in assets.

## MONEY MARKET FUNDS

A very important innovation for the investment industry has been the development of money market funds. *Money market funds* invest in short-term securities such as treasury bills, certificates of deposit, commercial paper and other money market instruments.

Since money market fund portfolios are entirely invested in short-term obligations, with average maturities usually less than 60 days, the shares of money market funds are very liquid and can be readily withdrawn by the investor and converted into cash with little risk of loss. Upon redemption, an investor receives the amount invested plus any dividends that have accrued in the account.

In addition to offering yields and liquidity, many money market mutual funds offer checking account-like services, allowing investors to write drafts against their investment accounts.

The seven-day annualized yields of money market funds are listed in Monday's *Wall Street Journal* and in *Barron's* as well as in many local newspapers.

During recent years, an entirely new type of money market fund has emerged: *tax-free money funds*. These funds combine the features of municipal bond funds with those of money market funds. Tax-free money funds invest exclusively in municipal bonds that are close to maturity, typically having only two to four months of remaining life, and in various types of short-term municipal notes. Excellent tax-

FIGURE 4–4
**The Average Yield and Total Assets of Money Market Funds for 1983 to March 1985**

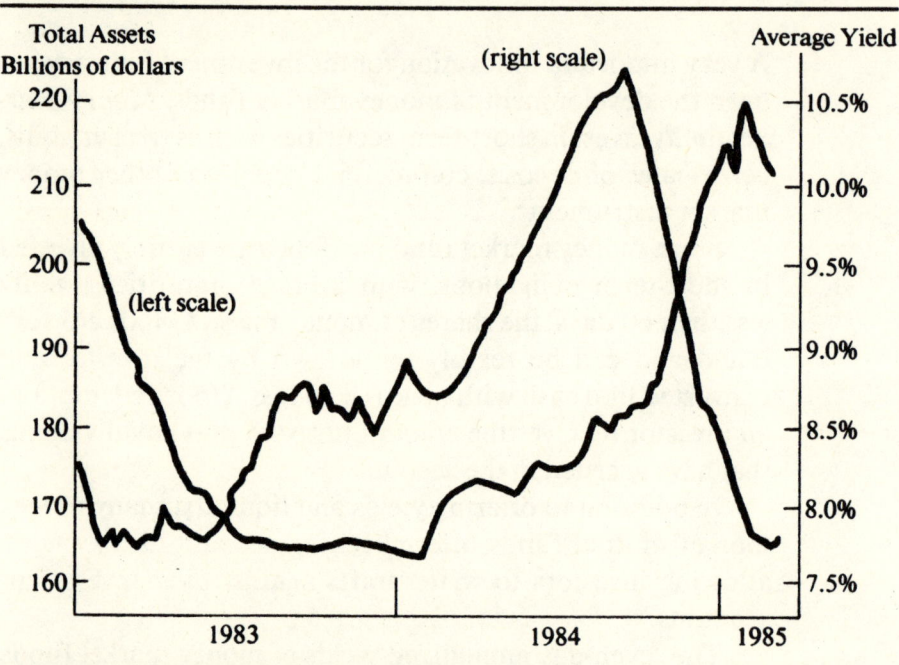

Source: Merrill Lynch Market Letter, March 4, 1985

free money funds are available from Dean Witter, Lehman, T. Rowe Price, and Vanguard. If an investor seeks extra secure yields and safety of principal, he or she can invest in money market funds that are made up entirely of short-term government securities.

Money market funds have grown from the first fund in 1971 to 230 funds by 1985, which together hold over $240 billion in assets. Total assets and average yields of money market funds are shown in Figure 4–4. Since money market fund risk is essentially negligible, you should look for a fund that offers a high, consistent yield. If you are investing in a family of funds, be sure to take their money market fund into account. Consistent yielding funds are offered by the Vanguard, T. Rowe Price, and the Kemper family of funds.

Examples of yields for several money-market, municipal money market and government securities money market funds are shown in Table 4–8. When comparing tax-free

TABLE 4–8
**Yields for Money Market Funds.**

| Type | Name | As of 2/28/85 1-Year Yield (%) | 3/19/85 30-Day Yield (%) | Assets (Millions $) |
|---|---|---|---|---|
| Money market | Kemper | 10.42 | 8.05 | 4,927 |
| Money market | Vanguard Prime | 10.38 | 8.31 | 1,703 |
| Tax free | Vanguard Municipal | 5.99 | 5.15 | 578 |
| Tax free | Calvert | 6.04 | 5.58 | 272 |
| Government only | Vanguard Federal | 10.03 | 8.17 | 498 |
| Government only | Shearson Government | 9.99 | 8.38 | 1,389 |

yields to taxable yields keep in mind that if you were in the 40 percent tax bracket, a tax-free yield of 6 percent would be equal to a taxable yield of 10 percent. Also note that the yields of the government funds are slightly below those of the regular money funds, but do not carry significantly less risk. An investor must decide whether the added security afforded by the government securities funds is worth a decrease in yield of almost one-half of one percent.

## SPECIALTY FUNDS

### Specialized Common Stock Funds

A *specialized common stock fund* seeks to achieve its objective by concentrating its holdings in a single industry or group of related industries, in a single geographical region, or in companies that have some common characteristic. These funds usually invest in the common stocks of high-quality companies that offer unique investment opportunities. Long-term capital growth is a common objective, although current dividend income is also sought. Specialty industries like electronics, gold, chemicals, and the health field are popular candidates for specialty funds.

For the twelve-month period ending March 31, 1985, several specialty funds had superior performance. Energy and Utility Fund and Fidelity Utilities both had twelve-month returns of 33.3 percent. Fidelity, in fact, offers a group of specialty funds that for the twelve-month period ending March 31, 1985 managed to place three funds in the top twenty performers: Utility (33.3 percent return), Financial Services (28.0 percent) and Health Care (27.5 percent). In addition, during that same twelve-month period, Century Shares Trust, which holds shares in insurance companies, gained 28.0 percent.

One must recognize that investing in a single industry involves unsystematic (*alpha*) risk that can be avoided with broader diversification. However, there are times when you may want to target your investments to a particular industry—perhaps one that you perceive as currently undervalued.

*Sector funds*, a form of specialty mutual funds, offer investors the opportunity to own portfolios concentrated in various segments of the stock market. Unlike well diversified funds that embrace many different industries, these funds focus on areas of the stock market that tend to be very active. If you think energy, technology or health stocks are ready for gains, this is a convenient way to buy that sector of the market and obtain a diversified, working portfolio of stocks that will benefit if that sector moves. If your hunch proves correct, the potential rewards can be great.

During periods of stagnant overall stock market activity, specific sectors within the market will still perform well. If you can choose the right sector fund, you can gain while the rest of the market is stalled. And, by using a family of specialized funds you can try to anticipate when market leadership begins to rotate from one sector to another and then switch to the more promising sector fund.

An investor can obtain sector funds that specialize in technology issues, utilities, banks, insurance companies, defense and aerospace firms, leisure and entertainment stocks, medical technology, government securities, regions of the United States and financial services.

Families of specialty funds are offered by Fidelity, Vanguard and Financial Programs. As discussed above, sector investing can be an attractive strategy. But because they carry somewhat higher risk, and require more involvement on your part, it may be best to allocate only a portion of your investments to these funds. My suggestion is no more than 10 percent.

Another way in which funds can specialize is by selecting stocks whose common characteristics are defined by how the market as a whole currently views those stocks, and whose characteristics place those stock under the general rubric of "special situations." For example, the Mutual Shares Fund specializes in stocks that are currently out of favor; that is, companies and firms involved in prospective mergers, consolidations, liquidations and reorganizations under the bankruptcy laws. The portfolio turnover of this fund was 70 percent in 1983 and 101 percent in 1984 and it grew at an 18 percent annual rate during the period 1980–1984.

About 30 percent of the $500 million portfolio of Mutual Shares is aggressively positioned in companies that are bankrupt, are in deep financial trouble or are about to be acquired. Because of the vast amount of research required to find these situations most investors could not engage in this type of specialized investing on their own and thus can benefit from a fund that does.

The final specialized stock funds we will consider are *index funds* whose objective is to duplicate the composite performance of the S&P 500 index. The returns of these funds match the S&P index and offer a *beta* coefficient of 1.00, which is equal to the market. If you accept the efficient market theory as we discussed in Chapter 1, then index funds will perform just as well as any of the other funds over the long term. One index fund is managed by the Vanguard group. Vanguard Index grew 110.4 percent over the five-year period 1979–1983 for an annual gain of 16.1 percent.

## Option, Commodity and Convertible Funds

Another group of specialty funds are those that write options against their stock positions to try to increase their yields. Some even trade options seeking capital gains. An *option fund* generally does well when the trend of the stock market is steady. During wavering years such as 1984, option funds perform less well. Option trading, of course, entails risks to match its rewards. If an option's underlying shares move in the wrong direction, the option holder ends up with nothing. Needless to say, using options aggressively requires a high level of expertise.

*Option income funds* "write" options—that is, they create and sell new options, as opposed to buying or selling them in the secondary market. One fund, Gateway Option, returned 13.5 percent during 1983, but only 3.6 percent in 1984. Over the period 1979 to 1983 it grew at an annual rate of 11.1 percent. In March 1985, Gateway changed its investment objective from trading listed stock options to trading S&P 100 Index Option contracts. The fund, which now has about $22 million in assets, uses the S&P 100 Index because its options are more heavily traded and have a much broader market than S&P 500 index options.

A *futures* or *commodity fund* is much like a stock mutual fund, except that it speculates solely in futures contracts. A futures contract gives its owner the opportunity to buy or sell a commodity, financial instrument or stock index contract at a specific price on a specific date in the future. The investor pays a price determined by open-market bidding prior to the settlement date. Many of the newest futures funds specialize in financial or cash type contracts, such as Treasury bond and stock index futures.

If an individual investor wishes to invest in commodities, he or she is advised to do so through a fund where losses are limited to the amount of the investment. Commodity funds, like option funds, do well when a clear, consistent trend is established in the market. Several commodity funds are sponsored by brokerage firms such as Thomson, McKinnon; A. G. Edwards; Paine Webber, and Prudential Bache. For the 1984 year, Thomson Financial Futures gained 70 percent while Prudential Bache Chancellor Futures declined 22 percent. This indicates, to some extent, how performance can differ among commodity funds during the same market.

Several specialty funds invest solely in *convertible securi-*

*ties*. Convertibles are hybrid securities. They are bonds or preferred stocks that can be exchanged for a specified number of a company's common shares. Convertibles offer many of the benefits of fixed-income securities, but still allow an investor to participate in any stock market advances through either conversion or appreciation of the bonds' aftermarket trading value. Yields on convertibles are usually higher and more predictable than those on common stocks and are made in the form of coupon interest or preferred dividends, which take precedence over common stock dividends. The prices of convertible issues also are less volatile than those of common stocks.

## Mortgage Funds

Funds recently have been established to invest in *real estate mortgage securities*. Most of these funds invest primarily in residential mortgage-backed securities, including obligations of the Government National Mortgage Association (Ginnie Maes), Federal National Mortgage Association (Fannie Maes), Federal Home Loan Mortgage Corp. (Freddie Macs) and various types of other mortgage securities, such as collateralized mortgage obligations (CMOs) and debt instruments secured by mortgages on residential property or commercial real estate.

Funds investing in mortgage-backed securities are attractive because they have higher yields and generally are of higher quality than other investments with similar returns. They also often offer yields comparable to those of long-term corporate bonds, but have the stability of bonds with much shorter maturities.

The greatest interest in the mid-1980's is in funds that specialize in investing in Government National Mortgage Association securities (GNMA), or Ginnie Maes, as they are referred to on Wall Street. These securities are packages of government-insured mortgages that are packaged or put together by lenders, such as banks or savings institutions and then sold to institutional or private investors in individual units. GNMA payments of principal and interest are guaranteed by the federal government.

GNMA funds, like bonds and other instruments, are subject to interest rate fluctuations. Although the average life of a Ginnie Mae mortgage is twelve years, it can vary depending on interest rates. If interest rates go up, homeowners tend to hang on to their low cost mortgages and the Ginnie Mae will fall in value. If interest rates fall, homeowners refinance to take advantage of lower rates, accelerating the maturity of the funds. GNMA funds are offered by the Fidelity, Vanguard, Kemper, and Twentieth Century fund families. In mid-1985 Ginnie Maes were offering returns above 12 percent—more than four percentage points greater than the returns on money-market funds. The Vanguard GNMA fund, a typical GNMA fund, returned 11 percent for all of 1984, ending the year with $280 million in assets.

## Government Securities Funds

It is the remarkable growth of *government securities funds* that provides the most up-to-date spotlight on investor preferences. Up from hardly anything a year ago to $12 billion in May 1985, their growth has been associated with the unusually high yields they offer. As their prospectuses clearly state, the value of their shares fluctuates directly with changes in interest rates. But it is clearly the secure feeling of having the U.S. Government stand behind these securities that has transformed them into mass market investment vehicles.

In March 1985, the Franklin U.S. Government Securities Fund, with $3.5 billion in assets, became the largest long-term mutual fund of all with more assets than any common stock or bond fund. Only a few money market funds are bigger. What's truly amazing is that it reached this level in only two years, growing from a modest $11 million in 1983.

### Tax-Managed Funds

Another form of specialized fund is the *tax-managed fund* which reinvests all of its income, pays no dividends or distributions and, therefore, is taxed on its earnings like a regular corporation. The basic objective of the tax-managed fund is to realize losses immediately while postponing the realization of gains. The advantage to the fund owner is that he will not have to pay any taxes until he sells his shares for a capital gain at a later date, such as at retirement. An example of a tax managed fund is Copley Tax Managed Fund of Fall River, Massachusetts. For the five-year period 1980 through 1984, the fund grew a total of 100 percent for an annualized return of 15 percent.

## GOLD FUNDS

*Gold funds* invest primarily in shares of gold or other mineral producing firms and sometimes directly in gold bullion. Purchased with care, they can provide excellent growth when other funds are faltering, since their growth and decline cycles are often opposite to those of the stock market. Gold funds generally increase when inflation heats up and serve as an excellent hedge against inflation. This effect is illustrated by Figure 4-5 which shows how both inflation and gold prices grew rapidly from 1975 to 1980, with both peaking in early 1980.

United Services Gold Shares is a fund that invests in firms that mine and sell gold. This fund is quite volatile as Figure 4-6 illustrates. Note the rapid rise in 1979 resulting in its late 1980 peak. The fund returned 488.4 percent over the

# FIGURE 4–5
## U.S. Price Inflation and London Gold Prices

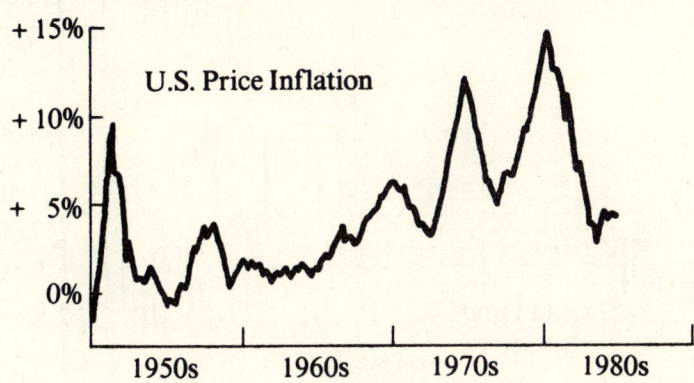

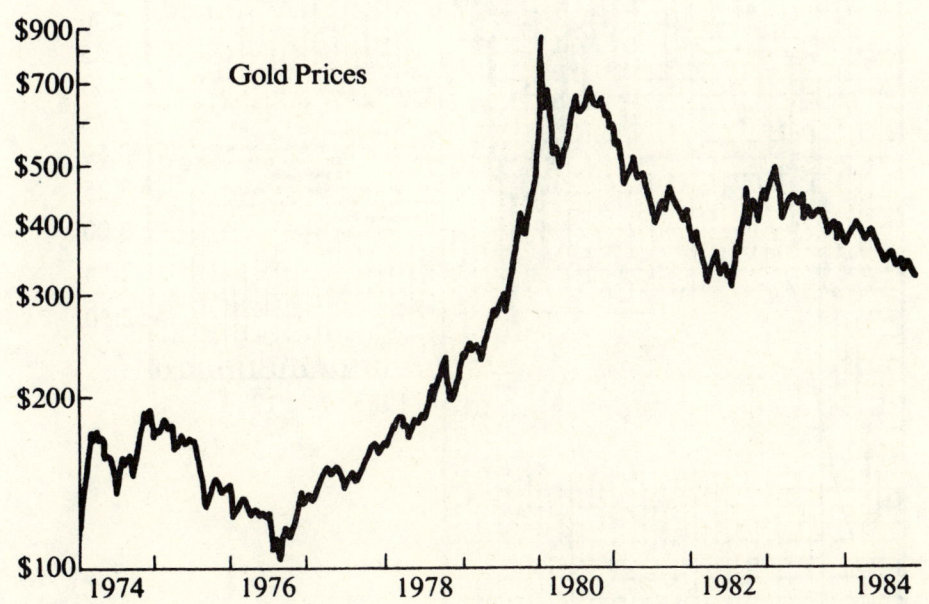

## FIGURE 4-6
**United Services Gold Shares for the Period 1979 to April 1985**

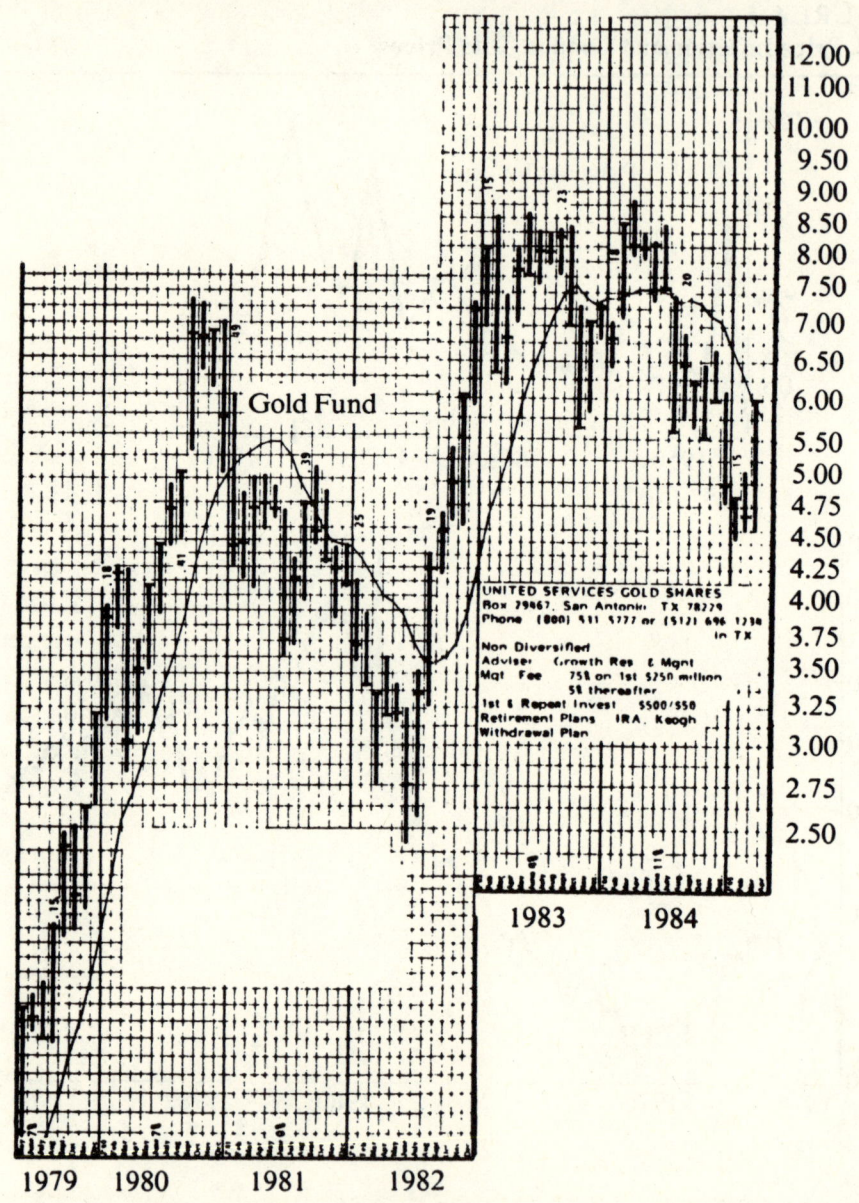

five-year period 1979–1983 for an annual return of 42.5 percent. However, it declined 28.5 percent in 1984, a period of low inflation. If you believe that high inflation will return in the late 1980s, it may be prudent to purchase shares in a gold fund. Table 4–9 shows the *beta* coefficients and 1983 and 1984 returns for two gold funds, United States Gold and Franklin Gold Fund, and average returns for all gold funds as a whole for those same two years.

## INTERNATIONAL FUNDS

*International funds* invest in the stocks of firms listed on stock markets in countries and regions outside the United States. It is wise to consider investing abroad since different economies experience intervals of prosperity and recession at different times. In the past, foreign markets have had periods where they have outperformed the U.S. market. The Japanese economy, for example, grew twice as fast as the American economy from 1953 to 1983. Another factor to consider is the value of the U.S. dollar relative to the currencies of other countries. As the dollar's value declines, the returns from international funds improve. Some funds such as Price International or Scudder International invest in

**TABLE 4–9**
**Gold Funds**

|  | Return (%) 1983 | 1984 | Beta | Assets (Millions $) |
|---|---|---|---|---|
| Gold Funds (average) | 1.0 | –27.0 | - | - |
| United Services Gold | 1.5 | –28.5 | 1.24 | 409 |
| Franklin Gold Fund | 8.8 | –24.0 | 1.09 | 130 |

TABLE 4-10
**International Funds**

|  | Return (%) 1983 | Return (%) 1984 | Beta | Assets (Millions $) |
|---|---|---|---|---|
| G. T. Pacific | 33.5 | -2.7 | .50 | 46 |
| Scudder International | -29.0 | -3.8 | .56 | 184 |
| T. Rowe International | 28.0 | -5.7 | .61 | 180 |

many regions, whereas others invest exclusively in one geographic area, such as G. T. Pacific which invests only in the Far East. For the five-year period 1980–1984, G. T. Pacific grew 68.2 percent for an annual gain of 11 percent. The fund holds stocks from Japan, Australia, Hong Kong, Singapore and Malaysia. The 1983 and 1984 annual returns for G. T. Pacific and two other international funds are shown in Table 4–10. Note that 1984 was a difficult year for international funds as the dollar strengthened against other currencies. Unfortunately, the strong U.S. dollar means that even when foreign stock markets do well, in terms of their own currencies, the good performances often do not compensate for the weakness of the local currency relative to the dollar. The widely-followed EAFE (Europe, Australia, Far East) market index was up 21.8 percent for 1984, which, however, translated into a much smaller 8.1 percent increase in U.S. dollar terms.

Risk and return performance for selected foreign stock markets for the five-year period ended September 30, 1983 is given on Figure 4–7. It shows that the U.S. stock market was less volatile during the period than the other markets shown. As the U.S. economic recovery moves overseas and the dollar begins to decline in value over the next couple of years, we can expect a significant increase in the value of international funds.

**FIGURE 4-7**
**The Risk and Return for International Stock Markets for the Five-Year Period Ending September 30, 1983**

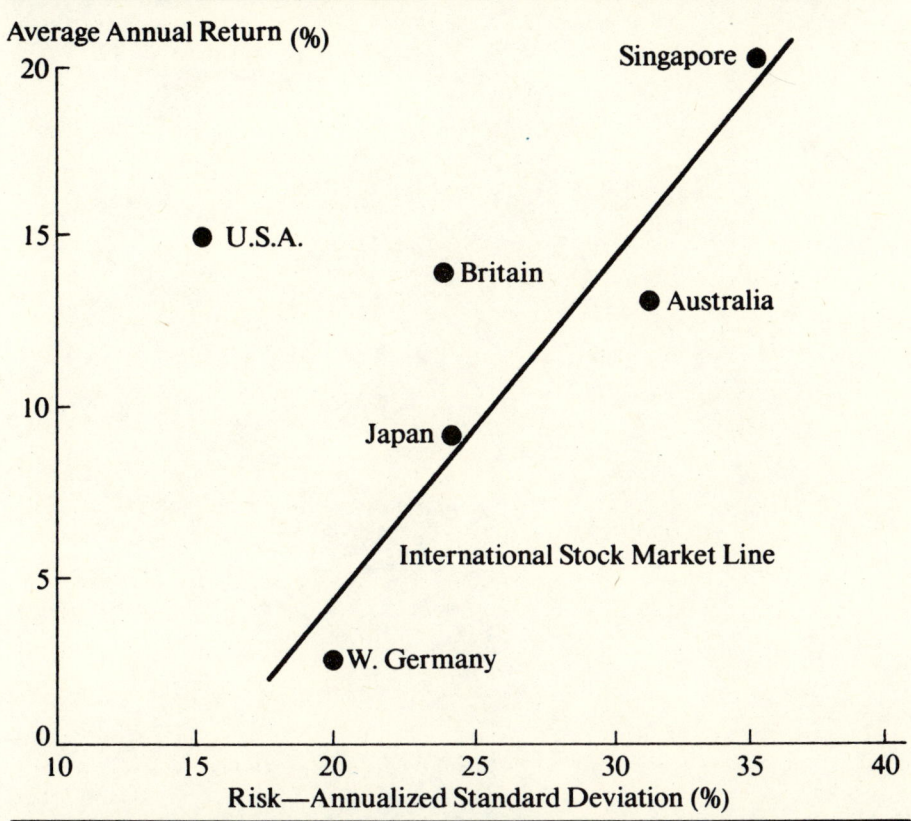

Source: The Economist, December 24, 1983, pg. 91

# Chapter 5

# Fund Performance

## INTRODUCTION

This chapter contains several calculations and equations with which you should familiarize yourself. Where the mathematics are less than obvious, I have tried to explain their purpose and sense in more understandable terms. However, if you are serious about your investments—as I assume you are—following the mathematics and carefully studying this chapter is strongly urged. The concepts presented here will enable you to better understand the relationship between investment risk and return. The calculations that I present are reported by many of the magazines, newsletters, annuals and technical reporting services that regularly track mutual fund performance—so at the very least, this chapter will enable you to better understand their reports. If you are the "independent–do–it–yourself type," a good business calculator or a microcomputer statistical software package is all you need to perform the necessary calculations. I suggest that you solve the equations as you read along using the sample data (or use your own data if you prefer).

## MODERN PORTFOLIO THEORY AND FUND INVESTING

Modern Portfolio Theory (MPT) provides a method of diversification that allows an investor to select the portfolio, or fund, that will produce the best return commensurate with the risk assumed. MPT assumes that:

1. the market is efficient;
2. investors are risk-averse;
3. investors prefer a higher rate of return; and
4. investors seek to maximize return while reducing risk for a given level of return.

Risk, as discussed in Chapter 1, is the variability of the rate of return and is measured by the standard deviation, the *beta* coefficient and *alpha*.

MPT assumes that investors try to minimize risk by minimizing deviations from their expected returns on an investment, and that this is done by means of portfolio diversification. It has been found that the standard deviation is reduced to acceptable levels when ten securities are assembled, and that fifteen securities reduce the standard deviation to ten percent, after which the standard deviation would decline very slightly with the addition of other securities. This suggests that a portfolio must have a minimum of ten securities to reduce its risk to the level of the market's risk, that fifteen securities in a portfolio would be optimum, and that, for large funds, no more than 25 to 35 issues would be necessary or make much of a difference.

We recall from Chapter 1 that *beta*, represents the systematic risk of a mutual fund's performance relative to the market's. And, *alpha*, represents the unsystematic risk of the market. If the systematic risk, as measured by *beta*, is higher than 1.00, the fund's returns are more volatile or riskier than the market's. Conversely, if *beta* is lower than 1.00, the fund is less risky than the market. If the market is expected to rise, then a high *beta* is desirable. If it is expected to fall, then a *beta* of less than one is desired. If *alpha* is positive, the fund performs better than expected given the market's performance. If it is negative, its performance is below expectations.

It is usually not possible to target a fund's *alpha* or *beta* coefficient once and for always. Some fund managers like to change market exposure periodically in attempts at improving market timing. Nevertheless, past risk exposure as indicated by a fund's *beta* and *alpha* seems to be a better guide to future risk exposure than the rather general statements found in a fund's prospectus.

*Alpha* is a somewhat more complex concept than the *beta* coefficient. It is a numerical statement of how well a fund has been doing, given its *beta*. A positive *alpha* is always desired. Thus, a fund with an *alpha* of zero is performing exactly as expected, and one with an *alpha* that is a negative number is doing less than might be expected. A positive alpha (say, 5.0) indicates that a fund has competent management, since it means that the fund has, in the past at least, performed 5.0 percent a year better on average than was warranted by the portfolio's characteristic volatility relative to the market.

## PERFORMANCE CALCULATIONS

The basic equation for measuring total return, R, for a stock or fund share price for a given period is:

$$R = \frac{P_1 - P_0 + D}{P_0} \times 100 \tag{5-1}$$

where $P_0$ is the price at the beginning of the period, $P_1$ is the price at the end of the period, and D represents the dividends paid during the period. If the price of a stock at the beginning of a year was $P_0 = \$100$ and at the end of the year $P_1 = \$111$ and the dividends paid during the year totaled $D = \$3$, then

$$R = \frac{111 - 100 + 3}{100} \times 100 = \frac{14}{100} \times 100 = 14 \qquad (5\text{-}2)$$

Thus the return for the year is 14 percent.

To calculate the return for a period of n years, we use the equation

$$P_0 = \frac{D_1}{(1+R)} + \frac{D_2}{(1+R)^2} + \cdots + \frac{D_n + P_n}{(1+R)^n} \qquad (5\text{-}3)$$

and solve iteratively for R. For example, for a three-year period where $P_3 = \$125$, $P_0 = \$100$ and $D_1$, $D_2$ and $D_3$ each equal \$3, then

$$P_0 = \frac{D_1}{(1+R)} + \frac{D_2}{(1+R)^2} + \frac{D_3 + P_n}{(1+R)^3} \qquad (5\text{-}4)$$

or

$$100 = \frac{3}{(1+R)} + \frac{3}{(1+R)^2} + \frac{3 + 125}{(1+R)^3}$$

After trying a few values for R, it is found that R, or the return, is 10.5 percent annually.

In a similar manner and, as we saw earlier, the performance of a fund is indicated by its annual percent return for a given year, which is represented as

$$R(i) = \frac{\text{Final NAV} + \text{distributions} - \text{initial NAV}}{\text{initial NAV}} \times 100 \qquad (5\text{-}5)$$

where NAV is the Net Asset Value.

If we want to find a fund's annual compound rate over a period of n years during which *there were no distributions* and we know what its value was at the start and at the end of the period in question, we would use

$$R = \left[\left(\frac{FV}{IV}\right)^{\frac{1}{n}} - 1\right] 100 \qquad (5\text{-}6)$$

where R = percentage return for a period of n years, FV = future or final value, IV = initial value and n = number

## Fund Performance

of years. The factor 1/n means we solve for the nth root. For example, let us consider a fund that had an initial net asset value of $10.00 and an ending net asset value of $14.00 after five years and there were no distributions made during the period. Then, its compound annual return for the five years was

$$R = \left[\left(\frac{14}{10}\right)^{\frac{1}{5}} - 1\right] 100 = 6.96\% \tag{5-7}$$

Now let us consider a fund that made *distributions each year* which we reinvested in additional shares of the fund. The progression of returns over the five years is shown in Table 5-1. The total return for the five-year period is:

$$R(5 \text{ years}) = R_1 R_2 R_3 R_4 R_5 \tag{5-8}$$

where $R_i = 1 + \frac{R(i)}{100}$ and R(i) is the percentage return for the ith year.

Calculating R(i) for year 2 in Table 5-1, using equation 5-5, we have:

$$R(2) = \frac{(12.50 + 1.50 - 11.00)}{11.00} \times 100 = 27.3\% \tag{5-9}$$

Then,

$$R_2 = 1 + \frac{27.3}{100} = 1.27.$$

**TABLE 5-1**
**Five-Year Return for a Fund**

| Year (i) | 1 | 2 | 3 | 4 | 5 |
|---|---|---|---|---|---|
| Initial NAV($) | 10.00 | 11.00 | 12.50 | 12.00 | 13.00 |
| Final NAV($) | 11.00 | 12.50 | 12.00 | 13.00 | 15.00 |
| Distributions($) | 1.00 | 1.50 | 0.10 | 1.00 | 2.00 |
| Annual return R(i)(%) | 20.00 | 27.30 | -3.20 | 16.70 | 30.80 |
| $R_i$ | 1.200 | 1.273 | 0.968 | 1.167 | 1.308 |

Similarly for the third year, we obtain:

$$R(3) = 100 \frac{(12.00 + .10 - 12.50)}{12.50} = -3.2\% \qquad (5\text{-}10)$$

Then, $R_3 = .968$. Calculating each annual return $R(i)$ and then obtaining $R_i$, for each year we can calculate R (5 years) from equation 5-8 as

$$R\,(5\text{ Years}) = R_1\, R_2\, R_3\, R_4\, R_5 = 1.200 \times 1.273 \times .968 \times 1.167 \times 1.308 = 2.257 \qquad (5\text{-}11)$$

To find the compound annual return for the five-year period, we use equation 5-7 as follows:

$$R = [(2.257)^{\frac{1}{5}} - 1]\,100 = 17.7\% \qquad (5\text{-}12)$$

If you do not have a calculator that computes nth roots, try multiplying different factors five times until you find the one that comes closest to R (5 years). Using this approach here, we would find that $(1.177)^5 = 2.259$.

The ten-year performance for the Nicholas fund for the years 1975–1984 is shown in Figure 5-1. The fund's initial value was $2.75 and its final value at the end of 1984 was $26 (adjusted for distributions). Applying the above equations, we can determine that FV/IV = 9.45 and its compound annual rate of growth for the 10 years was 25 percent.

(*Note*: When analyzing ten-year performance data, keep in mind that 1974 was a depressed year for most funds and, therefore, growth rates that are calculated using 1975 as the base year probably are overstated. For instance, Vanguard Windsor Fund gained 725 percent for the ten-year period 1975–1984, but only 475 percent for the 1974–1983 period.)

Calculating the *total return* of a bond fund is particularly important, since it is easy to be misled if you focus on just its yield. Consider the two bond funds shown in Table 5-2. Fund A would seem to be attractive due to its higher yield. But because its net asset value declined during the year, it had a total return of only 5.1 percent. Fund B had a lower yield but

## FIGURE 5-1
## The Performance of the Nicholas Fund for the Ten-Year Period 1975–1984

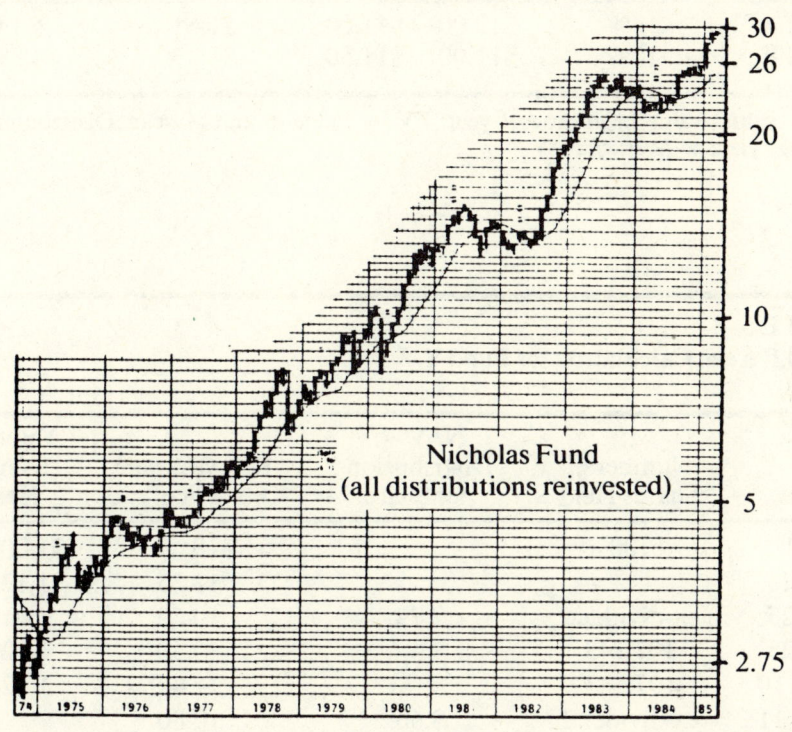

Source: Growth Fund Guide

**TABLE 5-2**
**Comparison of Fund A and Fund B**

| | Bond Fund Average Yield | IV | FV | Distribution | Annual Total Return |
|---|---|---|---|---|---|
| Fund A | 14% | $12.00 | $11.00 | $1.61 | 5.1% |
| Fund B | 10% | $11.00 | $11.50 | $1.13 | 14.8% |

IV = Initial value beginning of year; FV = Value at end of year; Distribution = Average yield × Average NAV

**TABLE 5-3**
**Total Return Calculation for Fund Y.**

| Date | Number of Shares Held | NAV = Distribution per Share | Reinvestment Price | Value of Shares Held |
|---|---|---|---|---|
| Jan. 1 | 100 | | $10.00 | $1,000.00 |
| Feb. 24 | | | 11.25 | 1,125.00 |
| Feb. 25 | ex-dividend | $.75 | 10.50 | |
| Feb. 25* | 107.143 | | 10.50 | 1,125.00 |
| Sept. 10 | 107.143 | | 11.40 | 1,121.43 |
| Sept. 11 | ex-dividend | $.60 | 10.80 | |
| Sept. 11* | 113.095 | | 10.80 | 1,221.43 |
| Dec. 31 | 113.095 | | 11.25 | 1,272.32 |

* = After reinvestment.

it realized a favorable 14.8 percent total annual return for the year.

Let us now see how we can calculate the total return for a fund that issues dividends and capital gains several times a year. Consider the fund in Table 5-3 where the investor held 100 shares valued at $10 a share at the beginning of the year. The fund price rises to $11.25 on February 24 when a distribution is made on February 25 thereby reducing the net asset value by the amount of the distribution. At that point, the fund is said to be ex-dividend. The investor received $75 as his share of the distribution and automatically reinvested in the fund, acquiring an additional 7.143 shares ($75/10.50). The value of his holding was $1,125 on the days both before and after the distribution. He received another distribution on September 11 for $64.29 (107.143 × $.60). And, after again reinvesting that distribution in the fund, he held 113.095 shares worth a total of $1,221.43. By the end of the year, his shares were worth $1,272.32, which provided him with a total return of 27.23 percent for the year on his initial $1000 holding.

## CALCULATING RISK

We have defined *risk* as the possibility of loss of future income. As we discussed earlier, one measure of risk is the standard deviation, which represents the variance of a fund's return around its expected average return over a period of time. The equation for calculating standard deviation is:

$$\sigma = \sqrt{\frac{\sum_{i=1}^{n}(R_i - Raver)^2}{n}} \quad (5\text{-}14)$$

where $\sigma$ = standard deviation, $R_i$ = return for the ith period and Raver = average or mean return for a period of time.

A stock that consistently realized its average return every year would have a standard deviation of zero. Consider the case of the mutual fund listed in Table 5–4. Using equation 5–14, its standard deviation is

$$\sigma = \sqrt{\frac{(.09-.10)^2+(.11-.10)^2+(.10-.10)^2+(.11-.10)^2+(.09-.10)^2}{4}}$$

$$\sigma = \sqrt{\frac{.0004}{4}} = \sqrt{.0001} = .01 \tag{5-15}$$

Therefore, for the sample fund, we see that its average return for the period is 10 percent and its volatility as measured by the standard deviation also is 10 percent, which would be an acceptable level of risk to many investors.

Two other measures of risk we discussed earlier are the *beta* coefficient, b, which can now be redefined as the slope of an investment's market line, and *alpha*, a, which is where the investment's market line intercepts the Y axis. The equation for the market line is

$$E(R) = a + b(R_m - R_f) \tag{5-16}$$

where $E(R)$ is the fund's expected return, $R_m$ is the market's return and $R_f$ is the return of a risk-free security.

Figure 5–2 shows the market line for five years of returns for the sample fund shown in Table 5–5. Using a linear

TABLE 5–4
**The Calculation of Standard Deviation of the Return for a Mutual Fund.**

| Year | Annual Returns | Expected Mean Return | $R_i$ – Raver | $(R_i - \text{Raver})^2$ |
|---|---|---|---|---|
| 1 | .09 | .10 | –.01 | .0001 |
| 2 | .11 | .10 | .01 | .0001 |
| 3 | .10 | .10 | .00 | .0000 |
| 4 | .11 | .10 | .01 | .0001 |
| 5 | .09 | .10 | –.01 | .0001 |

### FIGURE 5–2
**The Fund Return versus the Market Return**

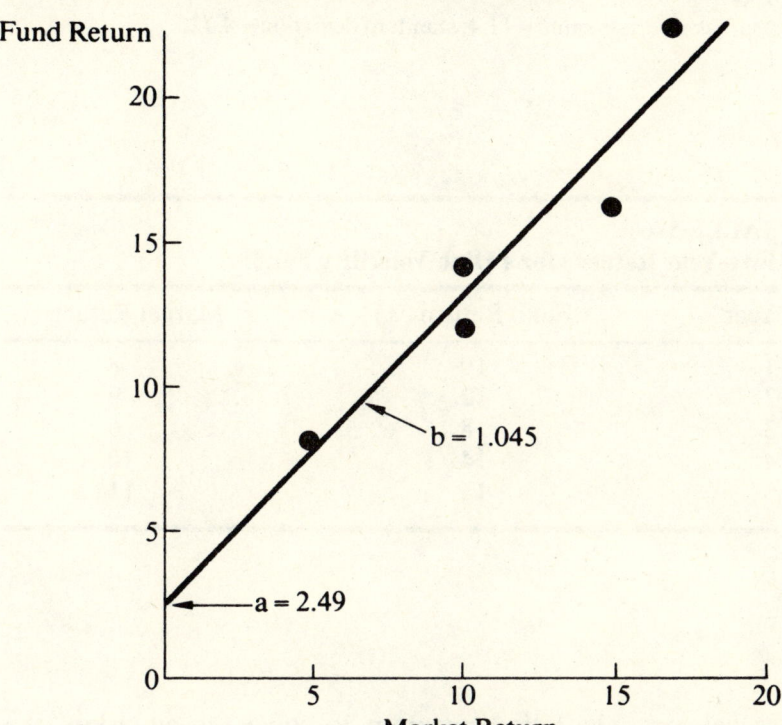

## TABLE 5-5
**The Return for a Fund over a Five-Year Period.**

| Year | 1 | 2 | 3 | 4 | 5 |
|---|---|---|---|---|---|
| Fund return | 22% | 12% | 16% | 8% | 14% |
| Market return | 17% | 10% | 15% | 5% | 10% |

Fund: Average value = 14.4; standard deviation = 5.18; b = 1.045; alpha = 2.49
Market: Average value = 11.4; standard deviation = 4.72

## TABLE 5-6
**Five-Year Returns for a High Volatility Fund.**

| Year | Fund Return (%) | Market Return (%) |
|---|---|---|
| 1 | 10 | 8 |
| 2 | 12 | 9 |
| 3 | 8 | 6 |
| 4 | 14 | 10 |
| 5 | 14 | 11 |

regression calculation program to solve the equation, the fund's *beta* is found to be 1.045. The fund's *alpha*, i.e. its Y intercept, is 2.49.

The five-year returns for a fund with high volatility is shown in Table 5-6. The *beta* for this fund is 1.32, i.e. its volatility was 32 percent higher than the market's. During the five-year period, the fund's return was also 32 percent greater than the market's (11.58 percent versus 8.79 percent). Therefore, for this fund, its higher risk resulted in a proportionally

# FIGURE 5-3
**The Expected Return versus Beta Where $R_f$ = Risk Free and $R_m$ = Market Return**

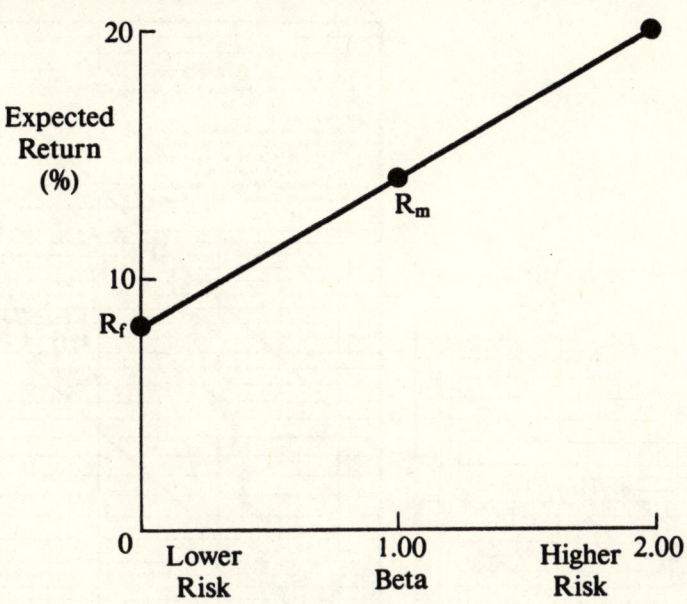

higher return than the market. Ideally, we expect a plot of expected returns and *betas* to appear as shown in Figure 5-3. As the Figure illustrates, when market risk, or *beta* is doubled, so is the expected return.

Another measure of risk for a fund is price volatility over a period of time. It can be calculated for a fund by obtaining an index of its volatility from its chart of prices. Let us consider the charts for the two funds and the New York Stock Exchange Index as shown in Figure 5-4. The New York Stock Exchange Index represents the measure of the market and can be assumed to have a *beta* equal to one. We can then

**FIGURE 5-4**
**Price Charts, including Reinvestments, for NYSE Select Investors and Mutual Shares**

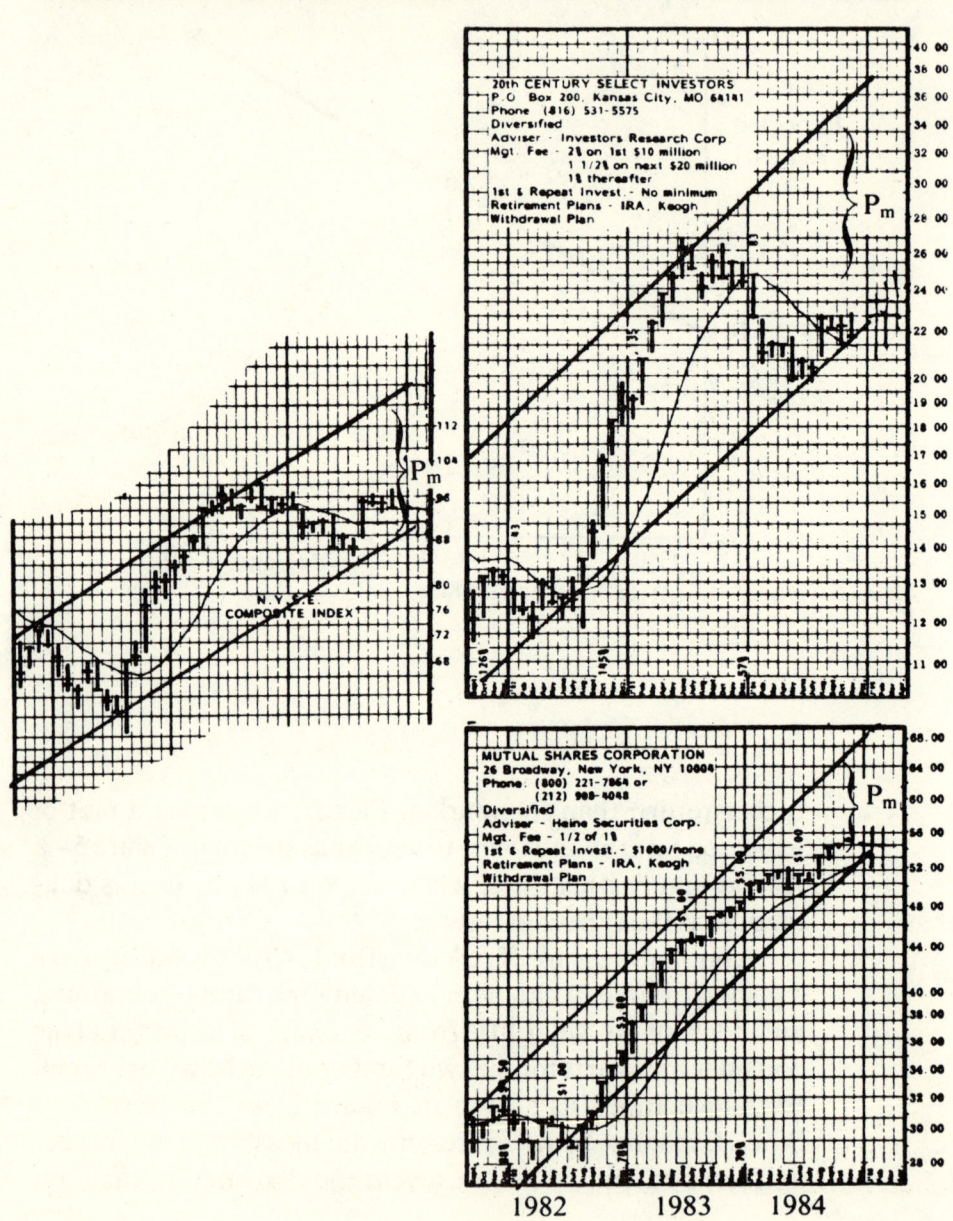

compare the volatility of each fund by calculating its *beta* on the basis of its relative price variation from the market. Using the price charts in Figure 5-4, which are from the Growth Fund Guide, we draw two trend lines for the three-year period. The width of the channel, dP, is then divided by the midchannel price, $P_m$ (the price at the highest point of the mean trend), to obtain the relative volatility V as follows:

$$V = \frac{dP}{P_m} \quad (5\text{-}22)$$

Similarly, calculating V for the market (the NYSE Index in our example), we obtain an approximate measure of the fund's *beta*:

$$b = \frac{V_{fund}}{V_{market}} \quad (5\text{-}23)$$

Using the price charts shown in Figure 5-4 and equations 5-22 and 5-23, we obtain the data shown in Table 5-7. Although these calculations are only approximations, comparing our calculated *beta* of 0.63 for Mutual Shares with its computer calculated *beta* of 0.62, we are quite satisfied with the results. Using our calculations, we learn that although Select and Mutual Shares both had an annual return of 27 percent during the period, the *beta* for Select was twice that for Mutual Shares.

TABLE 5-7
**The Calculation of Relative Volatility for a Mutual Fund**

| Fund or Index | Pm | dP | V | Beta | Return (%) |
|---|---|---|---|---|---|
| NYSE | 104 | 38.0 | .365 | 1.00 | 15 |
| Select Investors | 29 | 14.5 | .500 | 1.37 | 27 |
| Mutual Shares | 60 | 14.0 | .230 | 0.63 | 27 |

## THE RISK ADJUSTED RETURN

The theoretical market line for a fund is shown in Figure 5–5. Its equation becomes

$$E(R) = R_f + b(R_m - R_f) \qquad (5-17)$$

where $R_f$ = risk free return (the return from a Treasury Bill) and $R_m$ = market return (the S&P 500, for example). For the five-year period 1979–1983, $R_f$ was 8.5 percent and $R_m$ was 14.5 percent. The actual annual returns for several funds are also plotted on Figure 5–5. Clearly, some funds performed better than we might have expected from their *betas* and some performed less than expected. For example, T. Rowe Price Growth had a *beta* of 1.00 and, therefore, was expected to perform equal to the market, but it actually returned only 10 percent annually. On the other hand, Mutual Shares actually grew 23 percent annually, almost double its expected return of 12.2 percent based on its *beta* of .62.

Using equation 5–17 on data for the Constellation fund which had a *beta* of 1.8, we can calculate its expected return as

$$E(R) = 8.5 + 1.8(14.5 - 8.5) = 19.3 \qquad (5-18)$$

Since Constellation actually returned 29.0 percent annually during the 1979–83 period, it exceeded its expected return by 9.7 percentage points. The difference between a fund's actual return and its expected return is referred to as its *Risk Premium*.

We calculate the risk premium, RP, where

$$RP = R - E(R) \qquad (5-19)$$

or

$$RP = R - [R_f + b(R_m - R_f)] \qquad (5-20)$$

where R is the actual compounded annual return over the multi-year period.

**FIGURE 5–5**
**Annual Return versus Beta for Several Funds for the Period 1979–1983**

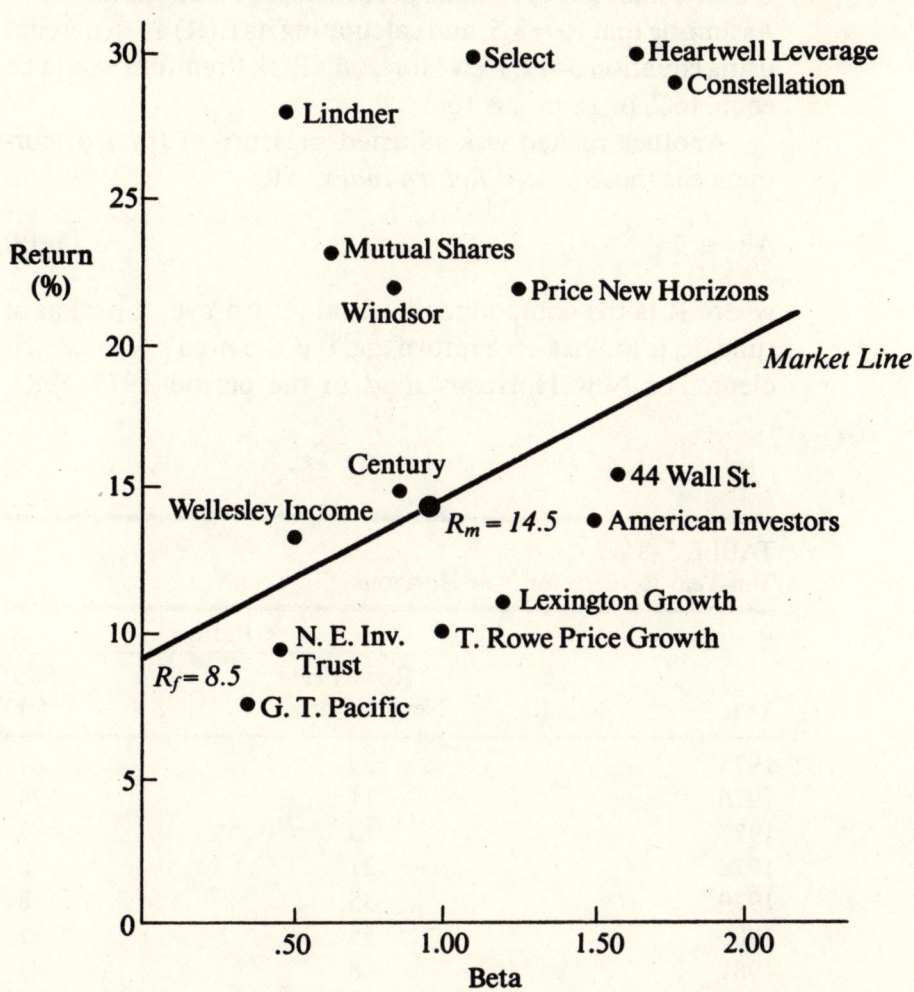

Annual returns for New Horizons fund and the S&P 500 are shown for the ten-year period 1975–1984 in Table 5–8. The New Horizons' ten-year compound return was 18 percent and the market's, 14.4 percent. We would expect the fund to provide a significantly higher rate of return than the market, since its *beta* was 26 percent higher than the market's. Assuming that $R_f = 8.5$, and calculating its $E(R)$ as 16 percent using equation 5–17, New Horizon's Risk Premium would be equal to 2, or 18 minus 16.

Another related risk-adjusted measure of fund performance is the *Adjusted Return Index*, AR,

$$AR = \frac{R - R_f}{b} \qquad (5\text{--}19)$$

where R is the compounded actual return over a period of time, $R_f$ is the risk-free return and b is the fund's *beta* coefficient. For New Horizons fund in the period 1979–1983,

TABLE 5–8
**Ten-Year Returns for New Horizons**

| | % Return | |
| --- | --- | --- |
| Year | T. Rowe Price New Horizons | S&P 500 |
| 1975 | 39 | 37 |
| 1976 | 11 | 24 |
| 1977 | 13 | −7 |
| 1978 | 21 | 6 |
| 1979 | 35 | 18 |
| 1980 | 55 | 31 |
| 1981 | −8 | −5 |
| 1982 | 17 | 20 |
| 1983 | 19 | 22 |
| 1984 | −7 | 6 |

$b = 1.26$, $R_f = 8.5$ percent and $R = 22.0$ percent. Therefore, $AR = 10.7$.

The two risk adjusted performance measures discussed above, the Risk Premium and Adjusted Return Index, are given in Table 5-9 for several funds over the period 1979-1983. They are ranked in descending order by their annual returns. Note, however, that the ranking order would change if we ranked them by one of the risk-adjusted return measures instead of by actual returns. For example, due to Constellation's relatively high level of risk compared to its return, it drops from 3rd down to 4th based on its Risk Premium and to 5th based on its Adjusted Return Index.

The Risk Premium and Adjusted Return Index can be plotted against *beta* as shown in Figure 5-6. The implications of this plot are represented by the regression line which

TABLE 5-9
**Risk Adjusted Performance Measures for the Period 1979-1983.**

| Rank Based on R | Fund | Annual Return R (%) | Beta | RP (%) | AR (%) |
|---|---|---|---|---|---|
| 1 | 20th Century Select | 30.0 | 1.10 | 14.8 | 19.5 |
| 2 | Hartwell Leverage | 30.0 | 1.67 | 11.5 | 12.9 |
| 3 | Constellation | 29.0 | 1.80 | 9.7 | 11.4 |
| 4 | Mutual Shares | 23.0 | 0.62 | 10.8 | 23.4 |
| 5 | Windsor | 22.0 | 0.82 | 8.4 | 16.5 |
| 6 | T. R. Price New Horizons | 22.0 | 1.26 | 6.0 | 10.7 |
| 7 | 44 Wall Street | 15.5 | 1.60 | -2.6 | 4.4 |
| 8 | T. R. Price Growth | 10.0 | 1.00 | -4.5 | 1.5 |

FIGURE 5-6
**Risk Premium and Adjusted Return Index for Selected Funds for the Period 1979–1983**

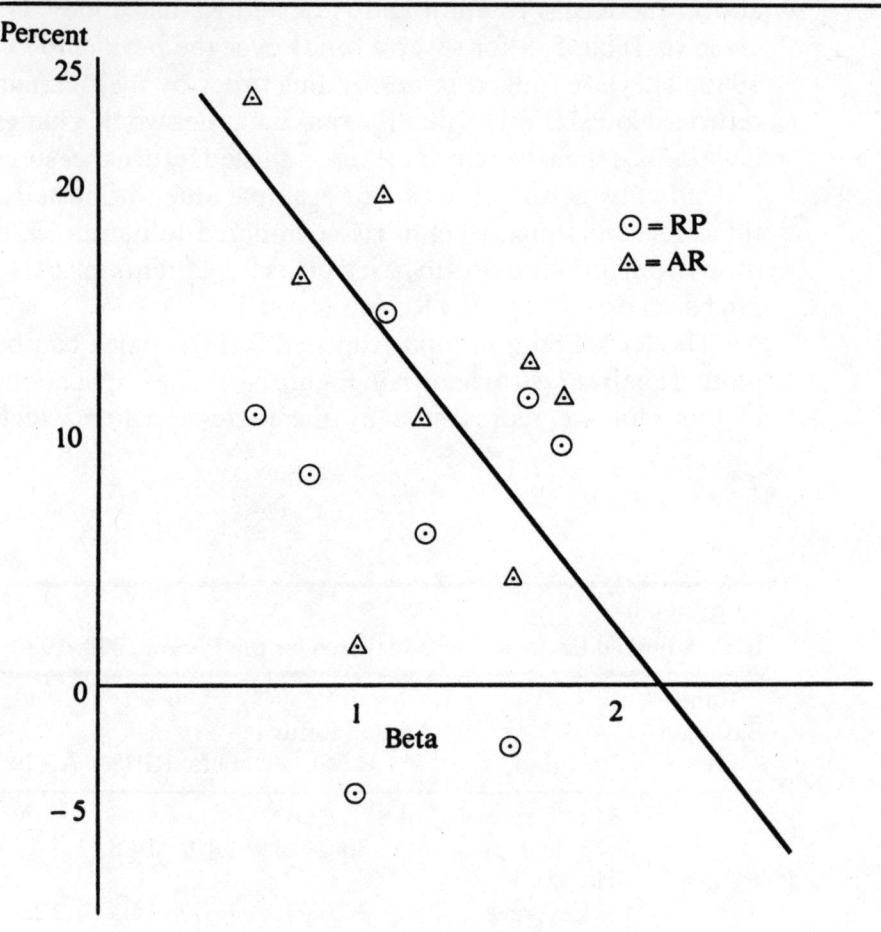

demonstrates how the Risk Premium and Adjusted Return Index decline with increasing *beta*. It suggests that, if you are risk adverse, you should try to select funds with *betas* of between 0.50 to 1.00 that have consistently provided a risk-adjusted return of 15 percent or higher annually. Candidates from Table 5–9 would include the Mutual Shares and Windsor funds.

# Chapter 6

# Selecting a Portfolio of Funds

## ADVANTAGES OF BUILDING A PORTFOLIO OF FUNDS

A well selected investment portfolio includes a selection of funds that will diversify the investor's risk. A portfolio should simultaneously meet three objectives:

1. liquidity for unexpected demand,
2. current income, and
3. the preservation and enhancement of wealth.

To meet these objectives, we have available three major categories of funds: money market and short-term income funds; income and bond funds; and growth funds. Every investor will want to hold some of all three types of funds.

An investor might hold five to ten different funds in order to obtain a diversified portfolio. Some of these funds will provide defensive protection while others will seek aggressive appreciation of capital. A mix of different types of investment approaches will do more to reduce total portfolio vari-

FIGURE 6-1
**The Rate of Return of Two Mutual Funds That Have a Low Correlation.**

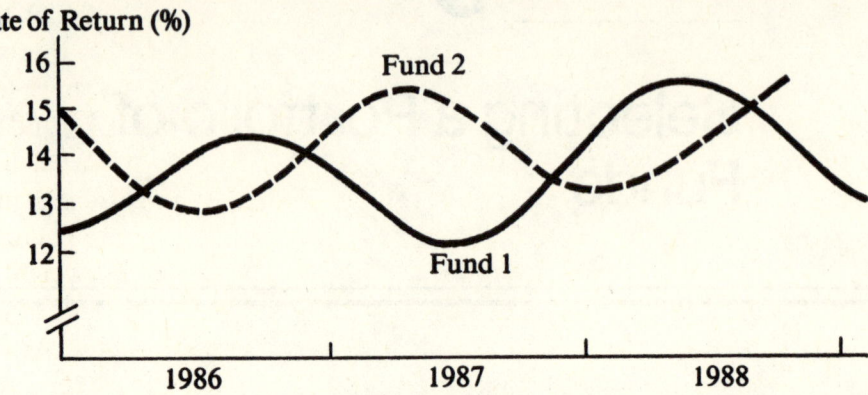

If you held an equal investment in each fund, the total return of the portfolio would be approximately constant.

ability than will a simple combination of several high-performing funds of the same basic type. The special situation funds can help an investor meet this requirement, as can a good international fund.

In order to achieve diversification, we must develop a portfolio of funds in which the *correlation* of price changes for the various funds in the portfolio is relatively low. For example, we may select an international fund that performs well in a period when our domestic growth fund is showing a decline in performance. Therefore, we would try to select funds that exhibit low or negative correlation with one another, such as shown in Figure 6-1. If we had an equal investment in each fund, we could expect an almost constant rate of return of approximately 14 percent.

An investor can structure a portfolio of funds to achieve a selected risk level by considering the expected returns and *beta* coefficients of the candidate funds. Let us consider the establishment of a portfolio from the three funds shown in Table 6–1.

If the investor desires a portfolio with a beta of 0.80, then he might select the portfolio shown in Table 6–2. In this case, he would hold 5 percent of his portfolio in the short term income fund, 55 percent in the growth and income fund and 40 percent in the aggressive growth fund. *Note:* We calculate the portfolio's beta by adding up the betas of the individual funds after they have been weighted according to the percentage each fund represents in the total portfolio. To weight the beta for each fund, simply take the total market value of your investment in the fund, divide it by the total market value of your portfolio, and then multiply that answer by the fund's beta.

Similarly, if we were more concerned with achieving a desired given rate of return, we could structure our portfolio using weighted expected returns of each fund to reach our targeted total portfolio return.

## ADJUSTING THE FUND PORTFOLIO TO MEET YOUR PERSONAL OBJECTIVES

Investors should select a portfolio of mutual funds based on personal needs and characteristics. Important factors will be age, marital situation, stability of employment income, net worth, inheritance or gifts, and many others. In addition, investors have their own inherent dispositions toward risk and the volatility of fund returns and share prices. An investor with a solid career and high earnings can expect to invest in low risk (low *beta*) funds during the first ten years of employment and then gradually increase both the risk and expected return of the portfolio as he approaches his mid-forties. As he or she approaches retirement in his mid-fifties, the investor, once again, will need to lower the overall risk (*beta*) of the portfolio.

**TABLE 6–1**
**A Portfolio of Three Funds.**

| Fund | Expected Return (%) | Beta |
|---|---|---|
| Short-term income fund | 9.0 | 0.10 |
| Growth and Income fund | 13.0 | 0.50 |
| Aggressive Growth fund | 16.0 | 1.30 |

**TABLE 6–2**
**Three-Fund Portfolio with a Beta of 0.80**

| Fund | Beta | Weight in Portfolio | Weighted Beta | Expected Return (%) | Weighted Expected Return (%) |
|---|---|---|---|---|---|
| Short term | 0.10 | 0.05 | 0.005 | 9 | 0.45 |
| Growth and income | 0.50 | 0.55 | 0.275 | 13 | 7.15 |
| Aggressive growth | 1.30 | 0.40 | 0.520 | 16 | 6.40 |
| Summation | | 1.00 | 0.800 | | 14.00 |

*Note:* Weighted beta = beta × weight in portfolio

Suggested portfolio *betas* for selected personal factors and ages are shown in Table 6–3. According to this table, the primary family wage earner with a moderate income and extensive family requirements would want to raise his portfolio *beta* as he matured and his family responsibilities declined. As he approaches retirement age, he will shift his funds towards low *beta* income funds to preserve capital, holding just a small percentage of growth funds if any at all. Of course, the risk levels presented in the table will have to be adjusted by one's own personal ability to handle risk.

The level of risk acceptable to an investor is referred to as *risk tolerance* and can be derived from asking the following question: assume that you invest in both risk-free Treasury bills that return 8 percent a year and a growth stock fund that has an annual return of 14 percent a year but carries a correlative level of risk with a *beta* coefficient of 1.00. What percentage of your total available funds would you be comfortable investing in the growth fund? If your answer is 50 percent, your risk tolerance can be said to be 50. The higher your risk tolerance, the greater should your investment be in growth funds. If your risk tolerance is equal to 100, your portfolio would contain only growth stock funds and would

TABLE 6–3
**Risk Portfolio for Individuals as Measured by Beta of the Overall Portfolio**

|  | Ages | | | |
| --- | --- | --- | --- | --- |
|  | 25–35 | 35–45 | 45–55 | 55+ |
| Personal Factors | | | | |
| High income, accelerating career | 0.60 | 0.90 | 1.20 | 0.80 |
| Moderate income, extensive family requirements | 0.40 | 0.50 | 0.60 | 0.50 |
| Moderate income, low family needs | 0.50 | 0.70 | 0.80 | 0.50 |
| Modest, but stable income with normal family obligations | 0.40 | 0.50 | 0.50 | 0.40 |

have a *beta* of 1.00. Thus, if you confidently answered the question and found, for instance, that your risk tolerance is 80 percent, you should seek to construct a portfolio with a *beta* of 0.80.

## TIME HORIZON

When constructing a portfolio of funds, you must take into account your expected future requirements for cash. If the assets may be needed in the near-term, it is best to keep them in short-term income funds with low volatility of returns or in a growth and income fund with a *beta* of 0.50 or less. An investor with a long-term horizon of seven years or more, should concentrate on long-term growth-oriented investments, keeping a small amount in safe investments for unexpected contingencies.

When investigating a fund you should look at the fund's return over a period that is comparable to your expected investment horizon. Thus, if you expect to buy and hold a fund in your portfolio for ten years, you should review the past ten-year performance of candidate funds.

In a recent study (Levy, 1978) the volatility of return versus the length of the holding period was examined for stocks and bonds. It was shown that risk, as represented by variability of return, declines with increasing holding periods as shown in Table 6–4 (page 102). The study clearly illustrates that a long term holding period helps to reduce the variability of return. You should also note that if you plan to hold an investment for ten years or more, the study indicates that you would be better off holding stocks than bonds. *In general, it has been demonstrated that investors with longer holding periods generally enjoy better investment returns than those with shorter investment horizons.* Patience really can be a virtue!

## AN EFFICIENT PORTFOLIO OF FUNDS

After you have determined your risk tolerance as represented by *beta*, you still must decide how to structure a fund portfolio to achieve the best expected return for your chosen level of risk. Let us return to the portfolio of three funds: (1) short-term bond fund; (2) growth and income fund; and (3) aggressive growth fund that is shown on Table 6–1. In Table 6–2, we constructed a portfolio of these three funds that yielded a *beta* equal to 0.80 and had a weighted expected return of 14.0 percent. We now want to determine if this is the best portfolio for these three funds given that we want a *beta* of 0.80 and the best return possible. The weighted portfolio *beta*, WB, is calculated by

$$WB = w_1 b_1 + w_2 b_2 + w_3 b_3 \qquad (6\text{–}1)$$

where $w_i$ = weight of the ith fund and $b_i$ = *beta* of fund i. The weighted portfolio return, WE(R), then is calculated by

$$WE(R) = w_1 R_1 + w_2 R_2 + w_3 R_3 \qquad (6\text{–}2)$$

The objective then is to maximize the portfolio return for a given portfolio risk, *beta* = 0.80, by adjusting the weights of each fund in the portfolio. Let us consider the portfolio mix we saw in Table 6–2. By substituting the 40 percent weight of the aggressive growth fund for $W_3$ in equation 6–2, it becomes

$$0.80 = 0.10 W_1 + 0.50 W_2 + 1.30(.40) \qquad (6\text{–}3)$$

Solving for $W_1$ and $W_2$, we find that $W_1 = 0.05$ and $W_2 = .55$ and we can calculate the weighted portfolio return as 14.0 percent. The three funds and their return and risk are graphically represented in Figure 6–2. The graph shows that the growth and income fund has a positive risk premium since it is above the market line, whereas the aggressive growth fund is slightly below the market line. This implies that we must weight the portfolio more heavily towards the growth and

## FIGURE 6–2
**Returns and Risk for Three-Fund Portfolio**

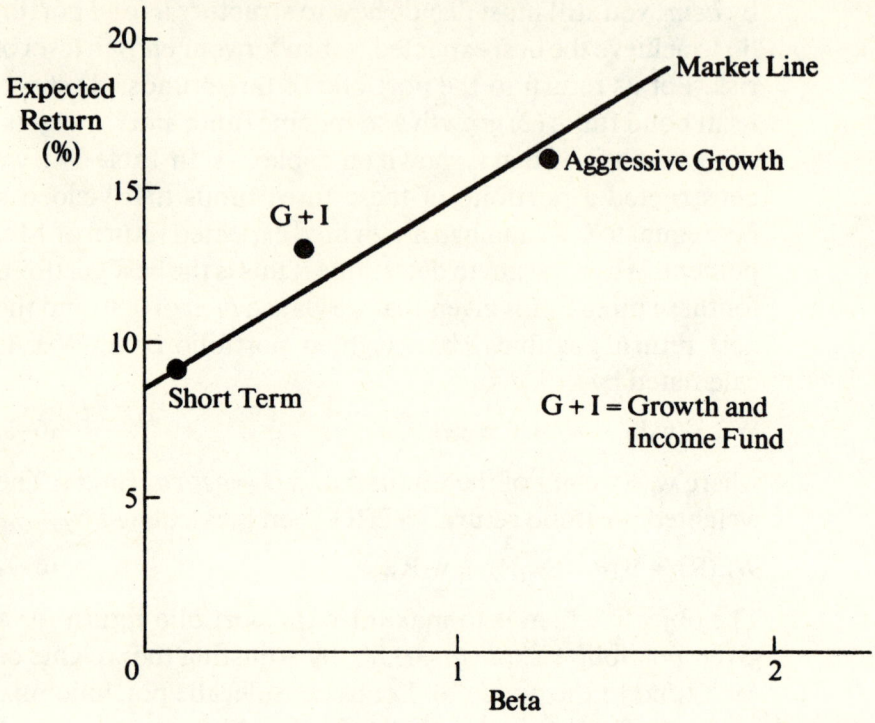

income fund to achieve maximum overall return. We do this by selecting a minimum contribution from the aggressive fund and then finding the weighted contribution of the other funds from the two equations

$$0.8 = .1 W_1 + .5 W_2 + 1.3 W_3 \tag{6-4}$$

and

$$W_1 + W_2 + W_3 = 1 \tag{6-5}$$

where we wish to minimize $W_3$. We solve this set of equations by noting that a minimum $W_3$ is obtained when $W_1 = 0$. Then,

$W_2 = 1 - W_3$ and substituting into equation 6–5 we have

$0.8 = .5(1 - W_3) + 1.3W_2$

then

$W_1 = 0, W_2 = .625$

and

$W_3 = .375$ \hfill (6–6)

as shown in Table 6–5. By completing the table, we find the weighted expected return for this new portfolio is 14.125 percent, which is slightly better than the 14.0 percent we achieved in Table 6–2.

Unless you are prepared to use a computer to calculate the optimal set of weighted investments, it would be helpful if you had a set of decision rules to allow you to construct a portfolio that will provide a nearly optimum combination of funds for a preselected risk level, or *beta*.

We suggest the following procedure for selecting and managing your portfolio of funds:

1. Select the risk level that you are comfortable with as represented by a portfolio *beta*, typically it will be between 0.50 and 1.50;
2. Select five to ten fund candidates for the portfolio based on their risk-adjusted return performance (the calculations for a fund's risk adjusted return were shown in Chapter 5);
3. Select a subset of the funds that provide acceptable risk-adjusted returns and that respond to market changes in uncorrelated ways with one another;
4. Establish a weight for each fund selected, emphasizing those funds that have *beta* coefficients that are close to your selected portfolio *beta*;
5. Calculate the portfolio's weighted expected return and *beta* coefficient.

**TABLE 6–4**
**Returns for Various Holding Periods.**

| Holding Period (Years) | 1 | 5 | 10 | 25 |
|---|---|---|---|---|
| Best annual return (%) | 53.9 | 23.9 | 20.1 | 14.7 |
| *Stocks* | | | | |
| Worst annual return (%) | −43.4 | −12.5 | −0.9 | 5.9 |
| Best annual return (%) | 18.6 | 10.3 | 7.1 | 4.8 |
| *Bonds* | | | | |
| Worst annual return (%) | −8.1 | −2.2 | 1.0 | 1.5 |

**TABLE 6–5**
**Optional Three-Fund Portfolio with Beta of 0.80**

| Fund | Weight | Beta | Weighted Beta | Expected Return(%) | Weighted Expected Return(%) |
|---|---|---|---|---|---|
| Short term | 0 | 0.10 | 0 | 9 | 0 |
| Growth and income | .625 | 0.50 | .3125 | 13 | 8.125 |
| Aggressive growth | .375 | 1.30 | .4875 | 16 | 6.000 |
| Summation | | | .8000 | | 14.125 |

TABLE 6-6
**Six Funds Performance for 1980–1984.**

| Fund | Beta | 5-Year Return (%) | Compounded Annual Return, R (%) | RP (%) | AR (%) |
|---|---|---|---|---|---|
| Aggressive growth (AG) | 1.30 | 110 | 16.0 | −0.3 | 5.8 |
| Growth (G) | 1.05 | 105 | 15.4 | 0.6 | 6.6 |
| Growth and income (GI) | 0.80 | 100 | 14.9 | 1.6 | 8.0 |
| Income (I) | 0.70 | 80 | 12.5 | −0.2 | 5.7 |
| Bond (B) | 0.50 | 85 | 13.1 | 1.6 | 9.2 |
| Money market (R) | 0 | 50 | 8.5 | 0 | NM |
| S&P 500 (B & P) | 1.00 | 97 | 14.5 | 0 | 6.0 |

Note that all portfolios should have a money market fund for holding cash (*beta* = 0) and at least one long-term aggressive fund (*beta* = 1.50 +) that will be held for long-term capital appreciation.

This process of allocating investor funds among several funds or assets is generally referred to as *asset allocation*. We will now use our 5-step model to construct our optimal portfolio using the six funds listed in Table 6-6. The annual returns and risk adjusted returns are graphically represented in Figure 6-3. The graph shows that during the 1980–1984 period for which these returns apply, the funds with lower *betas* outperformed the high-*beta* funds on a risk adjusted basis. If we assume that this past performance is indicative of the future, we will select those funds that came closest to

## FIGURE 6–3
**The Actual Return and Risk Adjusted Return for Six Funds and the S&P 500 for 1980–1984.**

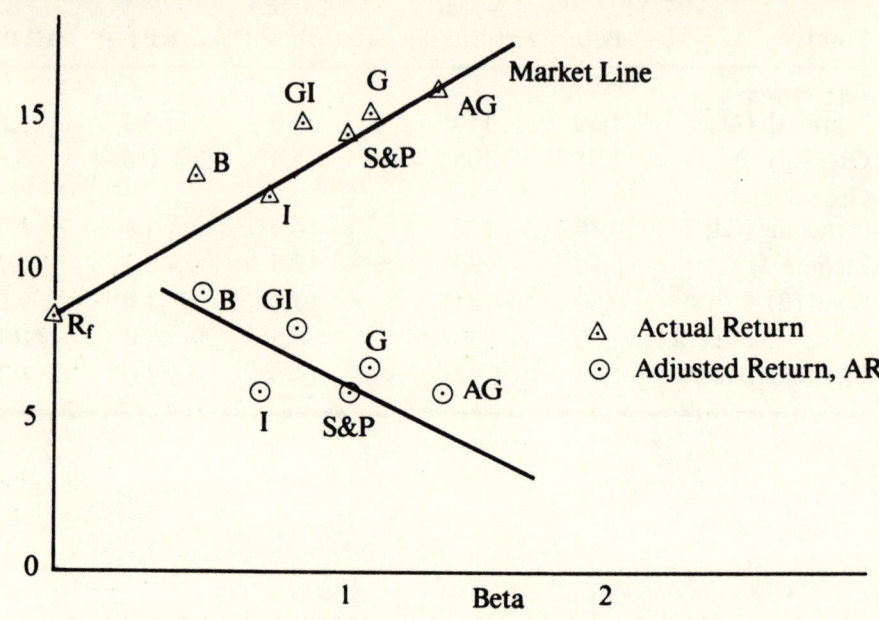

### TABLE 6–7
**Optimal Six Fund Portfolio**

| Fund | Weight | Beta | Weighted Beta | Expected Return (%) | Weighted Expected Return (%) |
|---|---|---|---|---|---|
| AG | .05 | 1.30 | .0650 | 16.0 | 0.800 |
| G | .15 | 1.05 | .1575 | 15.4 | 1.310 |
| GI | .50 | 0.80 | .4000 | 14.9 | 7.450 |
| I | .10 | 0.70 | .0700 | 12.5 | 1.250 |
| B | .15 | 0.50 | .0750 | 13.1 | 1.965 |
| R | .05 | 0 | 0 | 8.5 | 0.425 |
| Summation | | | .7675 | | 14.200 |

meeting our selected overall portfolio *beta* of .80, assigning a portfolio weight to each fund. Table 6–7 reflects the results of our calculation. It yields a portfolio *beta* of 0.77 and an expected return of 14.20 percent.

In many ways, the asset allocation problem is one of matching investments with the portfolio owner's future cash requirements.

In many ways, risk is a function of matching cash flows and not of volatility of returns. A person with substantial cash reserves can afford to maintain a portfolio with higher volatility (i.e., with fewer cash or near-to-cash assets in the portfolio) than another investor who is verging on insolvency. One useful strategy is to fund your cash requirements with the income stream from a high-quality, diversified equity fund portfolio that you dedicate solely to that purpose and forget about asset volatility entirely.

The ideal time to dedicate a portfolio to cover income requirements is when equity yields and interest rates are high. At those times, the highest current income and, therefore, the most cash flow insurance can be purchased for the lowest costs. Many portfolio owners inadvertently over-insure against volatility by over extending their holding periods for low-return, near-to-cash assets.

## HOW TO USE PAST PERFORMANCE TO SELECT FUNDS

Up to this point, we have used historical mutual fund performance as our basis for selecting funds for superior *future performance potential*. Numerous academic studies have attempted to show that very few funds can consistently perform in the top ranks year after year. The evidence indicates that observations of historical fund returns alone contain little predictive content with regard to future performance.

In some periods, specific mutual funds outperform the

market, while in others, they underperform. It also has been found that fund performance is not necessarily tied to the mutual fund's *beta* coefficient. Some high-*beta* funds outperform the market and some, underperform. The same is true for low-*beta* funds.

We, of course, are looking for funds that do better in both up and down markets, that have acceptable risk adjusted performance, and produce consistently superior returns. These funds do exist, although they number less than 25. The Mutual Shares Fund and Strong Total Return Fund are two examples of consistent superior performers with *betas* of less than 0.80.

Linder Fund is another good performer that returned 24 percent in 1983, 13 percent in 1984 and had a compound return of 25 percent for the period December 31, 1979 to March 31, 1985. This consistent performer has a *beta* equal to 0.50 and a risk return premium of 13.5 percent for this 63 month period. These are the kinds of funds we need to find to include in our portfolio.

## DOES FUND SIZE AFFECT PERFORMANCE?

Since we are interested in evaluating the performance of mutual funds, one factor we should take into account is the asset size of the fund. How important is a fund's size when assessing potential performance? A small, emerging fund may promise better future returns, but may also carry greater risk. On the other hand, an established, larger fund may be stable in performance, but also be less nimble and slower to react to market changes.

Consider a new emerging high-tech company that has a market capitalization of $50 million and a $20 million mutual fund that purchases $2 million worth of the company's shares. If the fund has total assets of $20 million, this purchase represents 10 percent of the fund's holdings and will have a significant impact on the fund's performance. At the same time, a $500 million fund also purchases $2 million in shares of the same emerging company, but it only constitutes 0.4 percent of the fund's total holdings. Any change in the firm's share value would have just a modest impact on this fund's performance. Large funds, therefore, generally provide diversification and stability, whereas small funds offer flexibility and higher volatility of performance.

A recent study demonstrated that small emerging companies provide a significant risk adjusted return premium for mutual funds. (Madden, 1984). The study showed that there exists an inverse relationship between returns and the relative sizes of the firms invested in by a fund. Presumably, a smaller fund responds more rapidly in selecting and purchasing these smaller, emerging firms and placing them in their portfolios. Small funds have fewer assets and, therefore, cannot invest in a very diversified list of stocks, making smaller firms more attractive.

Of course, a small fund with good performance will succeed by growing in assets and thus becoming a member of the large fund category. New investors rush to join the crowd and the fund swells in size. Often, but not always, this popularity hampers the fund's performance.

Windsor Fund, a member of the Vanguard Group, had $321 million in assets in 1974 and grew to $929 million in 1981. Then, in response to its superior performance, net cash inflows soared from $229 million in 1983 to $499 million in 1984, with an additional $700 million flowing in during the first half of fiscal 1985. As of this writing, Windsor Fund is now the largest equity mutual fund in the United States. Its net assets currently stand at more than $3.4 billion, compared to $2.5 billion at the end of 1984 and just $1.7 billion at the end of 1983. The fund's increasing asset base does not appear to have impaired Windsor Fund's performance at this point. Its results in 1984 and 1985 remain competitive relative to the investment results of the

S&P 500 Index. Nevertheless, the fund's trustees and its investment advisor are concerned that, at some point, uncontrolled growth could hamper the advisor's ability to meet the fund's investment objectives. Thus, effective May 15, 1985, the fund ceased offering shares to new or continuing investors.

Other funds besides Windsor (Lindner and Pennsylvania Mutual are two) have closed their funds to new purchasers in order to maintain consistent performance levels. On the other hand, Fidelity Magellan, a consistently good performer grew from $107 million in 1980 to $1.9 billion in 1985 and still remains open to new investors.

In terms of fund size, an investor should look for quality funds that perform well (with at least two years of performance), and that range in size from $10 million to $800 million. Funds smaller than $10 million probably will not be well followed and may not be listed in the newspaper. And funds over $1 billion may be reaching the point where they are unwieldy to manage, and thus slowing down in growth.

## THE TWO-FUND PORTFOLIO: A VIABLE ALTERNATIVE

One relatively easy way to assemble a fund portfolio is to limit your holdings to a money market fund and an index fund. Money market funds have a *beta* of zero and, since index funds attempt to duplicate the market, they have a *beta* of 1.00. Therefore, the maximum *beta* of such a two-fund portfolio would be 1.00. Consider the portfolio of an index and money market fund in Table 6–8. The proportion of the total portfolio invested in the index fund directly establishes the level of the portfolio's *beta* and return. However, keep in mind that the maximum return the portfolio can achieve is the market return, which certainly is limiting.

TABLE 6-8
**The Two-Fund Portfolio**

| Fund | Beta | Weight | Weighted Beta | Expected Return(%) | Weighted Expected Return(%) |
|---|---|---|---|---|---|
| Money Market | 0 | .2 | 0 | 8.5 | 1.7 |
| Index | 1.00 | .8 | .80 | 14.5 | 11.6 |
| Summation | | | .80 | | 13.3 |

## A FUND OF FUNDS

In this day of the fund, it is possible to purchase a fund of funds, which, simply put, is a mutual fund that purchases and holds the shares of other mutual funds. Some attractions of the fund of funds approach are the reduced risk inherent in its broad diversification and the increased likelihood that your investment will perform at least as well as the market as a whole.

One such fund is the Star Fund, offered by the Vanguard Group of mutual funds. Vanguard began marketing it in March, 1985. It invests in four other Vanguard funds: Windsor, a growth and income fund that accounts for 50–60 percent of Star's portfolio; Explorer Fund, a small-company growth fund that makes up no more than 10 percent of the portfolio; a GNMA fund, which represents 20–30 percent; and a money market fund, that accounts for 10–20 percent of the portfolio.

FundTrust, another fund-of-funds, began in November 1984 and is sponsored by broker Furman Selz with the Republic National Bank of New York serving as investment advisor. FundTrust offers four portfolios; aggressive growth,

growth, growth and income, and fixed income. The aggressive growth portfolio, for example is usually invested in ten or twelve funds.

One drawback to the fund-of-funds approach is the possibility of layered fees. Investors can be saddled with both the fund-of-funds fees and the management charges of the individual funds that make up the portfolio.

FundTrust's direct annual fees of about 0.85 percent include 0.5 percent to Republic National Bank as advisor, 0.15 percent to Furman and about 0.2 percent in miscellaneous expenses. But the funds within the fund also charge fees. Counting these "indirect" fees as well, the expense ratio for FundTrust is about 1.75 percent, compared to the average mutual fund's ratio of about 1 percent.

The expense ratio for Vanguard's Star Fund is about 0.62 percent, which includes the fees charged by the individual funds in which it invests as well as its own administrative fee.

# Chapter 7
# Market Timing

## TIMING MUTUAL FUND PURCHASES AND REDEMPTIONS

The essence of market timing in any investment is to buy low and sell high. While this is the dream of all investors, there is no fully guaranteed way to achieve it consistently; but there are methods that can be used to improve your timing of investment purchases and sales. Fluctuations in the investment markets and their corresponding reflections in fund price changes are difficult to discern. And hunches about future market changes are correct only 50 percent of the time, which is no better than the random walk that we discussed in Chapter 1.

*Market timing* is the "timely" shifting of assets into or out of the market in an attempt to take advantage of market rallies while avoiding major declines.

Many people use one or more indicators to help them determine when to sell or buy a fund. These indicators are some type of measure of stock market or economic activity.

The overall goal of market timing is represented graphically by Figure 7–1. The illustration shows how an investor

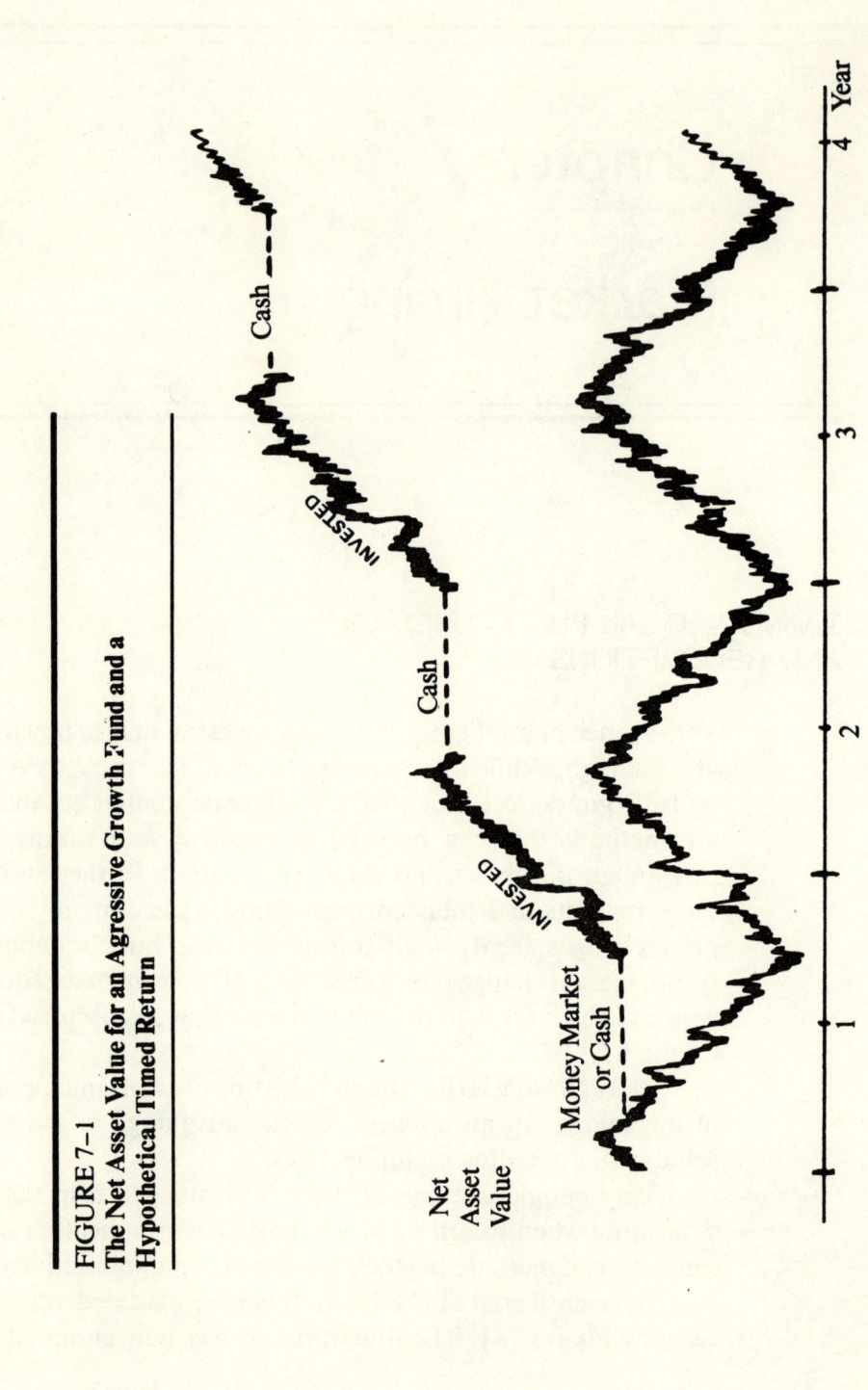

FIGURE 7-1
The Net Asset Value for an Agressive Growth Fund and a Hypothetical Timed Return

could improve returns in an aggressive growth fund if he perfectly timed his buys and redemptions to correspond to market changes. In the example, the investor switched to a money market fund or cash when the market declined and back into the fund when the market rose again. As this example illustrates, you can do very well in terms of overall return if you consistently time your investments.

Table 7-1 includes the major up and down trends of the Dow Jones Industrial Averages (DJIA) from 1969 to 1980. It shows that the market experienced extremely volatile swings during the period, rising as high as 80 percent (1975-76) and declining by as much as 54 percent (1973-74). For the period as a whole, the DJIA fell by almost 14 percent.

Table 7-2 illustrates what an investor's total return would have been at the end of each market movement if he invested $10,000 in 1969. The left hand column represents his return assuming a buy and hold strategy (without using timing in other words) and the right hand column indicates his return if he switched from stocks to a money market fund yielding 9 percent during the down markets and back into stocks at the start of each bull movement (again with perfect timing).

The results are quite clear. Excluding the effects of inflation, taxes and transactions costs, the buy and hold strategy would have resulted in a net loss of 13.7 percent for the period. Whereas, if the investor were able to apply perfect timing, he would have experienced a 435.8 percent gain in his initial investment for the period.

The purpose of this illustration is not to suggest that we can achieve perfect timing in our investment decisions, but to point out the stakes involved and to demonstrate that it certainly is worth our while to try to develop and improve our investment timing strategies.

Numerous studies of mutual fund timing strategies have attempted to demonstrate that good timing is not feasible. The ability to earn superior returns through superior forecasting is a violation of the efficient market theory that we

TABLE 7-1
**Advancing and Declining Markets of the Dow Jones Industrial Average**

| Movement of Market | Percentage Change | Period |
|---|---|---|
| Down | − 37 | 69–70 |
| Up | + 69 | 70–72 |
| Down | − 54 | 73–74 |
| Up | + 80 | 75–76 |
| Down | − 28 | 77 |
| Up | + 36 | 78–80 |
| | − 14 | 69–80 |

TABLE 7-2
**Performance without and with Perfect Timing (Assumes $10,000 Initial Investment)**

| | $ Value of Portfolio at the End of Each Period | |
|---|---|---|
| Period | Without Timing | With Perfect Timing |
| 69–70 | 6,300 | 10,900 |
| 70–72 | 10,647 | 18,421 |
| 73–74 | 4,898 | 20,079 |
| 75–76 | 8,816 | 36,142 |
| 77 | 6,348 | 39,395 |
| 78–80 | 8,633 | 53,577 |
| Total change for 12 years 1969–1980 | − 13.7% | 435.8% |

discussed in Chapter 1. As you may recall, according to the efficient-market hypothesis, it is unlikely that any investor can outperform the market over time, regardless of the strategy used. The competition is just too keen. In fact, investors who trade actively, trying to beat the market, probably will perform worse because of the high cost of commissions. The "modest" track record of professionals appears to confirm as much. Because the market is highly efficient, the theory states, the investor's best strategy is to buy and hold a portfolio that bears a degree of risk he is comfortable with.

As we saw in Chapter 1, current thinking has it that current market prices *represent a consensus of the varying expectations of all market participants*. If this is so, then it is the sudden, unexpected arrival of new information that causes prices to change. But this new information cannot, by its very nature, be predicted in advance. And only those future events that fall within the realm of the "reasonably expected" are reflected in current market prices.

I believe, however, that forecasting general market returns is more valuable and has a better success rate than forecasting the movement of individual stocks. One reason this is so is due to the fact the market forecaster's investment strategy and his buy and sell actions resulting from that strategy will have less of an effect on the price of stocks in the aggregate than it would on any individual stock.

Market timing is, in practice, a hybrid of fundamental and technical methodologies, blending business analysis with technical projections. Market timers track such economic conditions as the trend and level of interest rates, the degree and direction of business activity, corporate profits and industrial production.

Unfortunately, in the real world, market movements give dozens of signals, flashing buy, sell, and hold actions all at once. To further complicate the situation, institutions track each other's buy and sell actions as well as closely follow the same leading indicators. Thus, the major market players are all likely to react to the same information at about the same time.

Nevertheless, there are many investors and investment advisors that believe they can outperform the other investors because of the uniqueness of their indicators. And, of course, despite the efficient market theory, in the real world, there are actual inefficiencies in the market. And often, investment information or opinion is inaccurate and investment decisions are overly influenced by emotion and crowd psychology, thereby creating opportunities for beating the market.

Successful market timers strive to position their portfolios of funds to achieve higher *beta* values prior to market rises and lower *betas* before market declines. If that can be done and the resulting benefits are not outweighed by added transaction and tax costs, overall performance will be superior to that of a portfolio that maintains constant *beta* value irrespective of market movements.

Unsuccessful market timers, on the other hand, tend to alter their portfolios' *betas* in ways unrelated to market moves, adding costs but not benefits.

To take advantage of this approach, mutual fund investors can use a family of funds to quickly and easily switch between high *beta* and low *beta* funds as the market indicates. When the stock market is bullish, they would reallocate their fund investments to concentrate on those high *beta* funds within the family of funds that are geared toward equity appreciation through investment in common stocks with a high growth potential. In contrast, when the market becomes bearish, they would switch to funds within the family that seek preservation of capital and high current income such as offered by a money market fund. By switching to a near-cash fund they can still maintain decent earnings during bearish markets. The use of telephone switching options which are now offered by more than 300 funds is well suited to this approach. In order to apply this strategy, of course, it is important that an investor select a fund family

**FIGURE 7-2**
**The Return for the Fifteen Year Period 1969–1983**

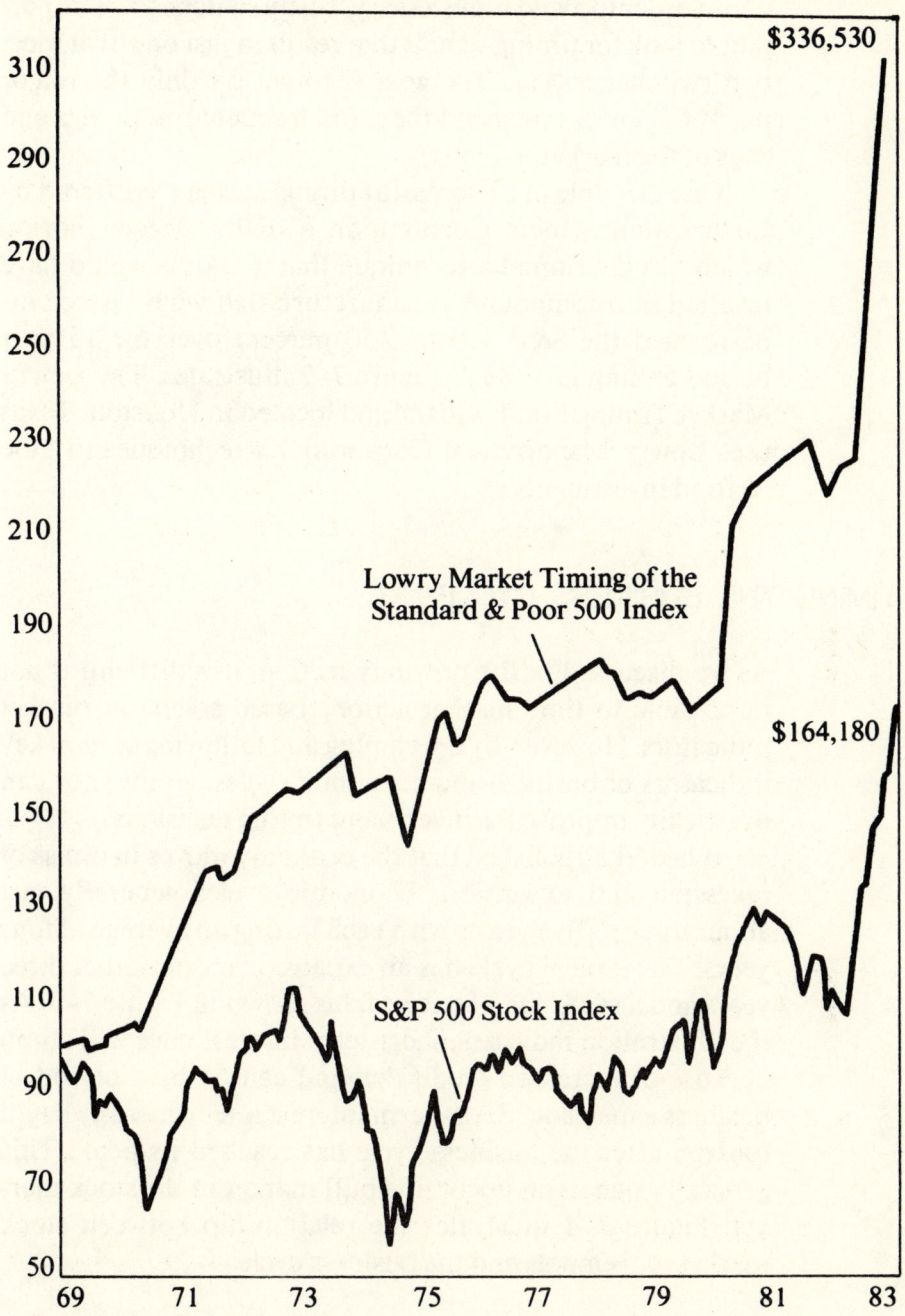

that offers a money market fund or a short-term bond fund.

In order to avoid unnecessary, costly switches, it is important to look for timing signals that result in just one or at most two switches a year. The goal is to act on only the major market changes and avoid the more frequent minor zigs and zags of the market.

One example of a successful timing strategy is offered by Lowry Management Corporation of Palm Beach, Florida which has developed a technique that it claims would have resulted in a compound annual return that would have outperformed the S&P 500 by 150 percent over the 15 year period ending in 1983 as Figure 7–2 illustrates. The Lowry Market Timing Fund, a load fund located in Houston, Texas uses Lowry Management Corporation's techniques to time its fund investments.

## TIMING THE BUSINESS CYCLE

As we discussed in the previous section, it is difficult if not impossible to time market actions based solely on market indicators. However, by developing and following several key indicators of business and economic cycles, an investor can drastically improve his investment timing decisions.

It is well established that the economy moves in cycles of recession and expansion. Economic cycles generally last about three to five years, with each lasting an average of four years. The typical cycle has an expansionary period of three years and a recession of one year, as shown in Figure 7–3. As the illustration indicates, short-term interest rates will climb because of increased credit demand caused by a period of business expansion. Short-term interest rates generally begin to drop after the business cycle has reached its peak. This generally signals an upcoming bull market in the stock market. Figure 7–4 illustrates the relationship between stock market movements and the business cycle.

**FIGURE 7–3
The Economic Cycle**

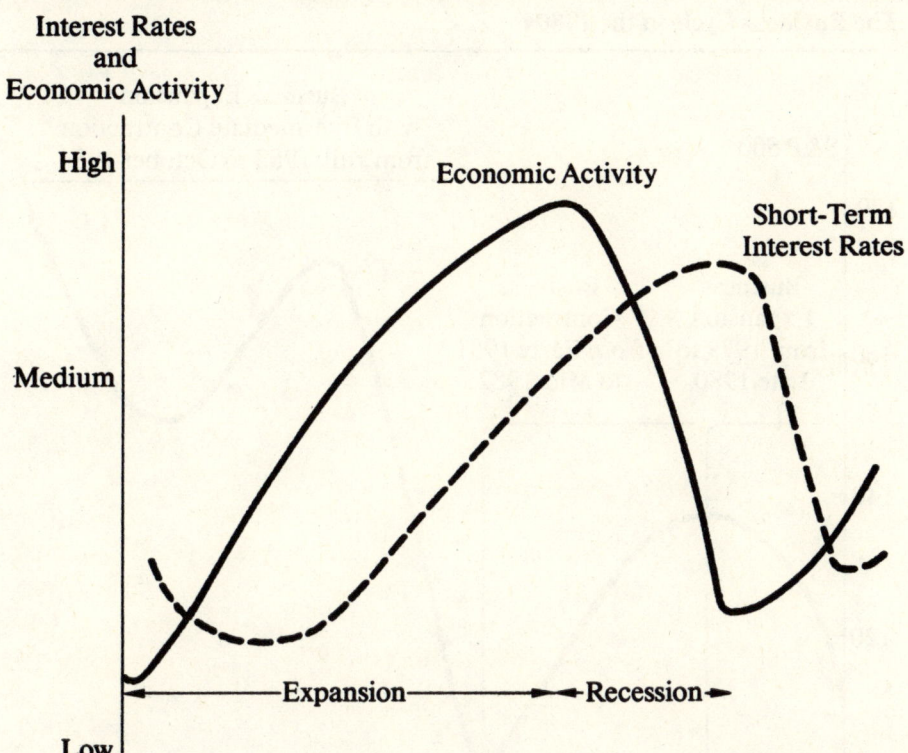

**FIGURE 7–4**
**The Business Cycle in the 1980s**

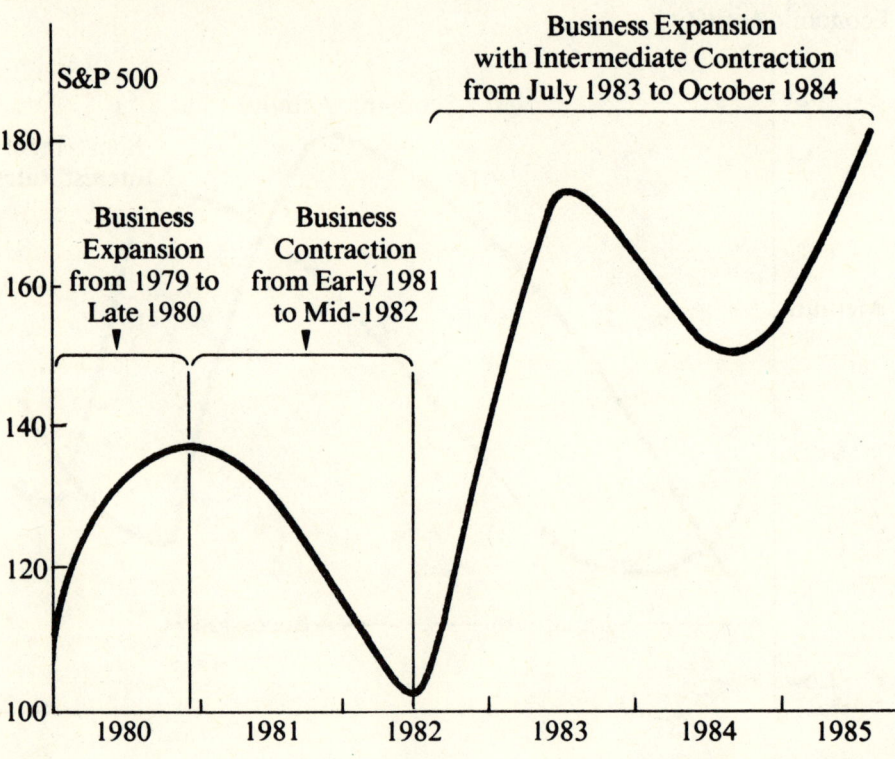

The economic cycle can be divided into four major phases:

1. recession bottom and turn around;
2. expansionary period;
3. expansion top, and;
4. recessionary period.

Representative economic conditions and appropriate fund portfolio strategies for each phase are outlined in Table 7–3. The goal is to maintain a portfolio *beta* of .70 to .80 throughout the cycle by holding growth and income funds while shifting aggressively between bond/money market funds and aggressive growth funds during the various phases of the cycle. We emphasize aggressive growth funds at the recession bottom and during the expansionary periods and bond/money market funds at the expansion top and during the recessionary periods.

One warning about this strategy is in order. To be successful, it requires that you overcome your natural inclination to

TABLE 7–3

| Phase | Average Length | Average S&P 500 P.E. Ratio | Proportion of Funds in Portfolio | | |
|---|---|---|---|---|---|
| | | | Bond and Money Market | Growth and Income | Aggresive Growth |
| 1 Recession bottom | 3 mos. | 5 | 40% | 40% | 20% |
| 2 Expansionary | 28 mos. | 10 | 10% | 50% | 40% |
| 3 Expansion top | 3 mos. | 14 | 20% | 50% | 30% |
| 4 Recessionary | 14 mos. | 7 | 50% | 40% | 10% |

continue to invest aggressively at the top of economic cycles and conservatively at the recession bottoms. This contrarian approach is not always easy to follow, but its rewards are worth the effort.

There are a number of indicators that can provide hints as to where we are in the business cycle and which direction the economy is likely to move. They include the sentiments of the business community, business and financial data, and economic activity measures.

When the economy is at or near a peak there usually is a general air of optimism in the economy that is evident everywhere. Friends talk about how well they are doing in real estate or in the stock market and newspapers carry articles about young geniuses who are making millions. There is a speculative mood in the air that everyone seems to share and wants to get in on.

At the bottom of the business cycle the opposite occurs. Friends talk about layoffs at their companies and losses in the stock market or on real estate. Newspapers write about large firms or prominent businessmen who are in serious financial difficulty and the general atmosphere is one of gloom and doom.

Of course, in the real world we all have to live in, nothing is ever clear cut. Even in expansionary times there will be government deficits, taxes, international crises and personal and business financial problems to reflect on, which of course will affect investment attitudes. Nevertheless, our goal is to develop a system that allows us to discern patterns in the economic cycle that will enable us to come reasonably close to determining investment market tops and bottoms and then adjust our portfolios accordingly. We may miss the ultimate tops and bottoms, but if we can come close we can still achieve enviable results. In fact, I do not believe that anyone can call all tops or bottoms perfectly and consistently.

## MOVING AVERAGES

In order to determine appropriate decision points in a business cycle many investors determine the trends of various economic indicators. *Moving average* is a useful statistical device that can be employed to smooth out data in order to more easily detect underlying longer-term trends. Intermediate trends (2–4 years) may be tracked with moving averages spanning from 50 to 90 days whereas long-term trends are usually tracked by averages spanning 100 to 300 days. Aggressive timing strategies use short or intermediate-term moving averages while those that are less aggressive use longer term averages.

A *straight* or *simple moving average* is calculated simply by adding up the data for the most recent series of events (e.g. a fund's daily closing prices for 10 days) you wish to average and dividing the total by the number of units involved.

A simple way of maintaining a moving average is to calculate the 10-day moving total for the initial 10-day period. On the 11th day, add in that day's data (i.e. the fund's closing price on the 11th day) and subtract the 1st day's data. On the 12th day, add in that day's data and subtract, again, the data from the 11th day back.

*Exponential moving average*, is a weighted moving average that also smooths out the minor fluctuations that occur within trends. However, it is designed to give more weight to recent data than to earlier data and, therefore, tends to be more reliable. The computations for calculating exponential moving averages are shown at the end of the chapter. (See Chapter Appendix.)

Examples of a four-week moving average using the weekly net asset values of a fund are illustrated in Table 7–4. Both the straight moving average and the exponential moving average are shown for twelve weeks of data. Plots of the actual net asset values as well as the straight and exponential moving

### TABLE 7-4
**Two Four-Week Moving Averages of a Fund**

| Week | Net Asset Value ($) | Straight Moving Average ($) | Exponential Moving Average ($) |
|---|---|---|---|
| 1 | 10.00 | 10.00 ⎫ | 10.00 ⎫ |
| 2 | 10.50 | 10.25 ⎬ Initialization | 10.20 ⎬ |
| 3 | 11.00 | 10.50 ⎭ Period | 10.52 ⎭ |
| 4 | 11.50 | 10.75 | 10.91 |
| 5 | 12.00 | 11.25 | 11.35 |
| 6 | 12.50 | 11.75 | 11.81 |
| 7 | 13.00 | 12.25 | 12.29 |
| 8 | 13.00 | 12.63 | 12.57 |
| 9 | 12.50 | 12.75 | 12.54 |
| 10 | 12.00 | 12.63 | 12.32 |
| 11 | 11.50 | 12.25 | 11.99 |
| 12 | 11.00 | 11.75 | 11.59 |

*Note:* The calculation of a straight moving average of N-period length does not become valid until the Nth period. Initialization of an exponential moving average is explained in the Appendix to this chapter.

averages are shown in Figure 7-5. Note how the exponential moving average tracks the recent movements of the net asset values more closely by weighting the recent values more highly.

The greatest benefit of a moving average is that it reduces the magnitude of all cyclic fluctuations within a trend that have a duration less than the span of the moving average and highlights those fluctuations with time spans greater than that of the moving average. In our example of a four-week moving average, fluctuations that occurred for less than four weeks would be significantly reduced, but those of five weeks or longer would be magnified.

Consider the chart of the Investor's Daily Fund Index which comprises six growth and aggressive growth funds shown in Figure 7-6. The 50-day and 200-day moving aver-

**FIGURE 7–5
Four-Week Straight and Exponential Moving Averages of the
Net Asset Value of a Fund over Twelve Weeks**

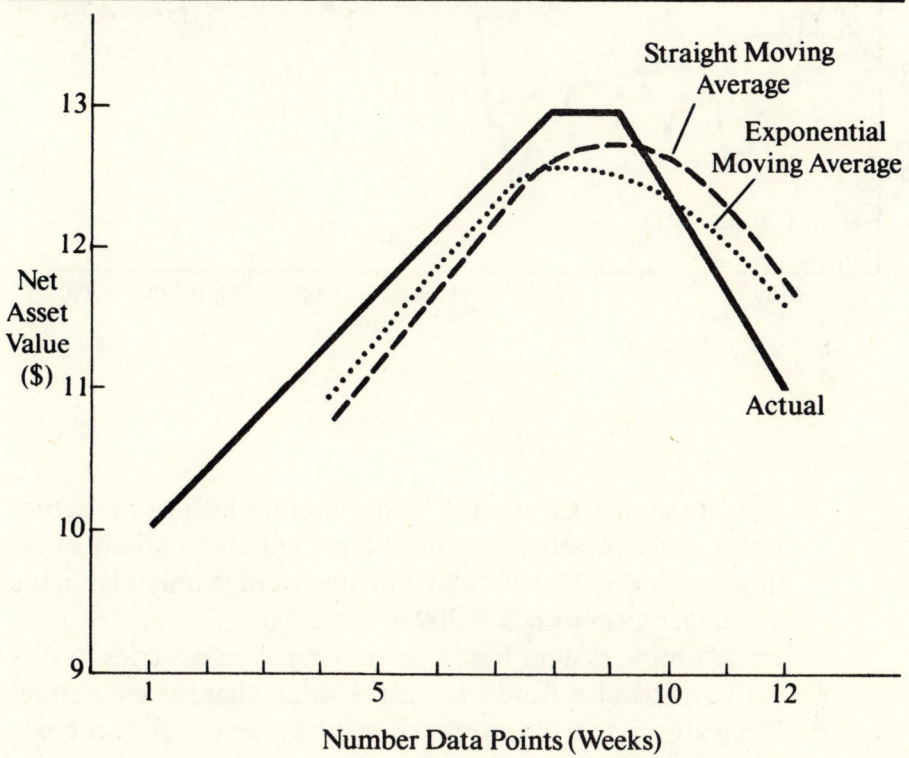

FIGURE 7–6
**The Investor's Daily Newspaper Mutual Fund Index for the Period May to November 1984.**

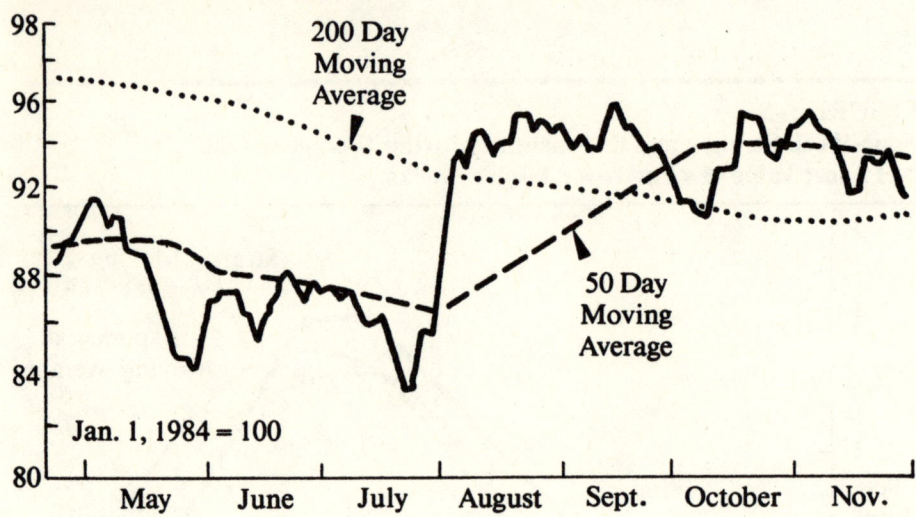

ages are shown. Clearly the 50-day average follows the actual index more closely and would highlight fluctuations of 50 days or longer. The 200-day moving average only highlights the longer term trends of 200 or more days.

A timing system based on moving averages tries to discern trends of a fund's net asset value changes over time. Typically, a moving average timing system uses two basic rules:

1. Buy signals are rendered whenever the price of the fund rises above the level of the moving average employed.
2. Sell signals are rendered whenever the price level of the fund falls below the level of the moving average employed.

Keep in mind that when you use moving averages, what you are looking for is actual, demonstrated long-term trends. Thus, you want to use moving averages that have relatively long time spans.

Table 7–5 shows the buy and sell signals for the 50 day moving average shown on Figure 7–6. The left-hand column is based on the two decision rules presented above.

One way of avoiding the whiplash buying and selling pattern caused by our decision rules is to modify them slightly to require that a fund's price would have to rise or fall at least 1 percent above or below the moving average before we take action. If we applied the adjusted decision rule to

TABLE 7–5
**Buy and Sell Signals for 50 Day Moving Average Shown on Figure 7–6**

|  | Basic Decision Rule | Modified 1% Decision Rule |
|---|---|---|
| April 27 | Buy | |
| May 1 | | Buy |
| May 11 | Sell | Sell |
| June 17 | Buy | |
| June 23 | Sell | |
| June 28 | Buy | |
| July 28 | | Buy |
| Sept. 28 | Sell | |
| Oct. 15 | Buy | |
| Oct. 25 | Sell | |
| Oct. 28 | Buy | |
| Nov. 10 | Sell | Sell |

our example, we would have responded only on May 1, May 11, July 28, and November 10 as the right-hand column in the table indicates. Avoiding the three other in and out moves would have reduced the number of trades to four instead of ten.

The preferred approach is to use our adjusted decision rules and a longer term moving average, such as the 200-day average also shown in Figure 7-6. Using this approach, we would have bought on April 3rd (not on the figure) and held throughout November with no trades in between. We would not have responded to the slight dip below the 200-day moving average in October, since we require a 1 percent change below the moving average to act.

Many market timers use moving averages to switch between equity funds and a money market fund. Their approach is to use a 200-day exponential moving average and limit the number of round trips (buys and sells) to one or two a year. Using the longer average and requiring that any buy or sell action must exceed a one percent movement above or below the trend line will accomplish this and provide significant timing opportunities.

A second approach to using moving averages is to use a system based on two averages of different lengths as shown in Figure 7-6. When two averages are employed, a buy signal is rendered when the shorter term moving average moves above the longer term average, indicating that shorter term trends are becoming more powerful than longer term ones. In contrast, sell signals are rendered when the shorter term average moves below the longer term one indicating that shorter term trends are weakening relative to longer term trends.

Although this approach will help prevent buy and sell whipsaws, one drawback is that the user would have to sacrifice early entry and exit opportunities.

Applying this approach to Figure 7-6, we would have had a buy signal on September 15th, when the short-term average passed above the long-term average. We would have missed the rise in late July, but it does avoid whipsaw actions.

A third approach using two moving averages is to use a confirmation method that renders a buy signal when the actual fund price being tracked moves above *both the shorter and the longer term averages employed.* If the fund price crosses above the shorter term average, you do not buy unless and until this signal is confirmed by the price's movement above the longer term moving average as well. The opposite, of course, holds true for sell signals. Applying this approach to Figure 7–6, we would have bought on August 2nd and sold on October 5th. And, if we used our adjusted decision rule, which requires that the fund price move beyond the trend line by 1 percent, we would not have sold on October 5th and would have retained the fund in our portfolio.

Several commercial mutual fund timing systems apply both a 52-week and a 26-week moving average to an index of mutual funds. They plot these averages for investors on a daily or monthly basis. One such index is offered by David Menashe (see Appendix C–4 for an address.). Menashe's system gives a confirmation signal when the short term aver- the fund index both break through the long-term 52-week composite index as shown in Figure 7–7. This method avoids large downturns and catches strong upturns.

Several newsletters, including Menashe's, provide short-term and long-term moving averages for selected funds. An example is shown for Constellation fund in Figure 7–8 for the period 1982 to 1984. Note the clarity of the signals provided.

A summary of the three moving average timing strategies discussed above and sources of moving average information are provided in Table 7–6.

**FIGURE 7–7**
**The Composite Fund Index for 1981 and 1982**

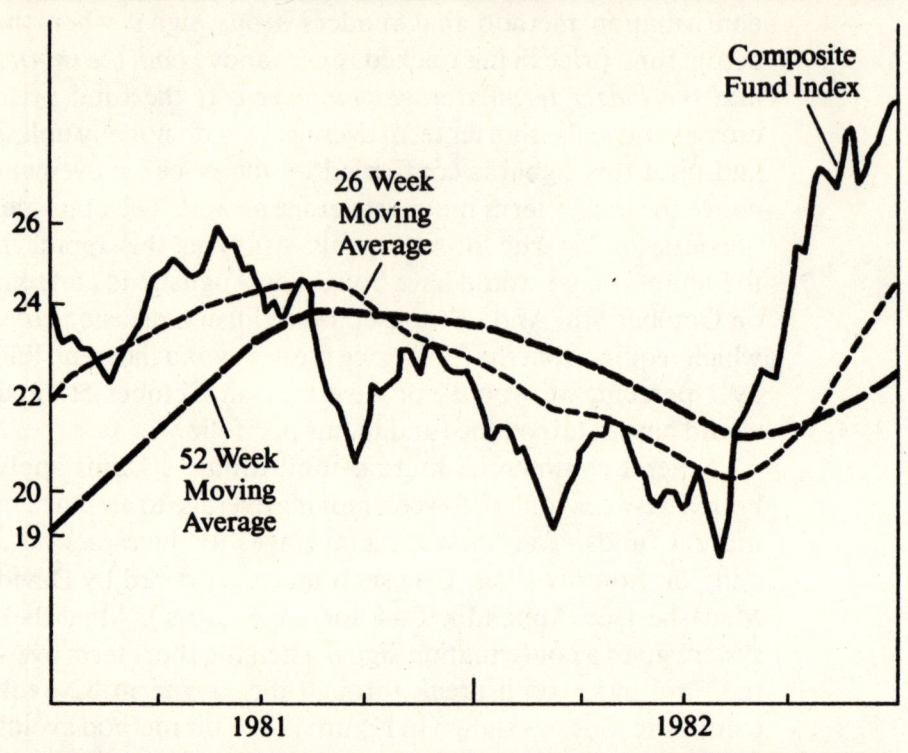

Source: Courtesy of David Menashe & Co.

# FIGURE 7-8
**Constellation Fund for 1982–1984 Showing a Buy Signal in August 1982 and a Sell Signal in November 1983**

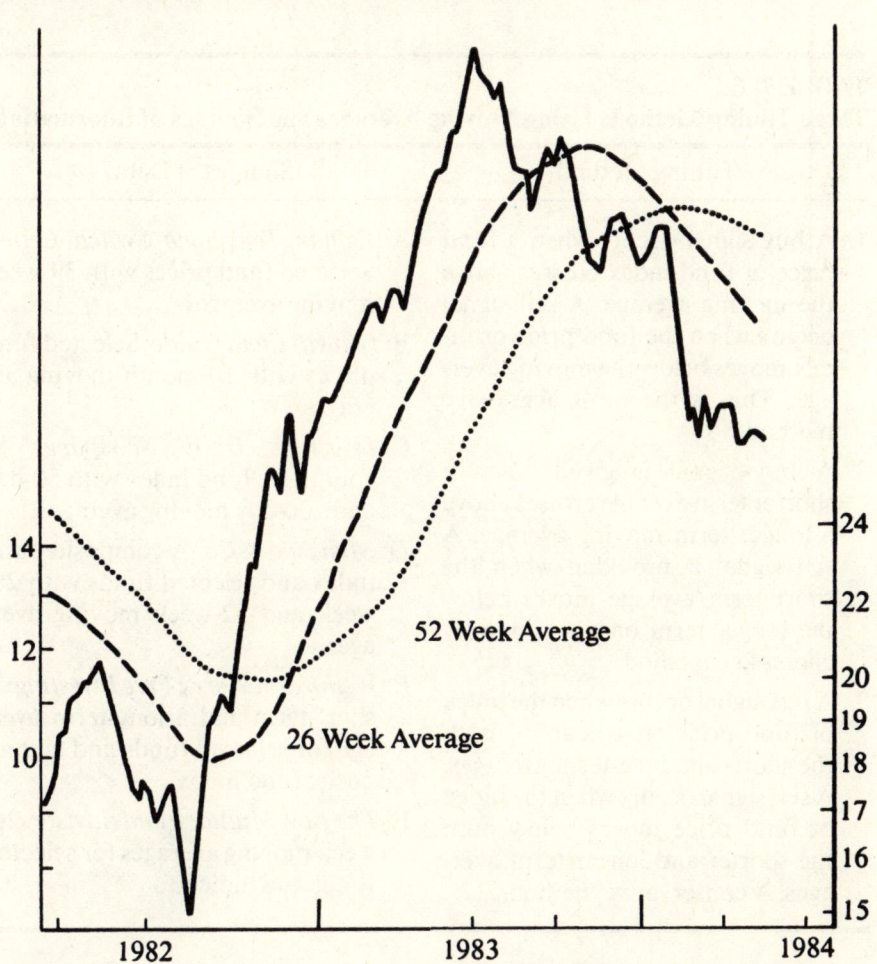

TABLE 7–6
**Three Timing Methods Using Moving Averages and Sources of Information**

| Timing Method | Sources of Data |
|---|---|
| 1. A buy signal occurs when a fund price or fund index crosses above the moving average. A sell signal occurs when the fund price or index moves below the moving average. This is the most aggressive method. | A: *Fabian Telephone Switch Letter:* Selected fund prices with 39-week moving averages.<br>B: *Growth Fund Guide:* Selected fund prices with 10-month moving averages.<br>C: *Investor's Daily Newspaper:* A composite fund index with 50-day and 200-day moving averages. |
| 2. A buy signal is given when a shorter term average crosses above a longer term moving average. A sell signal is provided when the short term average moves below the longer term one. A modestly aggressive method. | D: *Menashe & Co:* A composite fund index and selected funds with 26-week and 52-week moving averages.<br>E: *Wellington Worry Free Investing:* A short-term and a long-term average for selected funds and a composite fund index. |
| 3. A buy signal occurs when the index or fund price crosses above both the short- and long-term averages. A sell signal occurs when the index or fund price moves below both the shorter and longer term averages. A conservative method. | F: *The New Mutual Fund Advisor:* 26-week moving averages for selected funds and indices. |

## BUSINESS AND ECONOMIC INDICATORS

Many investors use a timing method that employs *technical analysis*. The presuppositions of technical analysis are that (1) the factors that affect the market from without (for example, economic news, world events etc.) are already reflected by and discounted in the market's current levels, and (2) that the market moves in discernable trends. It is the study of the phenomena internal to the market itself. The technician believes that price fluctuations reflect logical market forces that can be discerned accurately with the use of technical indicators.

A valuable set of indicators used by technical analysts is related to the flow of money in the economy. Changes in monetary conditions are one of the important indicators of stock market movement because of the effect they have on interest rates and economic activity.

*Money* is a financial asset that serves as a medium of exchange, a store of value and a unit of measure. New money in the form of newly issued currency is created by the federal government. During shorter periods of monetary constriction, interest rates tend to increase, and, it follows, in periods of monetary expansion, interest rates tend to fall. During protracted periods of monetary constriction, however, interest rates will fall since inflation will start to decline. On the other hand, after long periods of money expansion, inflation will increase, since the value of currency is decreased, and interest rates, therefore, also will increase. Two excellent measures of interest rates are the 90-day Treasury bill rate and the long-term corporate AAA bond rate. Treasury bill rates and corporate AAA rates for March, 1984 to May, 1985 are shown on Figure 7-9. Treasury bill rates and a 26-week moving average are on Figure 7-10 on a logarithmic scale for the two-year period May 1983-1985.

The stock market will be affected severely when both short-term and long-term interest rates reach new highs that

**FIGURE 7-9**
**The Treasury Bill and Corporate Bond Rates for the Period March 1984 to May 1985**

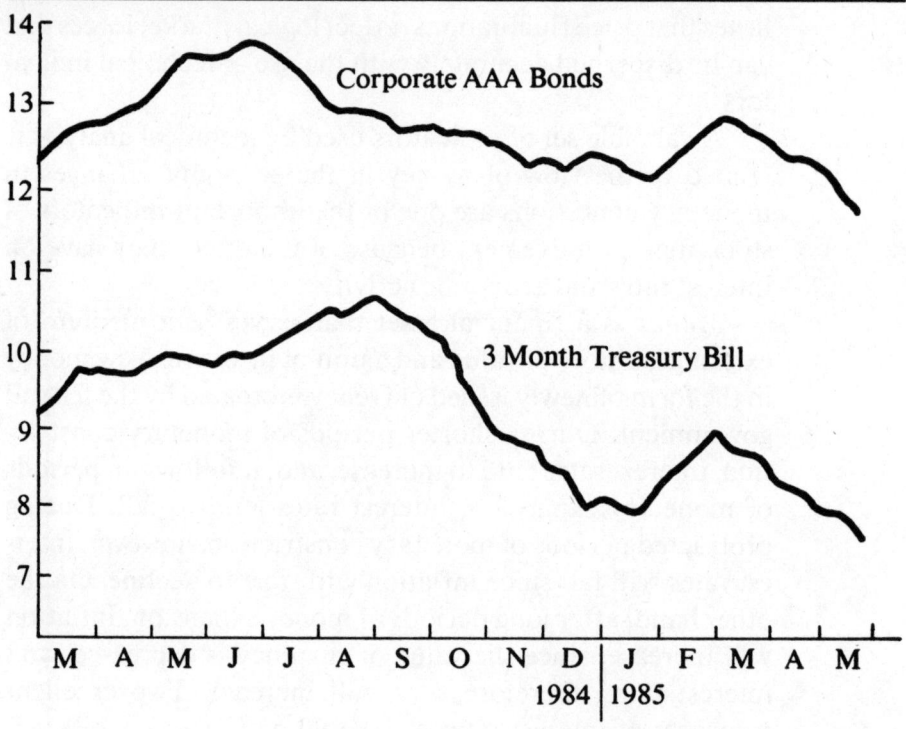

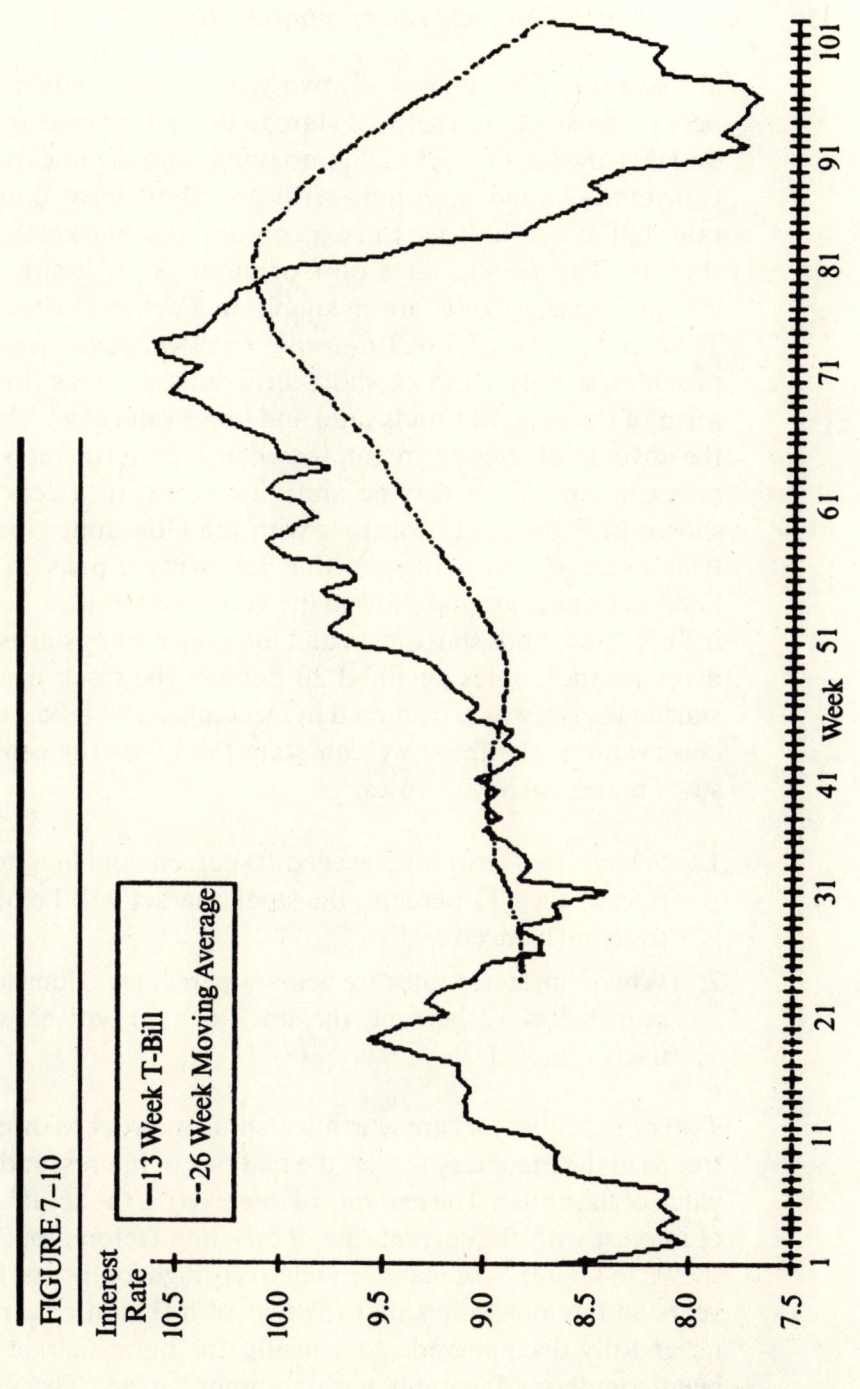

FIGURE 7-10

are sustained for a one- or two-year period. When this occurs the stock market will start to decline as investment dollars flow out of stocks and into bonds and income funds. Conversely, when both long-term and short-term interest rates fall to new lows we can expect the stock market to rise sharply. The weekly rates on Corporate AAA bonds and 90-day Treasury bills are available in *Barron's*, *Business Week* and *The Wall Street Journal*. *The Wall Street Journal* provides a daily chart of short-term interest rates (in the form of the Federal Funds rate) and bond values (which are the inverse of long-term rates—when long-term rates increase bond values decline and vice versa) in a chart as shown in Figure 7–11 together with the Dow Jones Industrial Average. You will note that following a peak in the Federal Funds rate and a low in the value of corporate bonds in July 1984, both short-term and long-term rates started to drop. As these rates declined 20 percent the stock market started to rise, which occurred in December 1984. Based on observations like these we can state the following general stock market behavior rules:

1. When short-term rates exceed 10 percent and long-term rates exceed 13 percent, the stock market will be negatively influenced and;
2. When short-term rates are below 8 percent and long-term rates below 12 percent, the stock market will be positively affected.

Two other indicators are worth watching in order to discern trends in the monetary sector, the real rate of interest and the value of the dollar. The real rate of interest (i.e. the actual rate of interest with the current rate of inflation factored out), as shown in Figure 7–12, has been relatively high for the last four years and demonstrates that the fear of inflation returning never fully disappeared. As a result, the bond market has been competing favorably with common stocks. The value

## FIGURE 7-11
**Monetary Indicators for 1983–1985**

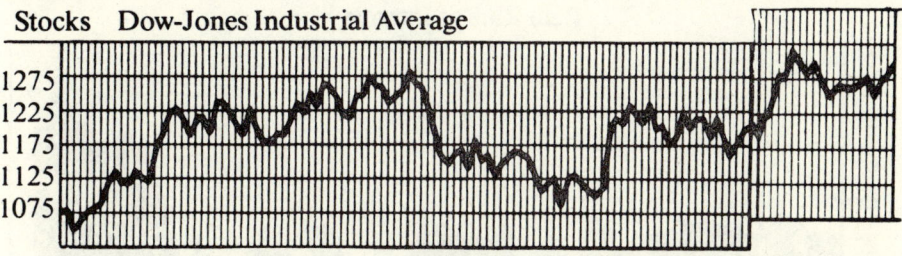
Stocks   Dow-Jones Industrial Average

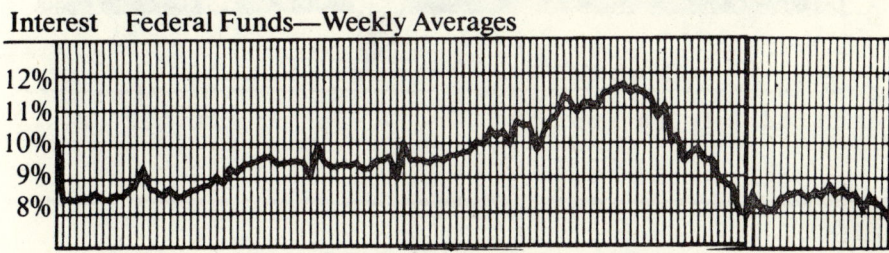
Interest   Federal Funds—Weekly Averages

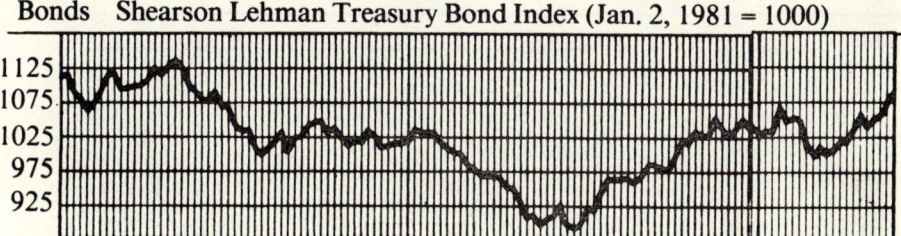
Bonds   Shearson Lehman Treasury Bond Index (Jan. 2, 1981 = 1000)

138    *The New Mutual Fund Investment Advisor*

FIGURE 7–12
**The Real Rate of Interest Represented by the Yield on a 20 Year Bond Minus the Inflation Deflator**

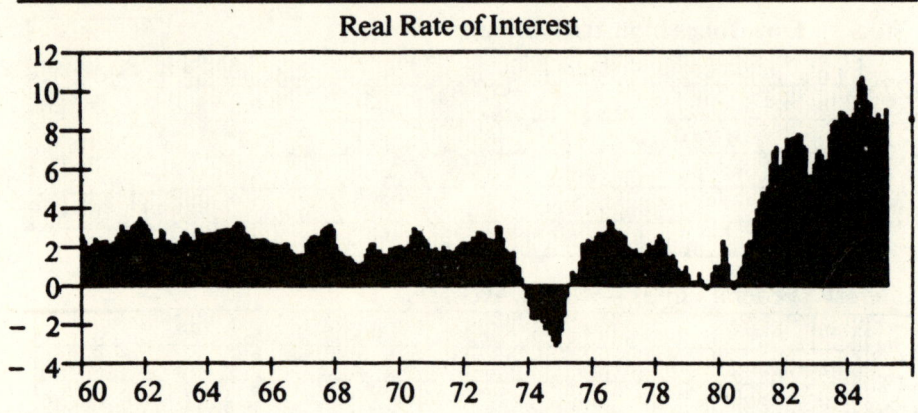

FIGURE 7–13
**The Trade Weighted Value of the Dollar (June 1982 = 100)**

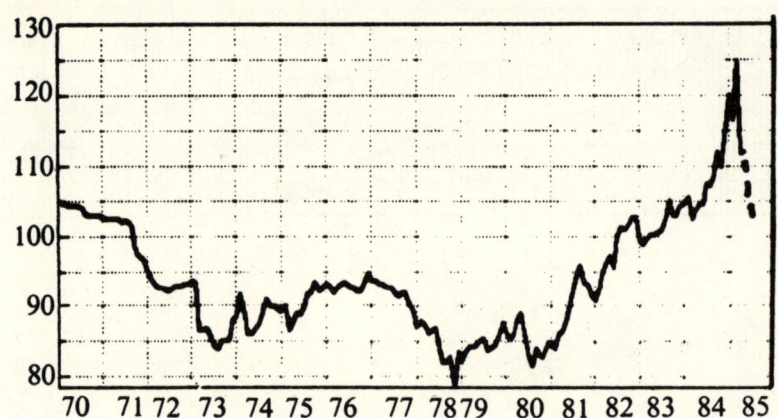

of the dollar as shown in Figure 7-13 increased 60 percent from its recent low in late 1978 to a high in early 1985. As the value of the dollar declines over the next several years, one can expect the value of international mutual funds to increase.

Another readily available indicator is the Business Week Leading Indicator which is published weekly in *Business Week* magazine. Applying a 26-week moving average to the Indicator, as shown in Figure 7-14, we can discern a significant indication of an improving economy registered in week 82 (December 10, 1984).

FIGURE 7-14
**The *Business Week* Leading Indicator for the Period April 9, 1983 to March 8, 1985**

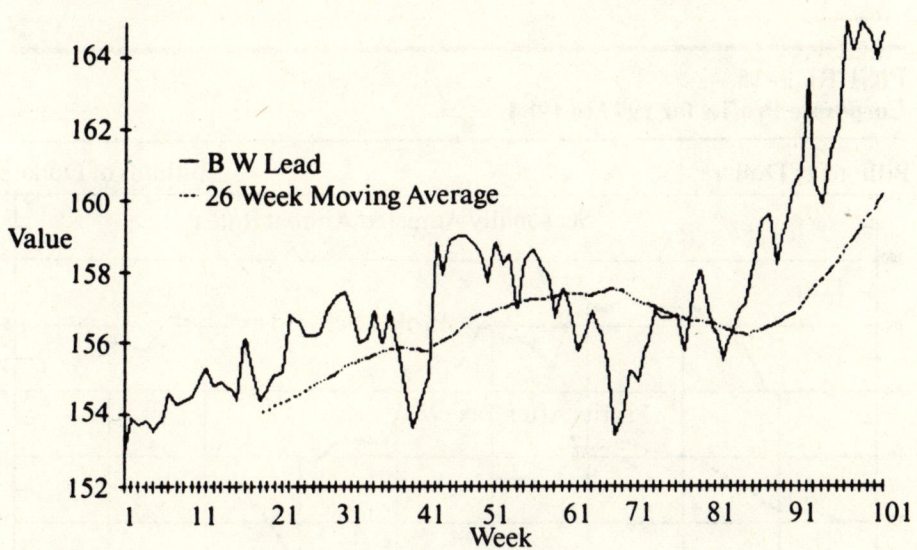

The simultaneous upward movement of The Business Week Leading Indicator (Figure 7-14) and downward movements of both short and long interest rates (Figure 7-9) in December 1984, signaled a rise in the S&P 500 (Figure 7-4).

Another useful economic indicator that technical analysts use is corporate profits as shown in Figure 7-15. As profits rise, we would expect common stocks also to rise. One can readily obtain information on corporate profits from Barron's or Business Week.

A technical indicator designed specifically for mutual funds is provided by the Growth Fund Guide as shown in Figure 7-16. It is the Growth Fund Corporate Oscillator, which consists of seven aggressive growth funds. When the composite is showing a long-term bullish signal or a rising market projection, the trend bar just above the oscillator is darkened. When it is providing a long-term bearish signal or a declining market projection, the trend bar below the oscillator is lightened.

**FIGURE 7-15**
**Corporate Profits for 1977 to 1984**

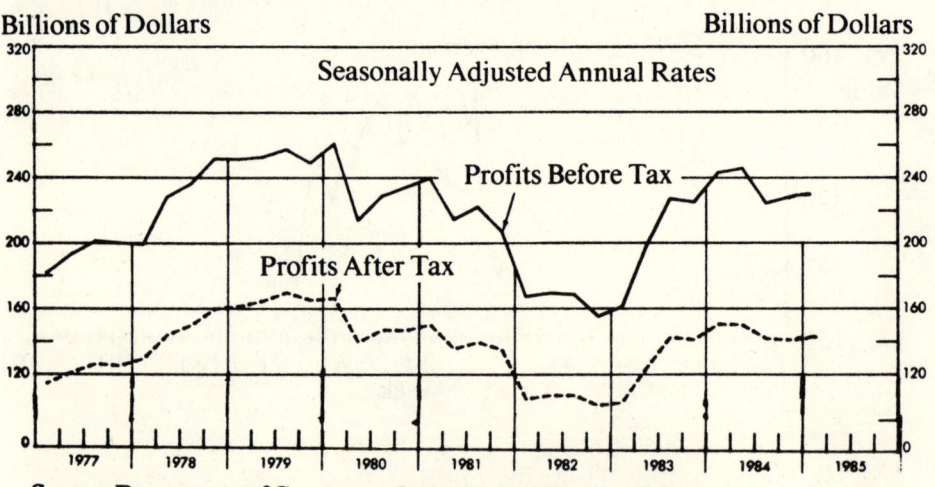

Source: Department of Commerce Council of Economic Advisers

# FIGURE 7-16
## The Growth Fund Guide Composite Oscillator

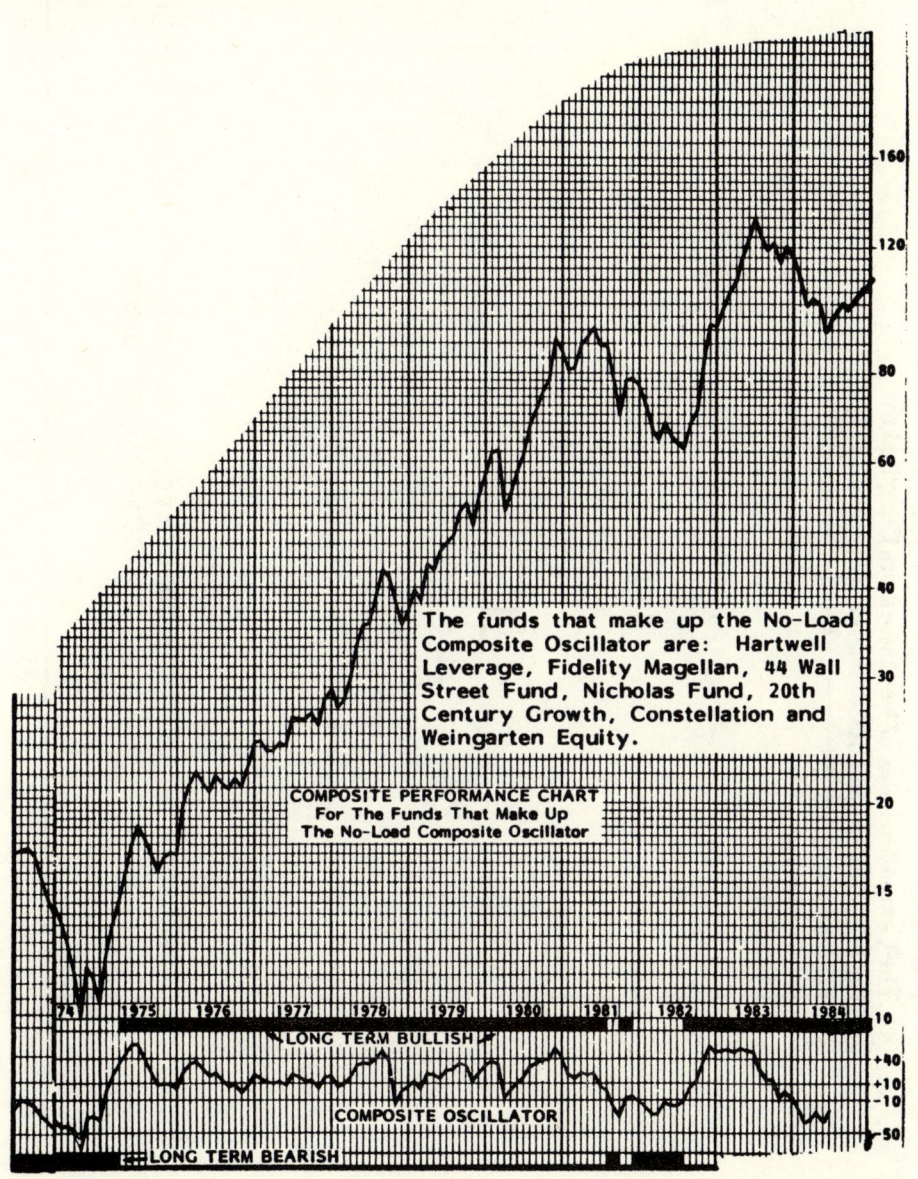

FIGURE 7-17
**The Composite Index of Key Indicators Compiled by the U.S. Department of Commerce**

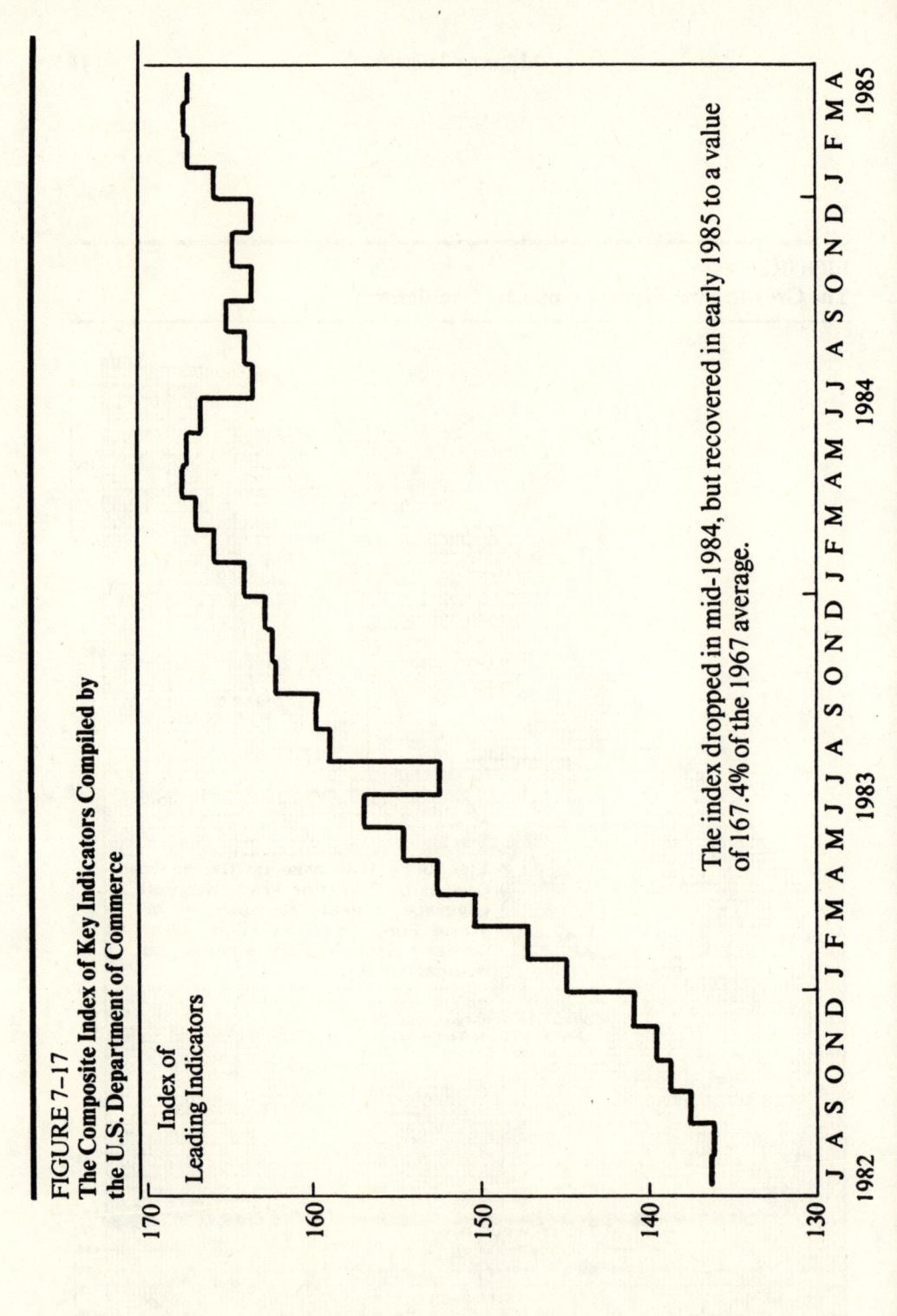

The index dropped in mid-1984, but recovered in early 1985 to a value of 167.4% of the 1967 average.

Finally, the corporate index of key indicators compiled by the U.S. Department of Commerce as shown in Figure 7-17 is frequently used by technical analysts as a predictor of economic activity. As this illustration shows, this indicator appeared to signal good economic improvement in 1983 with a leveling off during late 1984.

FIGURE 7-18
**The Percentage of Cash Held by Mutual Funds and the New York Stock Exchange Index for the Period 1970 to 1984**

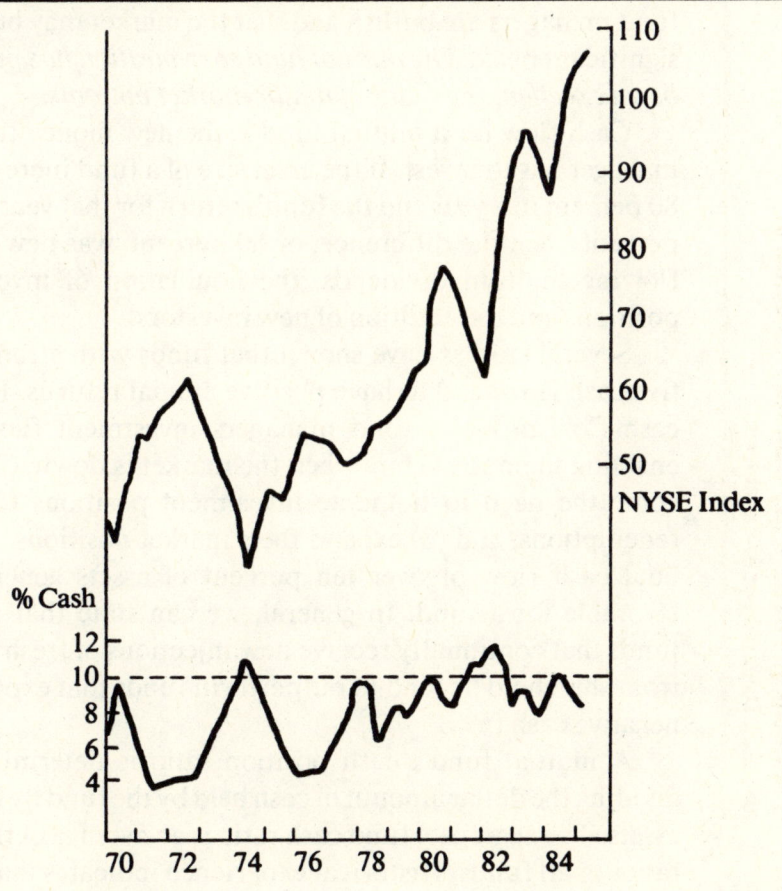

## THE CASH FLOW INDICATOR

The cash flow indicator is based on the concept of contrary thinking. This concept holds that the time to buy is when the majority of investors reach the peak of pessimism and, conversely, the time to sell when investor optimism reaches its peak. One contrarian indicator is the *mutual fund cash position*. It is the average percentage of cash held in mutual fund portfolios in the aggregate. A large increase in the percentage of mutual fund assets held in cash indicates that fund managers are bearish and that the market is probably near an important low. Conversely, a low cash position implies that fund managers are bullish and that the market may be near a significant peak. *The mutual fund cash position has proved to be an excellent indicator of major market bottoms.*

Cash flow for a mutual fund is the new money the fund manager has to invest. If the asset size of a fund increased by 80 percent in a year and the fund's return for that year was 20 percent, then the difference, or 60 percent, was new money flowing in from dividends, the liquidation of investment positions and the addition of new investors.

Several studies have shown that funds with strong positive cash flow tend to have positive annual returns. Positive cash flow provides fund managers investment flexibility, enabling them to (1) buy when the market is down; (2) overcome the need to liquidate investment positions to cover redemptions; and (3) expand their market positions. An annual cash flow of over ten percent of assets generally is favorable for a fund. In general, we can state that mutual funds that continually receive new injections of fresh money from shareholders tend to outperform funds that experience negative cash flow.

A mutual fund's cash position ratio is determined by dividing the dollar amount of cash held by the fund by its total assets. The aggregate fund cash ratio is an average of the cash ratios of all funds. Historical experience indicates that when the aggregate cash ratio rises above 10 percent, a major upward market move will soon occur. Conversely, when the mutual fund cash ratio falls below 8 percent, stock prices tend to fall by significant amounts. Over the last ten years, a normal cash ratio has been about 9 percent.

Figure 7-18 shows the aggregate mutual fund cash position ratio and the NYSE index for the period 1970-1984. It illustrates the negative correlation between the fund cash position ratio and the stock market. You will note that the cash position ratio exceeded 10 percent in mid-1974 and again in mid-1982, which, the graph shows, were both points of great opportunity to buy the market at the bottom. The monthly mutual fund cash position is available from *Barron's*. In general, the cash flow indicator can be used as a buy indicator when the cash position ratio exceeds 10 percent, which last occurred in July 1984 when it reached 10.2 percent.

## COST AVERAGING TIMING METHODS

As we have seen in the earlier sections of this chapter, most successful timing strategies require an inordinate amount of data gathering and tracking. Consequently most individual investors must rely on the services of an advisory firm or newsletter for compilation of the necessary data. Many investors, therefore, use other, easier methods to time the mutual fund market. Two useful alternatives are dollar cost averaging or a formula plan. Both techniques attempt to average the prices you pay for purchases of fund shares over time.

The basic idea behind cost averaging is that if we make several purchases of a fund's shares over an extended period of time, we will "average out" the unpredictable highs and lows and will end up with an average price that is more realistic than any single price we might have paid if we bought all the shares at once.

Of course, in using this approach, we will never be able to acquire a maximum number of shares when the fund price hits its low (if, in fact, we could predict when that occurs). While this is true, cost averaging assumes that we are willing to trade the possible gains we might realize from trying to buy the fund at its low for the losses we could sustain from unintentionally buying it at its high. In essence, we are compromising our investment position.

*Dollar cost averaging* is based on investing a fixed amount of money at fixed intervals in a given mutual fund. You invest and continue to invest on your pre-established schedule regardless of fluctuations in the fund price. This method tends to reduce the average cost of the fund shares you purchase because you will be buying more shares when the price is down than when it is up. When this scheme is practiced faithfully, losses during declining markets are limited, while the ability to participate in accelerating markets is maintained. The process of dollar averaging tends to eliminate the cyclical characteristics of a share price but retains its trend growth over time. Another important advantage of dollar cost averaging is that it forces you to plan an investment program more thoroughly and systematically than if commitments were made sporadically or all at one time.

A disadvantage of averaging is that although it helps provide a solution to the problem of timing purchases, it does not tell you when to sell your securities. Dollar averaging assumes that a fund, once purchased, will be sold only infrequently, and that the selling of fund shares is only incidental to the entire investment process. There certainly is an advantage in selecting a quality fund for a long-term investment and holding it. But the performance of funds do change and sometimes require that shares be sold.

Dollar cost averaging, is thus a long-term investment timing strategy. To be effective, it must be practiced over at least one full business cycle, and perhaps over as long as five years at minimum. Funds invested according to this strategy should not be considered liquid investments, since premature withdrawal may result in losses and really defeats the whole purpose of this timing approach anyway.

Dollar cost averaging performs better (i.e. results in a lower average per share cost) when the market and the fund price are volatile. Thus, using dollar cost averaging with a high *beta* fund in a fluctuating market environment has many advantages.

Let us consider an investor who selects Columbia Growth fund and decides to use dollar cost averaging to invest $2,000 during 1984 as shown in Table 7-7. Each investment of $166.67 is made on the last day of each month beginning January 31, 1984. Because of price fluctuations, the total

TABLE 7-7
**Dollar Cost Averaging in Columbia Growth Fund in 1984.**

| 1984 | Amount | Net Asset Value | Shares this Transaction | Total Shares | Account Value |
|---|---|---|---|---|---|
| Jan | $166.67 | $21.41 | 7.785 | 7.785 | $166.67 |
| Feb | 166.67 | 19.86 | 8.392 | 16.177 | 321.27 |
| Mar | 166.67 | 20.28 | 8.218 | 24.395 | 494.74 |
| April | 166.67 | 20.21 | 8.247 | 32.642 | 659.70 |
| May | 166.67 | 18.91 | 8.814 | 41.456 | 783.94 |
| June | 166.67 | 19.55 | 8.525 | 49.981 | 977.14 |
| July | 166.67 | 18.98 | 8.781 | 58.763 | 1115.32 |
| Aug | 166.67 | 21.15 | 7.880 | 66.643 | 1409.50 |
| Sept | 166.67 | 21.05 | 7.918 | 74.561 | 1589.51 |
| Oct | 166.67 | 21.26 | 7.840 | 82.401 | 1751.84 |
| Nov | 166.67 | 20.95 | 7.956 | 90.356 | 1892.96 |
| Dec | 166.63 | 21.52 | 7.743 | 98.099 | 2111.10 |
|  | $2000.00 |  | 98.099 |  |  |

shares purchased for the year was 98.1 at an average price of $20.39. If the investor had bought $2,000 worth of shares on January 31, 1984, he would have received only 93.4 shares at that time at an average price of $21.41. Table 7-7 shows another advantage of the plan: the investor only needed to have available $166.67 a month in cash using dollar cost averaging rather than the entire $2,000 if he bought once at the beginning of the year.

In another example, if a person had invested $1,000 in Fidelity Equity-Income Fund, Inc. on January 1, 1975, and each quarter thereafter invested another $250, the total value of the investment would have been $38,253.42 on December 31, 1984. He would have invested a total of $10,750 over the ten-year period at $1,000 per year.

A *formula method* of investing uses a growth fund investment with an associated money market fund to avoid market declines. The method is designed automatically to take you out of the growth fund and into the money market fund in declining markets and the reverse in rising markets. The method works as follows:

1. Record the weekly net asset values of the fund for each month;
2. Calculate the average of the weekly NAV's for the month;
3. Calculate the percentage change in the current month's average NAV from the previous month's;
4. If the percentage change equals or exceeds one percent, buy an amount of new shares in the fund equal to twice the percentage change when the percentage change is positive. If it is negative (the average NAV for the current month declined from previous month) then sell shares in the amount of twice the percentage change and invest the proceeds in a money market fund.

Thus, if the current month's average fund price declines by three percent, you would redeem 6 percent of the value of

TABLE 7-8
**The Double Percentage Adjustment Formula**

| Week | NAV | Monthly Average | Percentage Change | Fund Adjustment | Fund Value | Money Market Fund Value |
|---|---|---|---|---|---|---|
| 1 | $10.00 | | | | | |
| 2 | 9.90 | | | | | |
| 3 | 9.90 | | | | | |
| 4 | 9.80 | $9.90 | 0 | 0 | $10,000.00 | 0 |
| 5 | 9.85 | | | | | |
| 6 | 9.80 | | | | | |
| 7 | 9.80 | | | | | |
| 8 | 9.75 | $9.80 | −1% | −2% | $ 9,800.00 | $200.00 |
| 9 | 9.70 | | | | | |
| 10 | 9.65 | | | | | |
| 11 | 9.60 | | | | | |
| 12 | 9.55 | $9.625 | −1.8% | −3.6% | $ 9,447.20 | $544.80 |
| 13 | 9.60 | | | | | |
| 14 | 9.70 | | | | | |
| 15 | 9.60 | | | | | |
| 16 | 9.70 | $9.65 | −0.25% | 0 | $ 9,447.20 | $560.35 |
| 17 | 9.75 | | | | | |
| 18 | 9.82 | | | | | |
| 19 | 9.89 | | | | | |
| 20 | 9.94 | $9.85 | +2.1% | +4.2% | $ 9,843.98 | $169.17 |

*Note:* The money market fund earns 1 percent per month.

your current investment in the fund and use it to buy money market fund shares. This method helps you ease out of the market when it is declining and increase your commitment when it is increasing. Since you do not act when the percentage change is less than 1 percent, you will avoid the small fluctuations. Of course, if you wish, you could modify the rule to only act when the percentage change is below 1.5 percent or some other number you are more comfortable with.

An illustration of this formula plan is provided in Table 7-8. At the end of the second month it shows that the fund's percentage change in the monthly average is − 1 percent and therefore we reduce our investment in the fund by $200, or 2 percent of our $10,000 investment in the fund at that time. Similarly, at the end of the 5th month, the formula signals us to increase our holding in the fund by 4.2 percent. Thus, we reduce our money market fund investment by $396.78 and add that to our growth fund holdings.

This type of formula plan timing approach causes us to adjust our fund holdings twice as fast as the market changes. For example, if a market declined at a constant 2 percent a month, we would reduce our holdings by 4 percent a month. The method is particularly useful in periods of fluctuation and unpredictable cycles. Since growth funds traditionally rise sharply at the beginning of a market upswing, the system gets you back into the fund in time to enjoy the advancing market. And, because the system is so simple to apply, even novice fund switchers have no trouble using it.

## TIMING SERVICES VERSUS A BUY AND HOLD STRATEGY

Looking at charts of past performance, it becomes very clear when we should have bought and sold. The timing methods discussed earlier in this chapter certainly will help.

Yet many investors prefer to rely on newsletters or timing

services to provide timing signals rather to do it for themselves. A number of services are aimed at investors who use telephone switching services to move rapidly between equity and money-market funds within a no-load family. They track fund performance and recommend specific funds to buy in addition to providing timing signals.

A recent study demonstrated the performance of two popular newsletter timing services (Slater, 1984). The study used the Lipper Growth Fund Index to represent overall fund performance for the period January 1, 1977 to March 6, 1984. During the period, the Index grew 129 percent compared to 179 percent for the Telephone Switch Newsletter and 197 percent for Switch Fund Advisory. Of course, you would have to factor in the cost of the newsletters and the effects of taxes to determine the true value of their performance for you.

A related approach is to engage a timing service to make timing decisions for you. They usually require a minimum account of $25,000 and typically charge a management fee of one to two percent annually. One timing service, Greenwich Montrend, claimed a return of 19 percent annually, with below market risk, for the period from January 1, 1973 to December 31, 1982.

All timing services handle customers in much the same way. Before they begin managing your money you first invest in a fund. Your fund shares always remain in your name, and you can withdraw your investment at any time. However, you must sign a form empowering the timing service to move your money back and forth within the fund family of your choice.

As we discussed earlier, the burning question is whether, in fact, active traders or timers can do better than a simple buy and hold strategy without benefit of chance or hindsight. One sure answer to the question is that "it depends."

Performance measurements are strongly influenced by the period of comparison. For instance, we would expect a buy and hold strategy to do better in periods of upwardly trending markets. On the other hand, traders and timers seem to do better in declining markets when selling is more important than buying. In general, a buy and hold strategy is a generally bullish strategy that requires investing in only quality funds and that investments be made for the long term. However, as many of us have learned from experience, in down markets even the highest quality investments decline and, often, for various reasons, we cannot hold investments for the five years or more that a buy and hold strategy requires.

In good markets, we all can do well. In sideways markets, timing signals turn out to be false as often as true. And in down markets a sell signal, however it is obtained, is important so we can avoid riding the market to the bottom. A timing strategy or a timing service or newsletter, therefore, can help you cut your losses.

For example, as Figure 7-19 shows, if you could have switched in and out of the 44 Wall Street Fund using a simple moving average timing strategy, you could have avoided the terrible downturns that occurred in July 1982 and again in July 1983. In fact, if you had held from May 1979 to April 1985 the value of your investment would have declined 40 percent. On the other hand, if you could have missed the declines and temporarily placed your funds in a money fund paying 9 percent annually during those periods, your return for the six years would have been 230 percent. Thus, the switching system would have returned 22 percent annually, compared to a buy and hold negative return of 8 percent a year.

The returns for several funds for the June 30, 1982 to June 30, 1983 up market is compared to their performance during the June 30, 1983 to June 30, 1984 down market in Figure 7-20. The chart shows that the funds in the upper left-hand corner (Mutual Shares, Strong Investors and Windsor) performed positively in both the up and the down markets. On

## FIGURE 7-19
**The 44 Wall Street Fund**

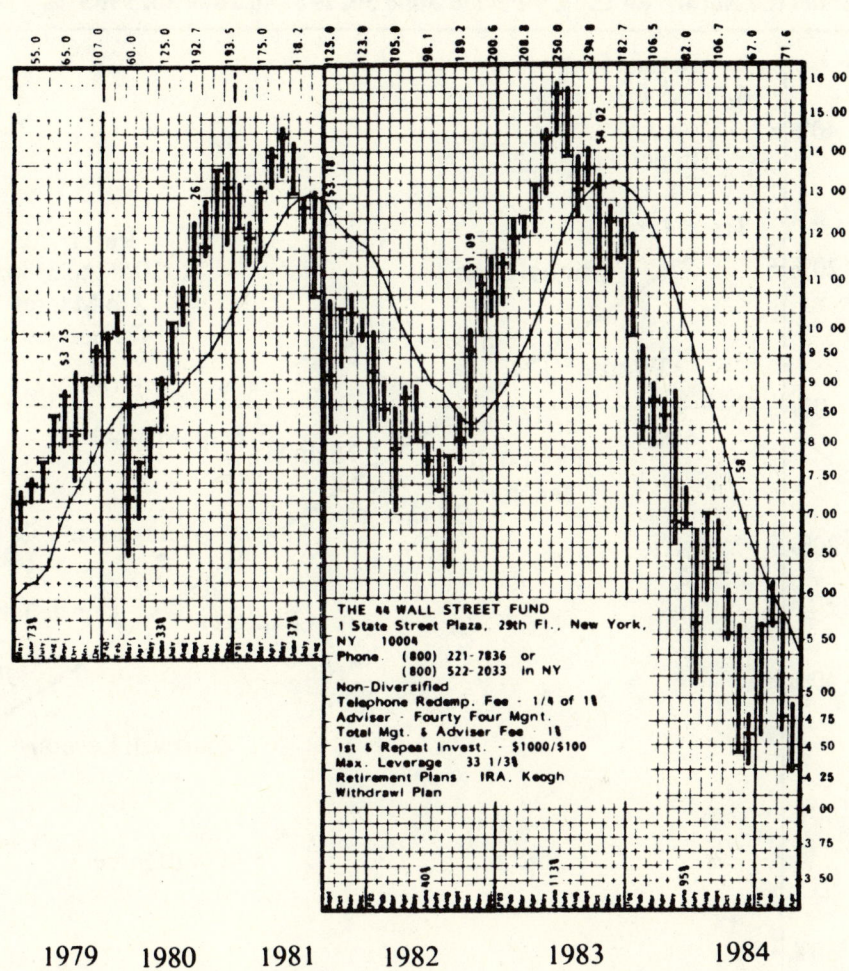

**FIGURE 7–20**
**The Return for the Down Period June 30, 1983 to June 30, 1984 versus the Return for the Up Period June 30, 1982 to June 30, 1983**

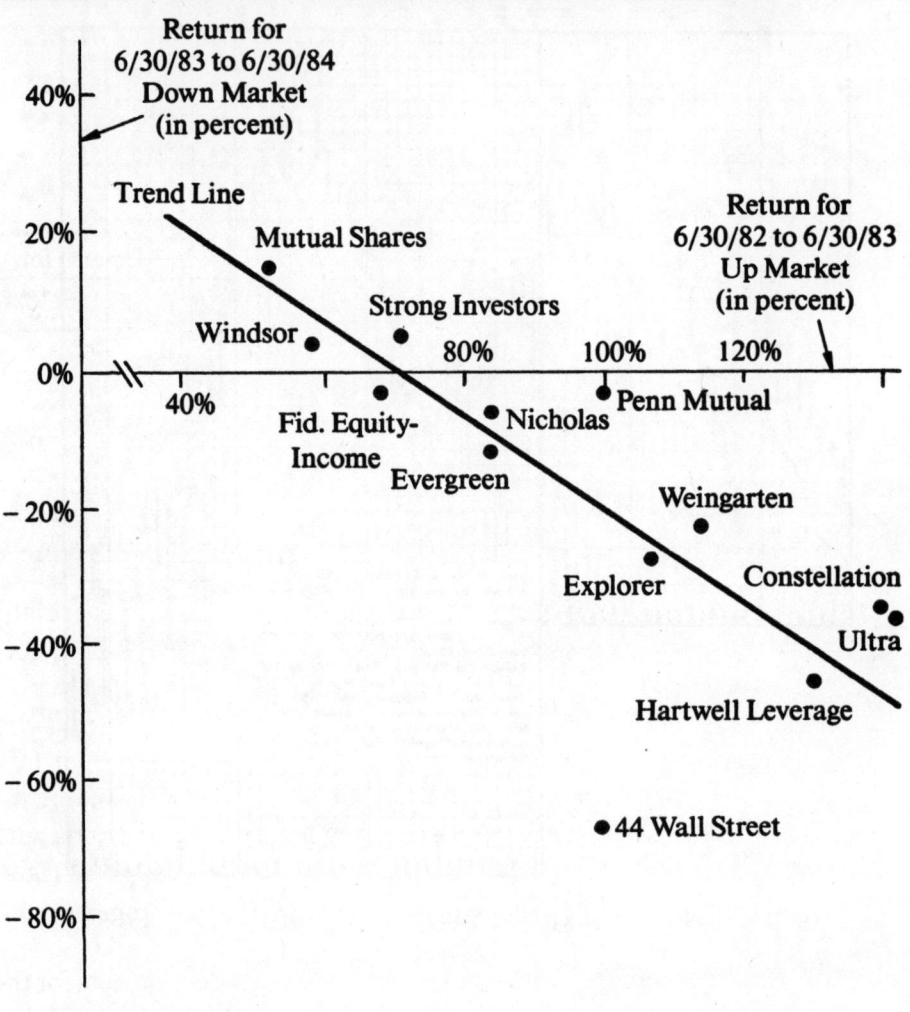

TABLE 7-9
**Funds for a Buy and Hold Strategy**

| Name | Beta | Total Return (Percent) for | |
|---|---|---|---|
| | | 1975-84 | 6/30/82-6/30/84 |
| Windsor | 0.85 | 685 | 66 |
| Evergreen | 0.99 | 1,135 | 61 |
| Pennsylvania Mutual | 0.90 | 1,323 | 94 |
| Nicholas | 0.83 | 830 | 72 |
| Mutual Shares | 0.55 | 831 | 78 |
| Fidelity Equity Income | 0.80 | 709 | 64 |

**Funds for a Timing Strategy**

| Name | Beta | Total Return (Percent) for | |
|---|---|---|---|
| | | 1975-84 | 6/30/82-6/30/84 |
| Constellation | 1.75 | 507 | 56 |
| 44 Wall Street | 2.03 | 430 | -11 |
| Weingarten Equity | 1.32 | 639 | 66 |
| Hartwell Leverage | 1.68 | 498 | 27 |
| Explorer | 1.08 | 542 | 50 |
| Twentieth Century Ultra | 1.50 | - | 57 |

the other hand funds on the lower right corner (especially Constellation, Hartwell Leverage and Ultra) performed very well in the up period, but gave up much of their gains during the down period. As Table 7-9 shows, the six funds with *betas* equal to less than 1.00 that were situated in the upper left-hand corner of Figure 7-20 are quite appropriate investments for a buy-hold strategy. On the other hand, the six funds with *betas* exceeding 1.00 that were situated in the lower right-hand corner of Figure 7-20 would be more appropriate investments for a timing strategy.

A buy and hold strategy can produce decent returns for the investor who selects good quality, low-*beta* funds and uses a guide, newsletter or annual report to track the performance. On the other hand, the investor who is prepared to select high-*beta* funds and commit to using one of the timing strategies we discussed in this chapter can achieve superior returns. If you feel that you can expend the time and effort and can muster the necessary discipline to commit to a timing strategy, I recommend that you do so with at least a portion of your fund investments. The rewards could be well worth the effort.

## APPENDIX: EXPONENTIAL MOVING AVERAGE CALCULATION

To compute an exponential average, you derive a smoothing constant for the exponential average you will be employing. This constant SC is determined by the equation

$$\text{Smoothing constant} = \frac{2}{\text{Number of units} + 1} \quad (7\text{-}1)$$

Thus, for an eight-week moving average of the weekly values of a fund, we have SC = 2/9 = .0222.

$$\text{Smoothing constant} = \frac{2}{8 + 1} = .0222$$

The exponential moving average (EA) is then calculated by

$$EA(n) = [V(n) - EA(n-1)]\,SC + EA(n-1) \quad (7\text{-}2)$$

for the nth period of time, where V (n) is the current value of the fund or indicator and EA (n − 1) is the most recently calculated value.

In calculating any exponential moving average of length N, one needs to calculate exponential moving averages for each of the first N periods to obtain a valid moving average from period N + 1 onward. This *initialization* is required to get the sequential calculation going.

Thus, in the example of an eight-week exponential moving average, although the averages obtained for the first eight periods will not be valid, they must be calculated (using equation 7-2, with a smoothing constant of .0222) to obtain a valid average for period 9 and onward.

An example of a four-week average is shown in Table 7-4.

# Chapter 8
# Monitoring Mutual Fund Performance

Most funds do not issue stock certificates, but do provide quarterly reports on distributions, capital gains and new investments. If for no other reason, keeping records of fund purchases, distributions and redemptions is necessary for paying taxes on the income and capital gains distributions. Careful and diligent record-keeping also can be helpful in enabling you to monitor your funds' performance on a regular basis.

Quarterly statements issued by funds typically record the beginning balance of shares, the activity in the account during the quarter and the total shares held at the end of the quarter. Using these reports, you can track the performance of each of your funds over time.

Let us consider the sample record for the fund shown in Table 8–1. This record is for one year, 1984. During the year, the fund owner received a dividend distribution in May and November and a capital gains distribution in November. All these distributions were reinvested as shown on the report.

In examining the sample statement, you will note that the

**TABLE 8-1**
**A Record of a Sample Fund for 1984.**

12/31/84                              Sample Fund

Mr. Customer
10 Apple Street
City, State 98765

| Confirm Date | Trade Date | Transaction | Dollar Amount | Share Price | Shares this Transaction | Total Shares Owned |
|---|---|---|---|---|---|---|
| | | Beginning Balance | | | | 341.00 |
| 2/13 | 1/12 | Purchase | $200.00 | $10.11 | 19.78 | 360.78 |
| 5/20 | 5/15 | Reinvest dividend $ .30 | $108.23 | $ 9.92 | 10.91 | 371.69 |
| 7/14 | 7/13 | Purchase | $300.00 | $10.81 | 27.75 | 399.44 |
| 11/25 | 11/5 | Reinvest dividend $ .46 | $183.74 | $11.07 | 16.60 | 416.04 |
| 11/25 | 11/5 | Capital gain reinvested $1.52 | $607.15 | $11.07 | 54.85 | 470.89 |

| | Current Year 1984 | | Shares You Own 470.89 |
|---|---|---|---|
| Total Distributions | Income Dividends | Capital Gains | Account Value |
| $889.12 | $291.97 | $607.15 | 470.89 shares at $11.22 = $5,283.35 |

price of each share in the fund decreases by the amount of every distribution on the day that it is made (trade date). For example, on May 15th, the price of each share dropped from $10.22 to $9.92 due to the $.30 distribution made on that date. The actual confirmation of the owner's automatic reinvestment of the dividend to purchase 10.910 new shares was issued on May 20th.

As we have seen earlier, the fund's return for the year can be obtained from the following calculation:

$$\text{Annual return} = \frac{\text{final NAV} + \text{distributions} - \text{initial NAV}}{\text{initial NAV}} \times 100 \quad (8\text{--}1)$$

or

$$\text{Return} = \frac{11.2 + 2.28 - 10.2}{10.2} \times 100 = 34.7\% \quad (8\text{--}2)$$

The initial net asset value is obtained from the previous year's final statement.

An investor should retain all his annual statements so he can record his fund's performance over time. One way of tracking fund performance is to track the value of a single share of the fund by recording its new value after every distribution. An example of how this can be done for a sample fund is shown in Table 8–2.

In order to calculate the adjusted or new number of shares held after a distribution, we have to calculate an *adjustment factor*

$$\text{Adjustment factor} = 1 + \frac{\text{per share distribution}}{\text{ex-dividend share price}} \quad (8\text{--}3)$$

Thus, as shown in Table 8–2, if we received a distribution of a $1.80 per share on February 8th and the share price after distribution was $20.22, the adjustment factor was

$$\text{Adjustment factor} = 1 + \frac{1.80}{20.22} = 1.0890 \quad (8\text{--}4)$$

We then multiply the number of shares prior to the distribu-

## TABLE 8-2
**Adjusting Future Share Values to Account for Fund Distributions**

| Week Ending | Share Price ($) | Distribution per Share | Adjustment Factor | Adjusted Number of Shares Held | Adjusted Value of Shares Held ($) |
|---|---|---|---|---|---|
| Dec. 28 | 14.00 | | | 1 | 14.00 |
| Jan. 4 | 15.00 | | | 1 | 15.00 |
| Jan. 11 | 15.90 | | | 1 | 15.90 |
| Jan. 18 | 16.75 | | | 1 | 16.75 |
| Jan. 25 | 18.52 | | | 1 | 18.52 |
| Feb. 1 | 21.45 | | | 1 | 21.45 |
| Feb. 8 | 20.22 | $1.80 | 1.0890 | 1.0890 | 22.02* |
| Feb. 15 | 21.70 | | 1.0890 | 1.0890 | 23.63 |
| Feb. 22 | 22.85 | | 1.0890 | 1.0890 | 24.88 |
| Mar. 1 | 22.05 | $1.45 | 1.0657 | 1.1605 | 25.59** |
| Mar. 8 | 23.42 | | 1.0657 | 1.1605 | 27.18*** |
| Mar. 15 | 25.65 | | 1.0657 | 1.1605 | 29.77 |
| Mar. 22 | 27.13 | | 1.0657 | 1.1605 | 31.48 |
| Mar. 29 | 30.05 | | 1.0657 | 1.1605 | 34.87 |
| | | | | Total Return = | 149.1% |

*Feb. 8    Adjusted number of shares = 1 share × 1.0890 = 1.0890
             Adjusted value of shares = 1.0890 shares × $20.22 = $22.02
**Mar. 1   Adjusted number of shares = 1.0890 shares × 1.0657 shares = 1.1605 shares
             Adjusted value of shares = 1.1605 shares × $22.05 = $25.59
***Mar. 8   Adjusted value of shares = 1.1605 shares × $23.42 = $27.18

tion by the adjustment factor to determine the adjusted number of shares held after the distribution.

$$\begin{matrix}\text{Adjusted no. of shares}\\ \text{after distribution}\end{matrix} = \begin{matrix}\text{Adjusted no. of shares}\\ \text{prior to distribution}\end{matrix} \times \text{Adjustment Factor}$$

or

Adjusted number of shares after distribution = 1 × 1.0890 = 1.0890

Similarly, the adjusted value of a fund share after the distribution is equal to the Adjustment Factor times the share price after the distribution or

Adjusted share value = 1.0890 × $20.22 = $22.02

The adjusted number of shares held remains 1.0890 until the next distribution, which was $1.45 per share on March 1. The new adjustment factor on March 1st then was

$$\text{Adjustment factor} = 1 + \frac{1.45}{22.05} = 1.0657 \qquad (8\text{-}6)$$

and the adjusted number of shares became 1.0657 × 1.0890 or 1.1605.

We now can calculate the fund's return for December 28 to March 29 period as follows:

$$\text{Return} = \frac{34.87 - 14.00}{14.00} \times 100 = 149.1\% \qquad (8\text{-}7)$$

There is an alternative method that can be used for tracking the performance of a single fund share over time. It, too, uses an adjustment factor that is calculated in the same manner as described above. However, with the second method, instead of adjusting *future* share values to account for each fund distribution, we would adjust *past* share values. This is done by dividing the adjustment factor into all share values prior to the time the distribution is made. As Table 8–3 shows, the second method may be easier to use on a daily basis, since new fund shares can be recorded directly from newspaper fund price listings without having to adjust them until a new distribution is made.

## TABLE 8-3
**Adjusting Past Share Values to Account for Fund Distributions**

| Week Ending | Share Price | Distribution Per Share | Adjustment Factor | Feb. 8 Adjusted Share Value | March 1 Adjusted Share Value |
|---|---|---|---|---|---|
| 12/28 | $14.00 |  |  | $12.86* | $12.07** |
| 1/4 | 15.00 |  |  | 13.77 | 12.92 |
| 1/11 | 15.90 |  |  | 14.60 | 13.70 |
| 1/18 | 16.75 |  |  | 15.38 | 14.43 |
| 1/25 | 18.52 |  |  | 17.01 | 15.96 |
| 2/1 | 21.45 |  |  | 19.70 | 18.49 |
| 2/8 | 20.22 | $1.80 | 1.0890 | 20.22 | 18.97 |
| 2/15 | 21.70 |  |  | 21.70 | 20.36 |
| 2/22 | 22.85 |  |  | 22.85 | 21.44 |
| 3/1 | 22.05 | $1.45 | 1.0657 |  | 22.05*** |
| 3/8 | 23.42 |  |  |  | 23.42 |
| 3/15 | 25.65 |  |  |  | 25.65 |
| 3/22 | 27.13 |  |  |  | 27.13 |
| 3/29 | 30.05 |  |  |  | 30.05 |
|  |  |  |  | Total Return = | 149.1% |

Note: The number of shares remains constant and equal to 1.
After Feb. 8 distribution:
  * 12/28 Adjusted Share Value = $14.00 ÷ 1.089 = $12.86
After Mar. 1 distribution:
  ** 12/28 Adjusted Share Value = $12.86 ÷ 1.066 = $12.07
  *** 3/1 Adjusted Share Value = $22.05 ÷ 1 share = $22.05

**TABLE 8–4**
**Adjusting for Distributions**

| Method 1 | Method 2 |
|---|---|
| Technique:<br>  Adjusts Future Share Values | Technique:<br>  Adjusts Past Share Values |
| Adjustment factor: same for both methods ||
| Adjustment factor = $1 + \dfrac{\text{Distribution}}{\text{Net asset value on distribution date}}$ ||
| Method:<br>  Multiply future share values by cumulative adjustment factor to obtain adjusted share values | Method:<br>  Divide prior adjusted share values by current adjustment factor to obtain adjusted share value |

Note: The cumulative adjustment factor = the product of all adjustment factors to date

The two methods are compared on Table 8–4. Either approach is acceptable and both will provide you with the information you need. As Tables 8–3 and 8–4 indicate, the two methods result in the same total return of 149.1 percent for the quarter.

## CHARTING FUND PERFORMANCE

An investor may want to illustrate the value of a fund over several years in order to assess its performance. The charted performance of the Templeton Growth Fund (an 8.5 percent load fund) is shown in Figure 8–1 for the 20-year period 1964–1983. A logarithmic scale is used on the vertical axis so that its percentage changes are reflected as constant incre-

**FIGURE 8-1**
**A Chart of Templeton Growth Fund for January 1, 1983 for an Initial $10,000 Investment**

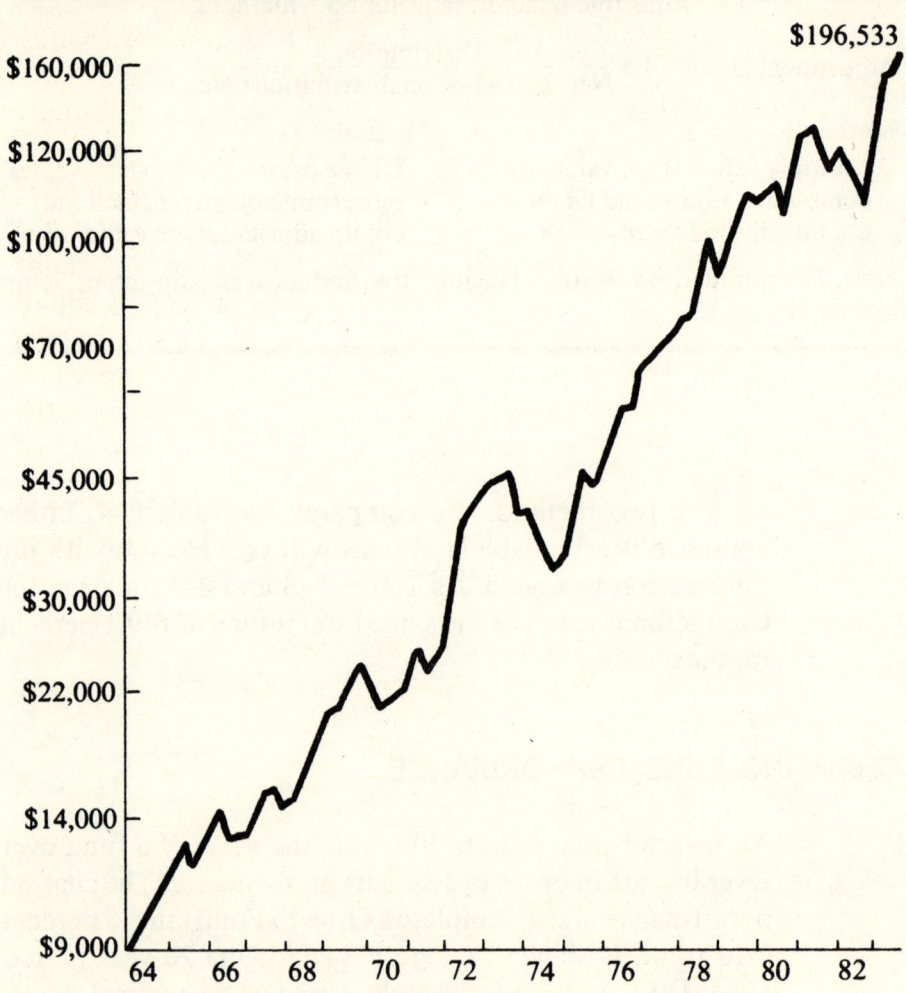

ments. The investor put $10,000 into the fund on January 1, 1964 and because of the 8.5 percent load held $9,150 at that point. During 1964, there were $121 in distributions and a $2,353 gain in the net asset value of the shares held. At the end of 20 years, the value of the holding grew to $196,533, for a compound annual return of 16.1 percent.

The chart for the fund is maintained by recording and plotting the value of the fund each quarter. If a more accurate accounting is needed, monthly data can be used. The Templeton chart in Figure 8-1 assumes the investor made a single purchase of $10,000 and held it over the entire 20-year period covered by the chart. This of course, is an oversimplified representation of most fund investments. Most investors would buy and sell shares continually over a 20-year holding period, especially if they are using a timing strategy. But it does illustrate how a fund's performance can be charted over several years.

Figure 8-2 shows a chart of the per-share values of the Seligman fund for 1974-83. For the ten-year period, we obtain its total return as

$$\text{10-year return} = \frac{(6.40 - 1.00)}{1.00} \times 100 = 540\% \qquad (8-8)$$

The 10-year compound annual return for Seligman is 20.4 percent. (See Chapter 5 for this calculation.) By drawing a trend line on Seligman's chart as shown on Figure 8-2, we calculate the annual return for the trend line as

$$\text{10-year return} = \frac{(5.80 - .58)}{.58} \times 100 = 900\% \qquad (8-9)$$

Again, by using the compound annual return calculation shown in Chapter 5, we find that the compound annual return of the trend line is 24.6 percent. The use of the trend line enables us to estimate expected future returns for the fund.

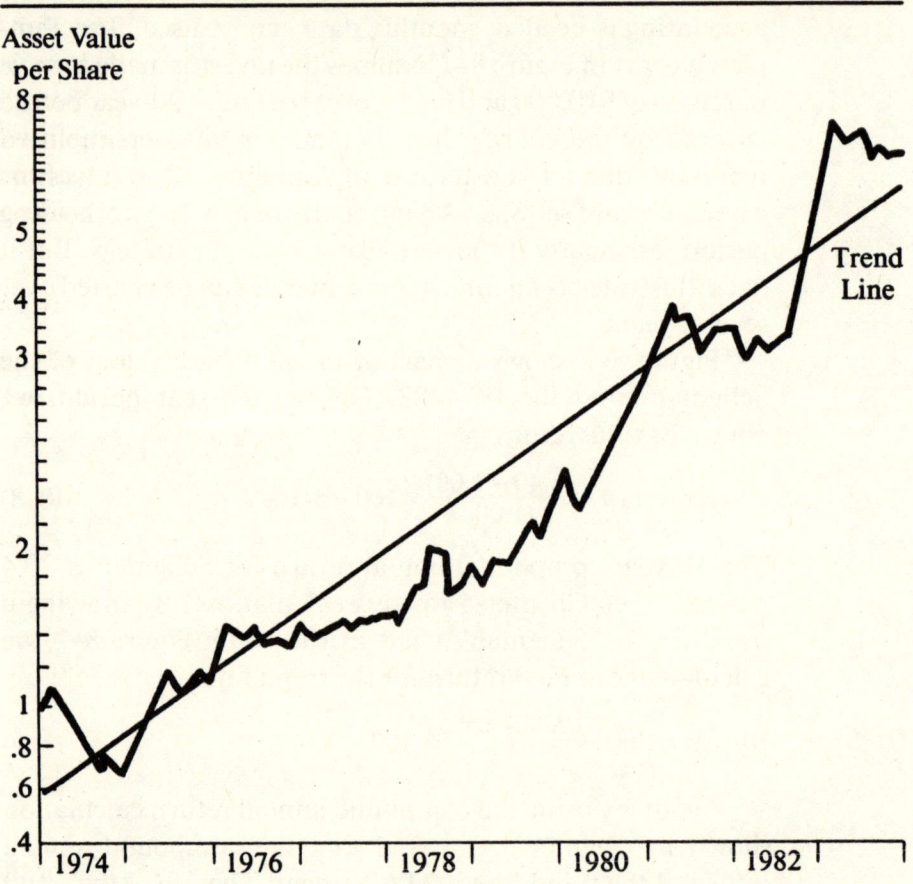

FIGURE 8-2
**Asset Value Per Share (January 1, 1974 = 1.00) for the Ten Year Period 1974–1983 for Seligman Capital Fund with all Distributions Reinvested**

## PORTFOLIO RECORDS

It is just as important to track the performance of a portfolio over time as it is to track individual funds. To do this, we must set up a recording system that tracks the asset values of each fund held in the portfolio. Then, as distributions and redemptions are made, we adjust the records of both the fund and the portfolio.

Let us consider a portfolio record for a set of three funds as shown in Table 8-5. We purchased fund A on June 30, 1982 and recorded a cumulative gain of 89 percent over the following two years. Thus, the compound annual gain was 37.5 percent for fund A. We then calculate the gains for funds B and C in a similar manner. The value of the portfolio on June 30, 1984 is

$$\text{Portfolio value} = \sum_{j=1}^{N} I_j G_j \qquad (8\text{-}10)$$

where $I_j$ = investment in the jth fund and $G_j$ = cumulative gain factor for the jth fund and $N$ = total number of funds. Thus, for Table 8-5, the portfolio value is

$$\text{Portfolio value} = (\$2,000 \times 1.89) + (\$3,000 \times 1.45) + (\$1,000 \times 1.19)$$
$$= \$9,320 \qquad (8\text{-}11)$$

To calculate the compound annual performance of the portfolio, we must account for the fact that each investment was held for a different amount of time. We would calculate the weighted average holding period from

$$\text{Weighted average holding period} = \frac{\sum_{j=1}^{N} I_j Q_j}{\sum_{j=1}^{N} I_j} \qquad (8\text{-}12)$$

where $Q$ = the number of quarters that fund j is held. For the funds in Table 8-5, we have

$$\text{Wgted aver. holding per.} = \frac{\$2,000 \times 8 \text{ quarters} + \$3,000 \times 7 \text{ quarters} + \$1,000 \times 6 \text{ quarters}}{\$2,000 + \$3,000 + \$1,000}$$
$$= 7.166 \text{ quarters} \qquad (8\text{-}13)$$

Since the total initial investment is $6000 and 7.166 quarters is 1.79 years, we find

$$\text{Annual return} = \left(1.79\sqrt{\frac{9{,}315}{6{,}000}} - 1\right)100 = 27.9\% \qquad (8\text{--}14)$$

TABLE 8–5

| Gain Factor for Quarter Ending | S&P 500 | Fund A (G) | Fund B (GI) | Fund C (I) |
|---|---|---|---|---|
| 6/30/82 | | Purchased $2,000 | | |
| 9/30/82 | 1.05 | 1.10 | Purchased $3,000 | |
| 12/30/82 | 1.04 | 1.08 | 1.06 | Purchased $1,000 |
| 3/30/83 | 1.05 | 1.06 | 1.05 | 1.03 |
| 6/30/83 | 1.05 | 1.08 | 1.07 | 1.03 |
| 9/30/83 | 1.06 | 1.11 | 1.06 | 1.03 |
| 12/30/83 | 1.04 | 1.02 | 1.04 | 1.03 |
| 3/30/84 | 1.04 | 1.12 | 1.05 | 1.03 |
| 6/30/84 | 1.03 | 1.09 | 1.05 | 1.03 |
| Cumulative gain factor | 1.422 | 1.890* | 1.447 | 1.194** |
| Annual gain | 19.2% | 37.5% | 23.5% | 12.5% |
| Number of quarters held | 8 | 8 | 7 | 6 |

G = Growth; GI = Growth and Income; and I = Income.

*Cumulative Gain Factor for Fund A =
$1.10 \times 1.08 \times 1.06 \times 1.08 \times 1.11 \times 1.02 \times 1.12 \times 1.09 = 1.890$

**Cumulative Gain Factor for Fund C = $(1.03)^6 = 1.194$

# Chapter 9

# Tax Considerations

## TAXES AND DISTRIBUTIONS

As we saw earlier, the income and capital gains realized by a fund is passed directly through to shareholders. Thus, all fund distributions create potential tax liabilities for shareholders.

Mutual fund capital gains income may be either *realized* (if the fund has disposed of securities during the tax year) or *unrealized* (if the securities continue to be held by the fund at the end of the tax year). Increases in fund income, whether realized or not, are transmitted to fund shareholders through increases in the value of total assets and are reflected in the fund's per-share net asset values.

When mutual fund distributions are made they become taxable to the shareholders who receive them. Taxes paid on these distributions reduce the fund's return.

Fund distributions are made in three forms:

1. current income;
2. short-term capital gains; and
3. long-term capital gains.

As we all know, the tax treatment of these three types of distributions is not the same. Income and short-term gains (i.e., gains from the sale of securities held six months or less) are taxed at regular tax rates. Long-term capital gains, on the other hand, receive preferential tax treatment (as of this writing, at least) and are taxed at 40 percent of the regular income tax rate. Thus income and short-term gains distributions are taxed more heavily than capital gains distributions.

When funds realize capital losses on the sale of securities during the year, they normally will carry them forward to offset gains in future years. Since capital gains cannot be taxed until they are realized (that is, until the security is sold), a fund that focuses on achieving its return from capital appreciation and not from dividends or interest payments is more attractive to high tax bracket individuals. Conversely, investors in low tax brackets tend to hold higher income paying funds.

The payments made to shareholders by mutual funds are distributions of realized income. On the *ex-distribution* date (the day the distribution is made), the per-share net asset value of the fund declines by the amount of the distribution. Thus, the income a fund shareholder receives from the distribution is offset exactly by a decrease in per-share net asset value.

Since the income distributed to shareholders represents realized income and is taxed accordingly, funds have an obligation to indicate the source of all distributions it makes during the year. Mutual funds annually provide every shareholder with tax form 1099-DIV (Statement for Recipients of Dividends and Distributions), which provides the necessary tax information on all distributions paid to the shareholder during the tax year.

To evaluate the true annual return of a mutual fund investment, an investor has to look at the after-tax return. Thus, every mutual fund shareholder must look at the fund's

## FIGURE 9-1
## Federal Income Tax Rates for 1985

Federal Income Tax Rates
(for taxable years beginning on January 1, 1985)
Exemptions
Single person (and each dependent)...............$1,040
Married persons: joint return....................  2,080
Additional exemption for taxpayer 65 or over ......  1,040
Additional exemption for spouse 65 or over ........  1,040
Additional exemption for blind taxpayer...........  1,040
Additional exemption for blind spouse ............  1,040

| Married Couples Filing Joint Returns | | | Married Couples Filing Separate Returns | | |
|---|---|---|---|---|---|
| Taxable Income | Pay | + % on Excess | Taxable Income | Pay | + % on Excess |
| 0– $3,540 | -0- | -0- | 0– $1,770 | -0- | -0- |
| $3,540– 5,720 | -0- | 11 | $1,770– 2,860 | -0- | 11 |
| 5,720– 7,910 | $239.80 | 12 | 2,860– 3,955 | $119.90 | 12 |
| 7,910– 12,390 | 502.60 | 14 | 6,195– 8,325 | 564.90 | 16 |
| 16,650– 21,020 | 1,811.40 | 18 | 8,325– 10,510 | 905.70 | 18 |
| 21,020– 25,600 | 2,598.00 | 22 | 10,510– 12,800 | 1,299.00 | 22 |
| 25,600– 31,120 | 3,605.60 | 25 | 12,800– 15,560 | 1,802.80 | 25 |
| 31,120– 36,630 | 4,985.60 | 28 | 15,560– 18,315 | 2,492.80 | 28 |
| 36,630– 47,670 | 6,528.40 | 33 | 18,315– 23,835 | 3,264.20 | 33 |
| 47,670– 62,450 | 10,171.60 | 38 | 23,835– 31,225 | 5,085.80 | 38 |
| 62,450– 89,090 | 15,788.00 | 42 | 31,225– 44,545 | 7,894.00 | 42 |
| 89,090–113,860 | 26,976.80 | 45 | 44,545– 56,930 | 13,488.40 | 45 |
| 113,860–169,020 | 38,123.30 | 49 | 56,930– 84,510 | 19,061.65 | 49 |
| 168,929–...... | 30,009.10 | 50 | 112,720–...... | 41,253.30 | 50 |

| Married Couples Filing Joint Returns | | | Married Couples Filing Separate Returns | | |
|---|---|---|---|---|---|
| Taxable Income | Pay | + % on Excess | Taxable Income | Pay | + % on Excess |
| 0– $2,390 | -0- | -0- | 0– $2,390 | -0- | -0- |
| $2,390– 3,540 | -0- | 11 | $2,390– 4,580 | -0- | 11 |
| 3,540– 4,580 | $126.50 | 12 | 4,580– 6,760 | $240.90 | 12 |
| 4,580– 6,760 | 251.30 | 14 | 6,760– 9,050 | 502.50 | 14 |
| 6,760– 8,850 | 556.50 | 15 | 9,050– 12,280 | 823.10 | 17 |
| 8,850– 11,240 | 870.00 | 16 | 12,280– 15,610 | 1,372.20 | 18 |
| 11,240– 13,430 | 1,252.40 | 18 | 15,610– 18,940 | 1,971.60 | 20 |
| 13,430– 15,610 | 1,646.60 | 20 | 18,940– 24,460 | 2,637.60 | 24 |
| 15,610– 18,940 | 2,082.60 | 23 | 24,460– 29,970 | 3,962.40 | 28 |
| 18,940– 24,460 | 2,848.50 | 26 | 29,970– 35,490 | 5,505.20 | 32 |
| 24,460– 29,970 | 4,283.70 | 30 | 35,490– 46,520 | 7,271.60 | 35 |
| 29,970– 35,490 | 5,936.70 | 34 | 46,520– 63,070 | 11,132.10 | 42 |
| 35,490– 43,190 | 7,813.50 | 38 | 63,070– 85,130 | 18,083.10 | 45 |
| 43,190– 57,550 | 10,739.50 | 42 | 85,130–112,720 | 28,010.10 | 48 |
| 57,550– 85,130 | 16,770.70 | 48 | 112,720–...... | 41,253.30 | 50 |
| 85,130– ...... | 30,009.10 | 50 | | | |

return in the context of his own marginal tax bracket. The federal income tax rates for 1985 are shown in Figure 9-1. However, remember that to get a true picture of your current tax rate, you have to add your state and/or city tax rates to your federal rate as determined from the table in Figure 9-1. As you can see when this is done, it is not difficult at all to reach the 35 percent total tax bracket or higher.

Let us consider the case of an individual in the 35 percent tax bracket and determine his after-tax return from a number of different funds. Table 9-1 lists the before and after-tax returns of a series of representative funds, which are graphically displayed on Figure 9-2. Given the marginal rate of 35 percent, we can calculate the after-tax return for a given fund as

$$\text{After-tax return} = \text{Before-tax return} \left[ 1 - (PI + .4\, CG) \times \frac{TR}{100} \right] \quad (9\text{-}1)$$

where PI = proportion of total distribution in income and PCG = proportion of total distribution in long term capital

TABLE 9-1
**The Before and After-Tax Returns for an Investor in the 35% Tax Bracket for a Series of Funds.**

| Fund | Fund Symbol | Before-Tax Return (%) | After-Tax Return (%) | Effective Tax Rate (%) |
|---|---|---|---|---|
| Money Market | MM | 8.5 | 5.5 | 35 |
| Income | I | 10.0 | 7.0 | 30 |
| Growth and Income | GI | 13.0 | 10.0 | 25 |
| Aggressive Growth | AG | 18.0 | 15.0 | 15 |
| Short term municipal bond | Muni | 7.5 | 7.5 | 0 |

**FIGURE 9-2**
**The Before and After Tax Return for a Person with a 35% Tax Bracket**

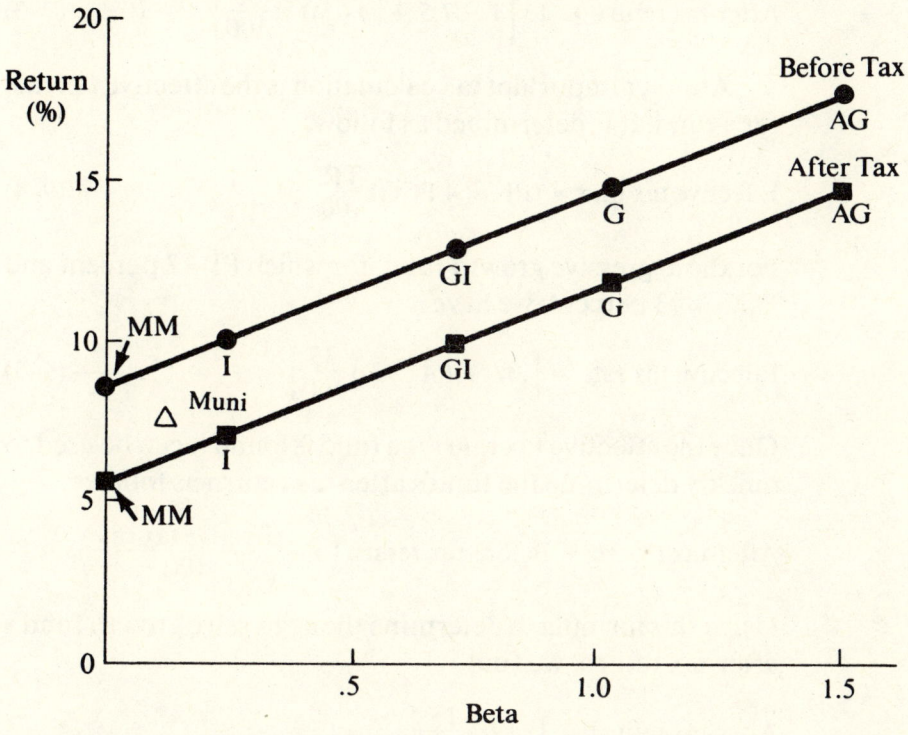

gains, and TR = marginal tax rate. First consider the money market fund with a before tax return of 8.5 percent. Since PI = 1 and PCG = 0 we have

$$\text{After-tax return} = 8.5\left[1 - (1 + .4(0)) \times \frac{35}{100}\right] = 5.5\% \quad (9\text{-}2)$$

For the growth and income fund, assuming PI = 50 percent and PCG = 50 percent, we find

$$\text{After-tax return} = 13\left[1 - (.5 + .4(.5)) \times \frac{35}{100}\right] = 10\% \quad (9\text{-}3)$$

Another important tax calculation is the effective tax rate for a fund. It is determined as follows

$$\text{Effective tax rate} = (\text{PI} + .4\,\text{PCG})\frac{\text{TR}}{100} \quad (9\text{-}4)$$

For the aggressive growth fund, for which PI = 7 percent and PCG = 93 percent, we have

$$\text{Effective tax rate} = \left[.07 + (.4(.93))\frac{35}{100}\right] = 15\% \quad (9\text{-}5)$$

Once the effective tax rate for a fund is found it can be used to quickly determine the fund's after-tax return as follows:

$$\text{After-tax return} = \text{Before-tax return}\left(1 - \frac{\text{effective tax rate}}{100}\right)$$

Using this formula to determine the aggressive growth fund's after-tax return, we find

$$\text{After-tax return} = 18\left(1 - \frac{15.5}{100}\right) = 15\%$$

Figure 9-3 shows the advantage of receiving capital gains distributions for high-bracket tax payers. The investor in the 50 percent bracket will have an effective tax rate of just 20

# FIGURE 9-3
**Effective Tax Rates as the Capital Gains Percentage Varies for Several Selected Individual Tax Rates**

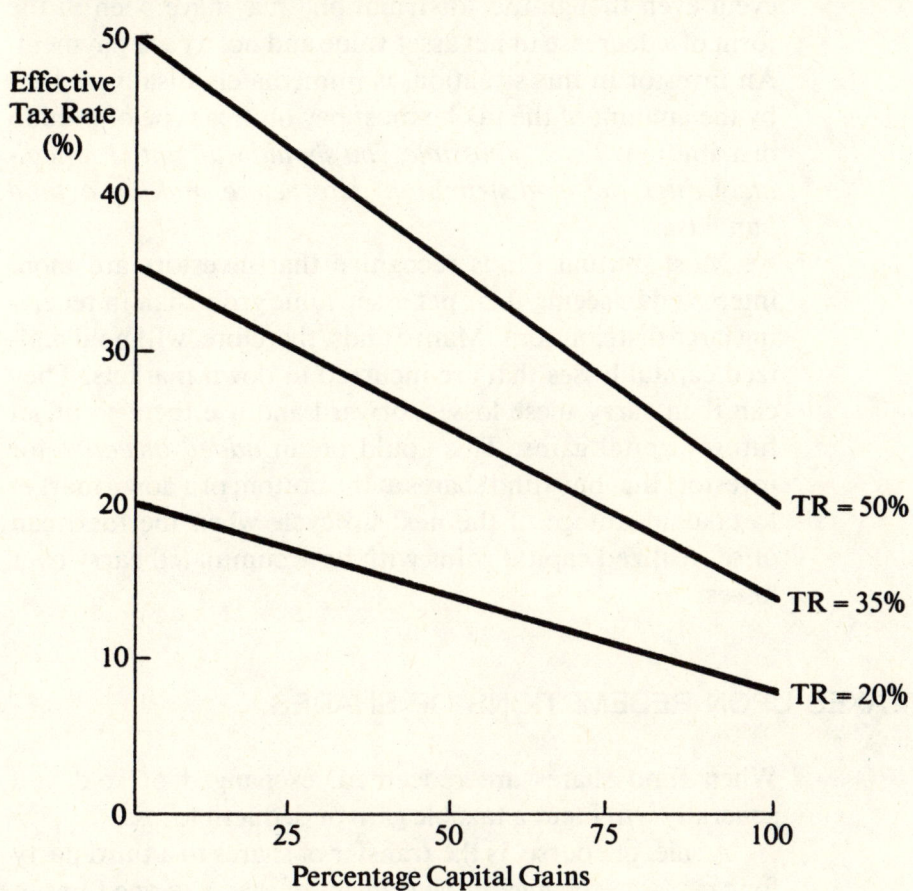

percent when all distributions are in the form of capital gains.

Since mutual fund distributions result in immediate declines in per-share asset values equal to the per share distribution, individuals who purchase shares right before a distribution immediately have a portion of their investment capital returned to them when the distribution is made. The IRS considers the distribution for the new shareholder a taxable event even though the "distribution" may have been in the form of a decrease in net asset value and not a cash payment. An investor in this situation, is immediately disadvantaged by the amount of the tax he must pay on this type of pseudo distribution. *Thus, if possible, you should wait until immediately after the ex-distribution date before making a fund purchase.*

Most mutual funds recognize that investors are more interested in seeing their net asset value grow than in receiving large distributions. Many funds, therefore, will hold realized capital losses that are incurred in down markets. They can then carry these losses forward and use them to offset future capital gains. This could be an *added incentive* for investors that buy fund shares at the bottom of a down market to take advantage of the next up cycle when the fund can offset realized capital gains with its accumulated carry over losses.

## TAXES UPON REDEMPTIONS OF SHARES

When fund shares are redeemed, exchanged or sold you generally will incur a taxable gain or deductible loss.

A sale, of course, is the transfer of shares to a third party for cash. An exchange is the transfer of shares of one fund in return for shares in another one. A redemption occurs when the fund reacquires its own shares. Gains or losses from fund share sales, exchanges, or redemptions are treated as taxable sales of capital assets and are subject to favorable long-term capital gains treatment if they were held for more than six months.

You can see the value of good record keeping since you will need to calculate your gain upon all liquidations of shares.

Let us consider the case where we invested $10,000 in a fund on January 1, 1980, which we then sold on December 31, 1984, and after having reinvested all distributions in the fund, the value of our fund shares increased 165.0 percent over the five-year period. Thus, our $10,000 investment grew to $26,500 and we realized a long-term gain of $16,500. However, during the period, we were credited with $1,500 in income distributions and $4,500 in capital gains distributions that we used to buy additional fund shares. Since, we already paid taxes on these distributions in the year they were credited to our account, we subtract them from our total gain to obtain our net capital gain of $10,500, which is the amount that is now taxable.

## FOUR METHODS OF CALCULATING CAPITAL GAINS

If we purchased shares on several different occasions, we would have to identify which of those shares we are selling. For example, consider the case shown in Table 9-2 where we purchase 100 fund shares on May 1, 1982 and then continued to increase our holdings over a two year period, when we sell all our shares of the fund. The pre-tax net capital gain is $3,088.15 (sales value) − $2,500.00 (our direct purchases) − $240.48 (our already taxed distributions) = $347.67.

If we sold less than our total holdings of these shares, we would have to identify the specific shares we sold. This requires accurate record keeping and the retention in our files of all quarterly account forms sent to us by the fund. In the

**TABLE 9-2**
**A Record of an Example Fund**

| Date | Transaction | Amount | Price | Number of Shares | Total Value |
|---|---|---|---|---|---|
| 5/1/82 | Purchase | $1,000.00 | $10.00 | 100.000 | $1,000.00 |
| 11/15/82 | Distribution at $.50 | $50.00 | $10.50 | 104.762 | $1,100.00 |
| 2/4/83 | Purchase | $1,500.00 | $11.25 | 238.095 | $2,678.57 |
| 10/15/83 | Distribution at $.80 | $190.48 | $11.85 | 254.169 | $3,011.90 |
| 5/1/84 | Sale | | $12.15 | 254.169 | $3,088.15 |

example above, suppose we redeemed only 100 shares on May 1, 1984 and received $1,215 in cash (100 × $12.15 share price). To identify the shares we are redeeming, we can use the *first in, first out* (FIFO) approach which assumes that we are selling the first 100 shares purchased on May 1, 1982. Since the cost of these shares was $1,000 we calculate a total capital gain of $215.

As an alternative, we could have used the *identifiable cost* method which requires that the shares sold be specifically identified as the ones acquired on a specific date. In our example, we could choose to redeem the 100 shares we purchased on February 4, 1983 which cost us $1,125. Then the net capital gain is $1,215 − $1,125 = $90.

In most cases it is best to use the *last in, first out* (LIFO) method of redemption, which assumes that we are selling the last shares we purchased. This results in the lowest net capital gain in our example. Of course, it simply postpones the eventual payment of taxes on those shares that we purchased earlier. If we use the LIFO method in our example, we identify the 16.07 shares we purchased on October 15, 1983 when we reinvested the distribution made on that date. These shares cost us $11.85 each. The remaining 83.93 shares we need to make up the 100 shares we are selling, we identify as belonging to that group of shares purchased on February 4, 1983 at a price of $11.25 for a total cost of $944.21. Thus, the total cost of the 100 shares was $1,134.69 and the net capital gain would be $1,215 - $1,134.69 = $80.31. Since all 100 shares were held more than six months, it would be a long-term capital gain.

Another way of calculating tax liability is to use the *average cost* method. It avoids the difficulty of having to identify specific shares purchased on different dates. First, we would have to calculate the total cost of purchasing all the shares we held on the date of sale. We then divide this total by the total number of shares purchased to obtain the average cost per share. For example, let us assume again that we redeemed 100 shares on May 1, 1984. On that date the average cost of all our shares is

$$\text{Average cost} = \frac{\text{purchases + distributions}}{\text{total shares}} \qquad (9\text{-}9)$$

$$= \frac{\$2{,}500 + \$240.48}{254.169}$$

$$= \$10.78$$

The average cost of the 100 shares we are selling was

$100 \times \$10.78 = \$1{,}078.00.$

Thus, the capital gain would be $1,215 - $1,078 = $137.

To determine the capital gains holding period for the average cost method, the first in, first out method applies (i.e. the shares sold are considered to be the shares acquired first). For a more detailed look at figuring your tax cost consult IRS publication No. 564 entitled "Mutual Fund Distributions." A summary of the four methods of calculating capital gains taxes on redeemed mutual funds is provided in Table 9-3.

**TABLE 9–3**
**Tax Methods for Redemption of Fund Shares.**

| Method | Comments |
| --- | --- |
| First In-First Out (FIFO): identifies shares sold as those purchased first. | Results in maximum capital gains tax if you have long-term gains. |
| Last In-First Out (LIFO): identifies shares sold as those purchased last. | Results in lowest capital gains taxes if share prices have continually increased over time. |
| Identified Shares: identifies specific shares as those sold. | Results in lowest capital gains tax if shares with highest purchase price are specified as sold. |
| Average Cost: calculates average cost of all shares held. | Easiest method of calculating capital gains. |

## TAX STRATEGIES: KEEPING YOUR TAX LIABILITY LOW AND AVOIDING UNNECESSARY TAXATION

The timing of a large purchase of a fund is important. As we described earlier, generally we do not want to purchase a fund just prior to a large capital gains distribution. On July 19, 1984, Lehman Capital Fund distributed $3.19 for each share held. The share price dropped that day from $18.44 to $15.25 reflecting the distribution. If you invested in the Lehman fund on July 18 you would have received a 17.3 percent distribution on your investment after just one day in the fund. If your investment was $10,000, the fund returned $1,730 to you and simultaneously reduced your total net asset value by the same amount. However, this distribution, which in effect was a partial refund of your $10,000 initial investment, created an immediate short-term tax liability of $1,730, the amount of the distribution. If you had waited until after the distribution, the price per-share would have been lower by the amount of the distribution and you would have been able to buy more shares for your $10,000 payment with no tax liability for the calendar year in which the investment was made.

Now, assume you have held a fund for longer than a year and are now eligible for the preferential long-term capital gains tax rate if you sell or redeem any shares. In this case, you should sell just before an income distribution. Then, all your profits will be capital gains. If you wait until after a dividend distribution, the income portion of the distribution would be taxed as ordinary income.

Thus, in summary, your tax timing strategy is:

1. Determine when a distribution is expected by consulting the fund itself or a newsletter service that reports distribution dates for your funds.
2. Make new purchases of fund shares just after a distribution;
3. Sell, redeem or exchange fund shares just prior to a distribution.

A popular year-end tax strategy is to hold onto fund shares that have appreciated, delaying sales of those shares until the next tax year, and sell in the current tax year any shares that have declined. Receipts from the sale of the depressed fund shares can then be reinvested in other mutual funds with similar objectives and investment characteristics.

This procedure is similar to tax-loss selling of common stocks at year-end. The basic difference is that you will incur no commission charges on your no-load fund transactions, and replacement assets with similar risk and return characteristics are readily available. *This switching strategy is most beneficial with aggressive growth funds.*

If you decide to use one or more of the timing strategies discussed in Chapter 8, it is important to keep tax consequences in mind, especially the six-month holding period requirement for preferential capital gains treatment, unless, of course, you are trading fund shares that are held in tax deferred accounts, such as IRA or Keogh accounts.

Finally, you should avoid funds with high turnover rates (over 100 percent) if you want to avoid paying excessive short-term gains taxes. (*Note:* We saw earlier how funds with excessively high turnover ratios also incur higher brokerage costs.) For example, Nova Fund had a turnover rate of 158 percent in 1983 and its long-term distributions in that year accounted for only 18 percent of the total. T. Rowe Price New Horizons Fund, on the other hand, had a turnover rate of only 45 percent, 88 percent of its distributions were in the form of long-term capital gains.

## TAX MANAGED FUNDS

*Tax managed funds* have a policy of making no distributions to shareholders and, thus, unlike other types of mutual funds that are required to distribute 90 percent of their income to shareholders, are subject to taxes on their investment income. Tax managed funds reinvest all income and capital gains. Shareholders of these funds, therefore, never have to pay taxes on distributed income. The only time they will owe taxes is when they sell fund shares at a gain and that is usually taxed at preferential long-term rates. The objective of a tax managed fund is to accumulate and compound income and capital gains on a tax deferred basis to the maximum extent possible.

There were two tax managed funds operating in mid-1985: Eaton Vance Tax Managed Trust and the Copley Tax Managed Fund. The Eaton Vance Trust is a 8.5 percent load fund that invests primarily in common stocks that pay dividends at relatively high rates and that qualify for the 85 percent corporate dividend deduction. The Trust retains and reinvests all its after-tax investment income and any realized after-tax capital gains, with no distributions made to shareholders. Also, taking advantage of the 85 percent corporate dividend deduction and other tax-management techniques, the Trust seeks to minimize its own federal tax liability. The fund appreciated 67.2 percent over the three year period, 1982–1984, for a compound return rate of 18.7 percent annually.

As a result of the 1984 Tax Reform Act, beginning in 1985, the Trust can no longer deduct capital losses from income that is subject to the accumulated earnings tax and, as a result, may experience greater accruals for such tax than it has in the past. Even so, the Trust will be able to compound its growth at a lower effective tax rate than most of its shareholders could do on their own through direct investments in dividend-paying or taxable interest-bearing securities.

The Copley Tax Managed Fund returned a compound annual return rate of 18.4 percent over the three-year period of 1982–1984. This fund attempts to distribute all its income and capital gains via redemptions. The fund holds stocks with high dividend income that create a flow of tax-free dividend income to the fund. It is structured so that investors receive an 85 percent federal tax exemption on all dividends received. The remaining 15 percent is usually used to cover the normal expenses of running the fund—thus no federal taxes are assessed to the shareholder.

## TAX-FREE BOND FUNDS

Tax-free bond funds hold municipal bonds issued by local, regional and state agencies and are free of federal taxes and, in some cases, state income taxes as well. A bond fund may be a tax free (1) money market fund (60 day average maturity); (2) short-term fund (2–3 years); (3) intermediate-term (4–10 years); and (4) long-term, high-yield (10–20 years). Many long-term tax-free bond funds may fluctuate widely in price, but over time they have been able to maintain before-tax yields above 8.5 percent. By contrast, short-term tax-free bond funds normally produce before-tax yields of only 6 percent annually.

The taxable equivalent yield is the yield an investor would have to earn on a taxable fund that would be equivalent to what he would earn from a tax-free fund. It can be calculated from the equation

$$\text{Taxable equivalent yield} = \frac{\text{tax-free yield}}{1 - \frac{\text{investor's tax rate}}{100}}$$

Table 9–4 gives taxable equivalent yields for different tax-free yields and three tax brackets. The table shows that if a person is in the 50 percent tax bracket and can attain 9 percent in a tax-free bond fund, he would have to earn 18 percent from a taxable investment to obtain the same net yield. As you can see, for high-bracket tax payers, tax-free bond funds are very attractive.

**TABLE 9–4**
**Sample Taxable Equivalent Yields.**

| Tax Free Yield (%) | Taxable Equivalent Yields in Percent | | |
|---|---|---|---|
| | 30% Tax Bracket | 40% Tax Bracket | 50% Tax Bracket |
| 5 | 7.14 | 8.33 | 10.00 |
| 6 | 8.57 | 10.00 | 12.00 |
| 7 | 10.00 | 11.67 | 14.00 |
| 8 | 11.43 | 13.33 | 16.00 |
| 9 | 12.86 | 15.00 | 18.00 |
| 10 | 14.29 | 16.67 | 20.00 |

## THE POSSIBLE EFFECTS OF THE PROPOSED TAX REFORM ACT OF 1986

The tax reform act proposed by the Treasury Department would have overall beneficial effects on the stock and bond fund markets due to proposed reductions in the top tax bracket to 35 percent from the current 50 percent and in the top capital gains rate to 17.5 percent from the current 20 percent.

Observers believe that the proposed tax reform act, by reducing marginal tax rates and lowering the capital gains tax, would make dividend income more attractive. And corporations, spurred by the proposed deduction of dividend payments, would be expected to begin paying higher dividends to shareholders. Cutting the highest marginal rate for individuals from 50 percent to 35 percent would mean that shareholders would retain 30 percent more on their after-tax income from dividends. Also, funds specializing in the entrepreneurial sector of the economy should benefit from the reduced tax rate for capital gains. Lower marginal rates would lift after-tax yields on both corporate and Treasury bonds, while tax-shelter reforms would lower returns on some competing investments, particularly real estate. The reduced competition from tax shelter investments also should boost the prices of municipal bonds, although their tax exemptions would be less valuable because of lower tax brackets. A summary of these and several other important effects of the proposed act is on Table 9–5.

TABLE 9-5
**Potential Effects of Tax Reform Plan.**

| Change | Impact |
| --- | --- |
| Reduce tax rates to three brackets: 15, 25 and 35 percent. | Maximum rate of 35 percent will reduce taxation on income distributions, thereby making income and growth and income funds more attractive. |
| Reduce maximum capital gains rate to 17.5 percent from current 20 percent with proposed 50 percent exclusion and top rate of 35 percent. | Reduce taxation of long-term capital gains, thereby improving after-tax return of fund gains. |
| Lowering marginal tax rates and reducing tax shelter incentives, also eliminating deductibility of state taxes. | Improve attraction of tax-free municipal bond funds, especially those that hold only bonds issued by the investor's state of residence. |

# Chapter 10

## Retirement Plans

### INVESTING FOR RETIREMENT

A person retiring at age 60 can expect to live another twenty years or so and will need to plan for a satisfactory stream of income during that period. Upon retirement, principal sources of income will consist of Social Security, pension benefits, and accumulated savings and investments. Very few of us can count solely on Social Security and our pensions to provide sufficient income for our retirement years. Therefore, it is important that we begin to develop a retirement investment plan as soon as possible.

I know you have probably heard it before, but I will say it again. *It is never too early to start your retirement investment plan*. Here is the reason why. If we could set aside $1,000 a year in a fund that yields an annual return of 10 percent, after 31 years the value of our holdings would be $164,494. For simplicity sake, this discussion ignores the effects of taxes and inflation. Then, assuming the fund continued to return 10 percent a year, we could draw out $19,321 annually for the next 20 years. By the end of that 20-year period, we will have drawn out a total of $386,429. This example illustrates the power of compounding and the importance of starting your investment program early in life.

Upon retirement, each individual's personal income requirements will vary depending upon his or her family obligations and life style. But whatever our particular situation may be, we should be able to live on one-half to two-thirds of our pre-retirement income. Let us assume that your pre-retirement salary is $40,000 a year. You should begin developing an investment program that would provide you with at least $20,000 a year in retirement income to supplement your pension and Social Security benefits. This can be achieved by consistently investing $1,000 each year for 32 years in a fund that returns 10 percent annually. Alternatively, you could reach this objective by investing $2,000 annually, for 24 years (in the same fund) and still achieve a retirement pay out of $20,000 annually for 20 years.

Social Security benefits, while helpful, never were intended to be the sole source of income at retirement. They have been aptly described as one leg of a three-legged stool, the remaining two legs being private pension benefits and investment income from savings. You need to calculate your expected income from each of these three sources. Surveys have shown that most Americans are not saving enough for their retirement despite their doubts about the long-term viability of the Social Security system and its programs.

Fortunately, the 1981 Tax Act expanded and enhanced the coverage of tax deferred retirement programs available to individuals. Mutual funds are especially suitable investments for these tax-deferred retirement programs, which include IRA, Keogh, and 401k plans.

## INDIVIDUAL RETIREMENT ACCOUNTS

Each year wage earners may invest up to $2,000 in an Individual Retirement Account. One must invest earned income (wages or salaries) and may not use unearned income in an IRA. Every dollar you contribute from compensation received during a year to an IRA up to the maximum $2,000 annual contribution ($4,000 for a working couple) is fully deductible from your current taxable income.

Every dollar your fund IRA earns grows and compounds on a tax-deferred basis. You pay no current taxes until you begin withdrawing funds from your account—any time between the age 59 1/2 and 70 1/2 (Withdrawals can be made prior to age 59 1/2; however, IRS penalties and tax payments are assessed when this occurs.). In retirement, your taxes may be significantly lower than they were when you were working as you probably will be in a lower tax bracket. But even if your tax bracket doesn't change, you still will enjoy greater after-tax income in an IRA thanks to the power of tax-free accumulation.

For example, if you earn income of $22,000 a year and contribute $2,000 to an IRA, your taxable income is reduced to $20,000 before you take into account any other deductions and credits. All the dividends, interest, and capital gains that accrue in your IRA are not taxable until you decide to withdraw funds from the account upon retirement or upon incurring permanent disability, should that happen before you retire. Should you die before receiving payments, accumulations in your IRA are distributed to your heirs.

You can transfer IRA deposits from one investment to another. You cannot, however, take personal receipt of your IRA monies before age $59\frac{1}{2}$ without forfeiting all tax advantages and paying an IRS penalty. Also, IRAs may not be used as collateral, under penalty of the forfeiture of all tax advantages.

One may transfer IRA assets from a bank IRA to a mutual fund and from one mutual fund to another without penalty. If you receive a lump-sum distribution from your employer's pension or profit-sharing plan, you may roll over within 60 days of receipt all or part of the distribution (minus any non-deductible employee contributions you made) to a mutual fund IRA, tax-free.

There are two ways to move an IRA. The most common is the direct transfer, in which the current sponsor (custodian or trustee) of your account shifts it directly to the new one. The alternative is the rollover, in which you close one IRA and personally shepherd the funds to the new account. Although there is no limit on the frequency of direct transfers you can take the rollover route just once every 12 months.

You have until tax filing time to make either your initial or subsequent IRA investments for each tax year, but it's best to do it right at the beginning of the tax year. If you make your IRA contribution in early January, you'll get tax-deferred growth all year. With an IRA you don't have to contribute the maximum and you can skip years.

Once you have reached $59\frac{1}{2}$ years of age all distributions from an IRA are taxed as ordinary income. At age $70\frac{1}{2}$ you can no longer contribute to your IRA and must begin taking money out each year based on your statistical life expectancy or the joint life expectancies of you and your spouse.

Consider an individual who, from age 30 to age 65, makes a contribution of $2,000 each year. If the mutual fund returns 15 percent annually, the value of the IRA will be $869,500. On the other hand, a non-IRA account with the same fund with identical contributions would be valued at $180,000 (if we assume the investor paid an average tax rate of 30 percent per year on each year's returns). The IRA investor does about five times as well because the compounding effect works on 100 percent of the dollars that accrue to the IRA, not just on the earnings of a non-IRA account after-tax.

Consider another example: a working couple at age 40 could invest $4,000 annually for 25 years. They would have $829,320 at age 65 if their investments returned 14 percent annually. They could withdraw $50,000 or more annually without ever depleting the principal in the fund. Of course, income tax must be paid on the withdrawals.

Although the maximum individual IRA contribution is $2,000 annually, there are numerous mutual funds that offer IRA accounts with minimum initial contributions of $250. By illustration, an annual contribution of $250 for 20 years, earning 10 percent a year, will accumulate to $14,319; at the end of 30 years, that same account will have mushroomed to $41,124. The power of compounding, even for small sums, should never be underestimated.

## MANAGING YOUR IRA FUNDS

In 1984, total IRA account assets grew to $132 billion from $26 billion in 1982. Since Congress liberalized eligibility rules in 1981, about 23 million households started IRAs. Currently, $16 billion of IRA money is invested in mutual funds. Despite the availability of IRAs as a universal tax shelter for working Americans at every income level, only about 25 percent of those eligible participate. The advantage of contributing each year to an IRA to reduce your current tax bill needs little elaboration: the benefit is an immediate tax savings. If you contribute $2,000 to an IRA and you are in the 40 percent tax bracket, you will save $800 on your current-tax bill. What does need some elaboration, however, is how your IRA can reach significant proportions and can be managed to produce even higher tax deferred gains with a risk/reward balance that is appropriate for your current stage of life.

In Chapter 7 we examined several market timing techniques and economic indicators that can be used to ensure that your IRA assets are always in economically advantageous mutual funds. Later on in this chapter, we will discuss how the fund mix should change in your IRA account as you move closer to retirement.

To the extent that IRA funds are intended for use during retirement, a note of caution is appropriate regarding active management of these assets. Approach all transfers of your IRA assets carefully: it does not pay to take risks on short-term market trends with retirement assets; nor does it pay to be blindly conservative. Holding assets in a fund yielding 7 percent when prevailing interest rates are stable at 11.5 percent is not, generally speaking, sound investing. It is, however, better to err on the conservative side.

## THE KEOGH RETIREMENT PLAN

A *Keogh* is an investment plan for self-employed individuals and eligible employees of companies that allow individuals to set up retirement funds consisting of tax-deductible contributions and tax-sheltered accumulations of income and capital gains. The Keogh plan was named after the legislator who sponsored the Employment Retirement Act of 1962. This bill was favorably modified by the Employment Retirement Income Security Act of 1974, which is commonly referred to as ERISA, and was once again modified by the Economic Recovery Tax Act of 1981.

To be eligible for a Keogh plan you must

1. work for yourself;
2. be unincorporated; and
3. file for self-employed Social Security.

You are not precluded from establishing a Keogh plan if you derive income from self-employment, even though you are an active participant as an employee in a corporate retirement plan. Thus, a consultant or a moonlighting professional can use this tax-deferred plan for his self-employment earnings.

The Keogh plan offers the same basic advantages as an IRA account. It lowers current income taxes—Keogh contributions are tax deductible—and it can defer any income or capital gains that are realized until withdrawals from the plan are made. Most rules concerning IRAs also apply to Keogh plans. One exception is that Keogh contributions may be made beyond the age of 70 1/2.

Despite their significant benefits, very few people are apparently aware of the advantages offered by Keogh plans. According to recent statistics, less than 15 percent of eligible individuals have established such plans.

The mutual fund share of the Keogh market is substantially greater than its current penetration of the IRA market (about 28 percent of the $21.5 billion in Keoghs is invested in mutual funds *versus* about 12 percent of the $132 billion in IRA assets outstanding in 1984.)

If you are self-employed, you can contribute the lesser of $30,000 a year or 25 percent of your income into a Keogh account. It's all right to have both a Keogh and an IRA. One tax shelter doesn't eliminate the other.

One form of Keogh plan, known as "defined benefit," is set up to yield a specific target income in future years. Contributions to defined benefit Keoghs are based on assumptions about how much money you need to invest now to fund the future target benefit. Taxpayers who set up such a plan can target retirement income as high as $90,000 a year, and fund the plan with tax deferred money accordingly.

## SEP, 401 AND 403 PLANS

One popular type of plan which may be offered by either corporate or noncorporate entities is the 401(k) plan. A 401(k) plan is a tax-qualified profit-sharing plan which includes a "cash or deferred" arrangement. The cash or deferred arrangement permits an employee to have a portion of his compensation contributed to a tax-sheltered plan on his behalf or paid to him directly as additional taxable compensation. Thus an employee may elect to reduce his taxable compensation with contributions to a 401(k) plan where those amounts will accumulate tax-free.

Section 403(b) of the Internal Revenue Code permits employees of certain charitable organizations and public school systems to establish tax-sheltered retirement programs similar to those in the 401(k) plan.

Theoretically, an individual can have an IRA, a 401(k) plan at work and a Keogh for free-lance income. For all but the highest-paid individuals, the limitations simply depend on how much income a taxpayer can afford to put aside in retirement plans.

Under a 401(k) plan, an employee can have his contribution matched by his employer. But even without a matching contribution, a 401(k) plan allows you to invest up to $30,000 a year or 25 percent of your salary, which ever is less. For the most part, 401(k) or 403(b) plans are salary reduction arrangements.

Over one-half of all major U.S. companies have instituted 401(k) plans for their employees.

A *Simplified Employee Pension Plan* (SEP) is an IRA account to which both employees and employers may contribute. It is an alternative to a 401(k) or 403(b) plan. The employee may deduct up to $30,000 or 20 percent of compensation, which ever is less, for employer contributions to the account. In addition, the employee may deduct his or her own contribution to the account up to $2,000. SEP accounts provide a mechanism for owners of small incorporated or unincorporated businesses, consultants and free-lancers to provide themselves, as well as their employees, with pension and tax benefits, without the complicated paperwork of qualified pension and Keogh plans. Also, a SEP can be established without help from an attorney or accountant.

The value of a SEP, IRA and Keogh account contrasts greatly with that of taxable accounts. Table 10–1 shows that tax deferred accounts can have a final value three times that of a taxable account.

**TABLE 10-1**
**The Value of a Mutual Fund Investment if You Invest $1,000 a Year at 10 Percent Return.**

| End of Years | Value of Taxable Account* | Value of IRA, Keogh or SEP | 401 (k) with 50% Employer Contribution |
|---|---|---|---|
| 5  | $ 3,585 | $ 6,716 | $ 10,073 |
| 10 | 8,383   | 17,531  | 26,297   |
| 15 | 14,804  | 34,950  | 52,245   |
| 20 | 23,396  | 63,002  | 94,504   |
| 25 | 34,894  | 108,182 | 162,273  |

*Assuming a 40 percent tax bracket

## CHOOSING A PORTFOLIO OF MUTUAL FUNDS FOR A RETIREMENT PLAN

With any retirement investment plan, you want to benefit from (1) the tax deferral of your contributions; and (2) the profits from your investments.

Investment income is deferred until after retirement and is then taxed as regular income. You normally expect to hold this investment for a long period, even though you can switch between fund investments each year. Since you can defer the tax consequences, you should seek maximum yield and generally ignore the volatility of fund net asset values, since you do not plan to withdraw monies until retirement. You should look for a mutual fund that provides the best total return (current yield plus price appreciation) over a holding period of ten years or more.

The selection of a fund for a tax deferred account should meet the regular test of past performance, consistent return, and a clear objective for a good total return in excess of 12 percent compounded annually.

As you approach retirement you should move your portfolio towards less volatile funds. By age 60, 70 percent of your mutual fund investments should be in current income producing funds, 20 percent in growth and income funds and 10 percent in aggressive growth funds. The aggressive growth funds provide some potential participation in the future growth of the economy.

One method to diversify a retirement portfolio is to buy a different mutual fund for each year's successive IRA or Keogh contribution. Another way to diversify is to hold a portfolio of funds and distribute each year's investment among several funds. As an investor you should be counting on the benefits of both portfolio diversification and holding time (horizon). For example, a good candidate for a tax deferred account in January 1, 1974 would have been the no-load Nicholas Fund. It lost 33.3 percent in 1974 and then increased every year through 1984, providing a compounded annual return over that 11-year period of 18.0 percent.

Tax deferred accumulation linked with dollar cost averaging is yet another method that should be considered for building IRA assets with mutual funds. The advantage of this method can be illustrated with the Massachusetts Capital Development Fund, a load growth fund. If you had purchased $1,000 worth of shares monthly in a Keogh or 401(k) plan at a 7.25 percent load for the period January 1, 1974 to May 31, 1985 the value of your holdings would be $492,271. The compound rate of return of your investment over the 137 months would have been 19.3 percent. You would have purchased these shares for a total cost of $137,000. Besides showing the value of dollar cost averaging, this illustration showing the value of dollar cost averaging, this illustration shows that a good performing fund with a load charge can effectively meet your objectives.

Table 10–2 illustrates how to determine retirement capital requirements given specific rates of return and expected retirement years. For example, a person with a life expectancy of 20 years holding an income fund with a total annual return of 10% would obtain a withdrawal factor equal to 9.4

from Table 10–2. Then, if he desires a yearly income of $15,000, he will need 9.4 × $15,000 = $141,000 in capital invested in the fund upon retirement.

## Taking Inflation into Account

As you near retirement you should adjust your portfolio to stress income, safety and preservation of capital. Intermediate term bond funds and low volatility growth and income funds are well suited for meeting this objective. However, you also must anticipate the erosion of purchasing power to inflation. It is important to determine what your retirement income requirements will be in future dollars.

For example, consider a couple with an annual budget of $30,000. If they expect to retire in 20 years and we assume that inflation will average 5 percent until that time, they will need $79,500 ($1.05^{20} \times \$30,000 = 79,500$) as an annual income upon retirement to maintain the same level of purchasing power as $30,000 gives them in today's dollars. If they wish to maintain the income of $79,500 for another twenty years after they retire, they will need 8.4 times $79,500 or $667,800 in capital upon retirement assuming their mutual fund portfolio yields 12 percent annually over the 20-year period.

**TABLE 10–2**
**Withdrawal Factors**

| Return on Fund (%) | Years Capital Will Last | | | |
|---|---|---|---|---|
| | 15 | 20 | 25 | Indefinitely |
| 8 | 9.2 | 10.6 | 11.5 | 12.5 |
| 10 | 8.4 | 9.4 | 10.0 | 10.0 |
| 12 | 7.6 | 8.4 | 8.8 | 8.3 |
| 15 | 6.7 | 7.2 | 7.4 | 6.7 |

*Note:* Multiply the withdrawal factor (obtained for a given period and return) by the expected annual income to determine the required capital upon retirement.

# Chapter 11

# Withdrawal Plans

Mutual fund withdrawal programs are a systematic means for investors to obtain regular payments of dividends and invested principal. They are offered as a service by most mutual funds.

Withdrawal plans usually are flexible and convenient. Regular payment amounts can be changed or terminated at any time and lump sums can be obtained for special purposes, such as making large purchases. The disbursements may be sent directly to the shareholder, to a bank for deposit, or to a third party.

Retirees use mutual fund withdrawal plans to provide monthly living expenses. The simplicity of such a system for retirees is very attractive. And they also can be used for dependents, for the payment of a child's college expenses or even for making rent or mortgage payments.

The number of years that annual fund withdrawals can be made for various fund return levels and annual inflation adjusted withdrawal percentages is shown in Table 11-1.

For example, assume that we expect inflation to grow 4

**TABLE 11-1**
**Number of Years that Payments Can Be Made.**

| Inflation Adjusted Rate of Return (Annual Percent) | Rate of Withdrawal (Annual Percent) | | | |
|---|---|---|---|---|
| | 4% | 6% | 8% | 10% |
| 4 | I | 28 | 17 | 13 |
| 5 | I | 36 | 20 | 14 |
| 6 | I | I | 23 | 15 |
| 7 | I | I | 30 | 17 |
| 8 | I | I | I | 20 |

I = indefinitely

percent a year for the next twenty years and our annual fund return is 10 percent. Then the inflation adjusted rate of return would be 6 percent. Using Table 11-1, we see that, at a 4 percent inflation adjusted return rate, we could withdraw 8 percent of our net asset value each year for 17 years. Thus, if we wished to receive $10,000 per year in today's dollars and wanted to withdraw at an 8 percent rate, we would have to invest $125,000 in the fund at the start of the first year. We would receive $10,000 the first year, $10,400 the second year and so forth for 17 years, with each subsequent year's payment adjusted up 4 percent for inflation.

In another example, suppose we want to obtain $20,000 a year (adjusted for inflation) over an expected twenty years of retirement. We can obtain this inflation adjusted amount each year for 20 years by withdrawing at a 10 percent rate each year if our mutual fund maintains an inflation adjusted rate of return of 8 percent a year. If inflation is expected to be 4 percent a year, we must invest in a fund that returns 12 percent a year. To maintain a $20,000 payment each year in current dollars, our initial investment in the fund must be at least $200,000.

The *inflation adjusted* or real return of a fund is the critical performance measure. To illustrate, if we expect 5 percent inflation over the foreseeable future, with a portfolio of mutual funds that returns 12 percent annually, our real rate of return is actually only 7 percent. If we invest $2,000 annually in this portfolio, it will grow to an inflation adjusted value of $220,436 after 31 years. We then can begin withdrawing $20,800 annually at that point, with each annual payment increasing by 5 percent a year to account for inflation.

Unfortunately, most funds provide limited information regarding systematic withdrawal plans. So you may have to contact your fund directly to find out what the requirements are for its withdrawal plan. For most funds offering withdrawal programs, a minimum initial investment is required. In addition, there usually is a minimum withdrawal payment, typically $100, and annual withdrawal rates may be allowed up to 12 percent a year. Normally, you start withdrawing immediately upon investing in a fund provided you meet these other requirements. Also, you generally are given great latitude in setting up your payment program. You may withdraw on a monthly or a quarterly basis and you may request fixed-dollar, fixed-share or fixed-percentage withdrawals.

Of course, one alternative to a systematic withdrawal plan is simply to redeem fund shares as you need them, or you could maintain a portion of your investment in a money market fund and use its check writing privilege to withdraw what you need when you need it.

## WITHDRAWALS FROM IRAs AND KEOGH PLANS

Tax rules require us to withdraw our investments in IRAs and Keogh plans according to actuarial tables prepared by the

Internal Revenue Service. Failure to do so can lead to a tax penalty. However, while the IRS can dictate a withdrawal schedule, it does not require us to spend the funds we withdraw. We can reinvest our required IRA and Keogh withdrawals right back into a regular tax-bearing mutual fund account.

The IRS would require a seventy year old man with a sixty-five year old wife, to draw down his IRA or Keogh investments over a twenty year period. Since the investment will continue to grow even as it is being drawn down because of annual fund returns, he will have to withdraw 1/20th of his fund value in the first year, 1/19th of the value of the fund in the second year and so on. For example, he would withdraw $5,000, or 1/20th (5.0 percent), of his $100,000 fund investment at the end of the first year. In the second year because the $95,000 balance earned a return he would have to withdraw 5.3 percent. By the tenth year he would have to withdraw 1/5th of his remaining fund value and, at the end of the twentieth year, he would withdraw all the remaining funds.

As we saw in Chapter 10, IRA withdrawals cannot begin until you reach age 59 1/2 without incurring a penalty. And, they must begin by December 31st of the year you reach 70 1/2 years of age. If at all possible you should use other non-IRA sources of income or capital before withdrawing your IRA funds. You should never liquidate your tax-sheltered IRA or Keogh assets until you have to.

## DOLLAR COST AVERAGING WITHDRAWALS

As an alternative to withdrawing a fixed dollar amount from your fund, you could redeem or sell a fixed number of shares periodically. Although using this dollar cost averaging withdrawal plan may result in uneven payments in terms of the cash you will receive from each share redemption, over time fewer shares will have to be redeemed to attain essentially the

### TABLE 11-2
**Dollar Cost Averaging Withdrawal Plan.**

| Month | Price/ Share | Fixed Payment | | Cost Averaging | |
|---|---|---|---|---|---|
| | | Shares Redeemed | Remittance | Shares Redeemed | Remittance |
| 1 | $10 | 10.00 | $100 | 10 | $100 |
| 2 | 6 | 16.67 | 100 | 10 | 60 |
| 3 | 8 | 12.50 | 100 | 10 | 80 |
| 4 | 12 | 8.33 | 100 | 10 | 120 |
| 5 | 14 | 7.14 | 100 | 10 | 140 |
| 6 | 8 | 12.50 | 100 | 10 | 80 |
| 7 | 6 | 16.67 | 100 | 10 | 60 |
| 8 | 4 | 25.00 | 100 | 10 | 40 |
| | Total | 108.81 | $800 | 80 | $680 |
| Average Number of Shares to provide $100 | | | 13.60 | | 11.76 |

same total amount of dollar withdrawals as the fixed payment withdrawal plan. Table 11-2 shows how the dollar cost averaging method works and compares it to a fixed payment withdrawal plan. It also illustrates the benefits of a dollar cost averaging withdrawal plan. This method is especially attractive when you expect the fund's share price to fluctuate widely over time.

# Chapter 12

# Estate Planning

## MUTUAL FUNDS AND ESTATE PLANNING

Most of us have accumulated some wealth during our lifetimes and want to be sure that this wealth is passed on unencumbered to our designated heirs and survivors. To ensure that this will occur, we must establish an estate plan that minimizes the federal and state taxes that are paid upon transfer of property to our heirs and legatees.

Under the Tax Act of 1981, it is possible to leave a large portion of your estate to heirs on a tax-free basis. Your estate plans should be established and recorded in your *will*, which will guarantee that your estate goes to whom you want, when you want, and with minimal taxation. A will is necessary to dispose of any property.

States have differing laws regarding the property of spouses. In community property states, any assets acquired during marriage are jointly owned by both partners—except for gifts and inheritances. In common law states, assets are owned by whomever buys them. Ownership of mutual funds can in this case, be individual or joint with right of survivorship.

In addition, under the Tax Act of 1981, you may leave all your estate to your spouse tax free. By setting up a trust, you can ensure that your spouse will have an income from the estate as long as he or she lives, and that your children will receive whatever is left after your spouse dies. Should you be unmarried at the time of death, the maximum amount of your estate that is exempt from federal estate taxes is $500,000. This will be raised to $600,000 in 1987.

## TAKING TITLE OF MUTUAL FUNDS

Most people rarely give any thought to how to take legal title to their mutual funds. *Title* is evidence of ownership of an asset. Inappropriate forms of ownership can severely complicate an otherwise well designed estate plan. There are two forms of ownership: individual and co-ownership. Holding title to a mutual fund as an individual is a clear form of ownership, although if you are married in a community property state, the ownership is actually joint with your spouse.

There are three commonly used forms of co-ownership:

1. joint tenancy with right of survivorship;
2. community property; and
3. tenancy in common.

In *joint tenancy*, joint ownership is combined with the right of survivorship. At the death of one owner, the property passes automatically and completely to the surviving joint owner or owners. The advantages of joint tenancy are (1) avoidance of probate; (2) protection of ownership and; (3) convenience. The primary disadvantage of the joint tenancy form of ownership may be increased estate taxes in certain circumstances.

*Community property* only exists between husband and wife and exists in eight states that follow community property laws: Arizona, California, Idaho, Louisiana, Nevada, New Mexico, Texas and Washington. Community property is created automatically when either one of the spouses is employed. Either spouse can control community property without the other's consent. At death, each spouse controls his one-half of community property. It passes at his/her death to the person designated in the respective will or trust. Inheritances, gifts, and property brought to the marriage by one spouse is not considered community property. Community property is subject to probate when one or both spouses die. This disadvantage, however, can be overcome by placing the property in a revocable trust, which is not subject to probate.

Community property receives favorable income tax treatment when the surviving spouse elects to sell the property. The cost basis is stepped-up to fair market value to determine the capital gain on the sale at the date of death. This stepped-up basis applies to all community property and not just to the one-half included in the deceased spouse's estate.

Where property is owned by *tenants-in-common*, each tenant owns a proportionate interest in the entire property. Tenants-in-common may hold equal or unequal shares in the property. The most important distinction between a joint tenancy and a tenancy-in-common lies in the right of survivorship, which is characteristic only of joint tenancy. When a tenant-in-common dies, interest passes to the estate and heirs and not to the surviving owners.

The primary characteristics of the three forms of ownership are shown in Table 12-1. Everyone should consult an attorney and establish an estate plan and a will. Generally, you should hold mutual funds in individual ownership or, if married, in joint tenancy with right of survivorship.

## TABLE 12-1
## Forms of Ownership of Mutual Funds

|  | Tenancy In Common | Joint Tenancy | Community Property |
|---|---|---|---|
| Parties | Any number of persons (can be husband & wife). | Any number of persons (can be husband & wife). | Only husband & wife. |
| Division | Ownership can be divided into any number of interests, equal or unequal. | Ownership interest must be equal. | Ownership interests are equal. Managerial responsibility is with the husband in several states. |
| Title | Each co-owner has a separate legal title to his undivided interest. | There is only one title to the whole property. | Title is in the "community." Each interest is separate but management is unified. |
| Possession | Equal right of possession. | Equal right of possession. | Wife's rights may be subject to husband's managerial perogatives. |
| Conveyance | Each co-owner's interest may be conveyed separately by its owner. | Conveyance by one co-owner without the other's breaks the joint tenancy, except where it is community property held in joint tenancy merely for purposes of convenience. | One co-owner may convey ownership of the property. |
| Death | On co-owner's death, his interest passes by will to his heirs. No right of survivorship. | On co-owner's death, interest ends and cannot be disposed of by will. Survivor owns the property by rights of survivorship. | On co-owner's death, half belongs to surviving spouse. |

## MUTUAL FUNDS IN TRUSTS

A *trust* has legal title to property held by one party, the trustee, for the benefit of another, the beneficiary. Mutual funds are particularly suitable for trusts. The trustee serves as the monitor and steward of the ownership of the fund while the investment manager takes care of the management of the stock and bond portfolio. The trustee is responsible for selecting and transferring from one fund to another as prudence requires.

There are two basic forms of trusts: testamentary and living trusts. *Testamentary trusts* become effective upon death. *Living trusts*, often called *inter vivos* (between the living), are effective for any desired period. Establishing a trust requires the naming of four parties: the trustee, who carries out the instructions of the trust; the person who makes the trust, called the grantor; the person who receives the income from the trust, called the income beneficiary; and the person who gets what's left of the trust when it terminates, called the principal beneficiary.

You may purchase a mutual fund, enhance its value over time and then place it in a testamentary trust to be managed by a trustee of your selection. In this case, you are the grantor, your spouse or child, the income beneficiary, and your final surviving child or heir, the principal beneficiary. You can also set up a trust that pays income to several beneficiaries, continuing until all beneficiaries are deceased. You or your trustee may set the withdrawal rate or pre-establish the rate of payment to each beneficiary. The establishment of a simple trust with mutual funds is accomplished easily by executing a trust agreement with the assistance of your attorney, selecting a trustee who is knowledgeable of the mutual fund market, and then transferring title in the fund to the trust.

There are two types of living trusts: revocable and irrevocable. A revocable trust is one that can be revoked, usually at the option of the person who created it. In other words, its provisions can be changed, and it can be terminated in whole or in part, at any time. An irrevocable trust on the other hand ordinarily cannot be changed after it has been established. Current tax benefits are available only through an irrevocable trust. The disadvantage of tying one's hands forever, or for a stated period, must be measured carefully against the value of the anticipated tax savings.

Through the judicious use of irrevocable trusts it is possible to reduce both income taxes and estate taxes. Income taxes are reduced when the income of the trust is taxable to an individual beneficiary in a lower tax bracket than the grantor. Death taxes are avoided when the property is removed permanently from the estate of the creator of the trust.

## GIFTS TO MINORS

When selecting a mutual fund for a child be certain that it can be held for the long term, and be certain to gift the fund to the child. Outright gifts of mutual funds to minors are now possible in every state under legislation known as the Uniform Gifts to Minors Act. These state statutes provide for the registration of the shares in the giver's name, or in the names of the child's specified adult relatives as "custodian" of the securities.

All that is required under the Uniform Gifts to Minors Act is registration of the securities in the name of the donor, an adult member of the minor's family, a guardian of the minor, or a trust company, followed in substance by the words "as custodian for (name of minor) under the (name of state) Uniform Gifts to Minors Act."

Gifts of mutual fund shares to minor children should be made as early as possible in the child's life so that the fund's income will grow in the child's estate and be taxed at his or her rate, not yours.

The custodian may exercise all management rights over

the funds and move from fund to fund as appropriate. While you cannot use fund income to pay regular living expenses for a child, you can use the fund to pay for the cost of a college education.

To establish a gift to minor account, no trust document or lawyer is required. Simply complete the application form for the fund with you as the custodian and the child as the beneficiary. When the minor becomes of age, the fund is his without a formal accounting or the payment of taxes or fees. No gift taxes are involved unless you exceed the allowed exemptions.

Under the Uniform Gifts to Minors Act, you can give up to $10,000 per year in securities or money to each child (or any minor) without paying any Federal gift taxes.

Because all income or capital gains earned on the gift property is taxable to the minor who is, most likely, in a substantially lower tax bracket than you, the tax savings can be considerable.

For example, if you invested $3,000 a year in a custodial account for a minor and earned a 10 percent annual rate of return, the child's account after ten years would total $52,594, (if the child paid no taxes). If you were in a 40 percent tax bracket and invested the same amount over the identical period, and earned the same return, the after-tax total in your account would be $41,915—or $10,679 less.

In addition, if you have fund shares that have appreciated above your initial cost in a non-gifted fund, you can place these shares in your child's custodial account and thereby avoid capital gains taxes.

# Chapter 13

# Strategies for Investing in Mutual Funds

## CHALLENGES OF THE ECONOMY

In June 1984, the economy was booming, interest rates were rising rapidly and economists were generally pleased with the pace of capital investment in the United States. By June 1985, however, economic growth abated, interest rates fell and growth in business investment slowed dramatically. Despite the stimulative monetary and fiscal policies of the federal government, unemployment held at 7.25 percent, inflation hovered at about 4 percent, and consumers exhibited tentative confidence in the economy.

From these indicators, what conclusions can we draw regarding what happened to the U.S. economy?

One problem that we can isolate is the *foreign trade deficit*. In mid-1980, the dollar began to rise in foreign exchange markets as foreign investors realized the Federal Reserve was serious about fighting inflation. By March 1985, it had risen some 80 percent in value, declined somewhat, but nevertheless remained at record levels. Although the strong dollar has made foreign goods and travel more affordable to Americans, it also has made it difficult for U.S. businesses to sell its products abroad. Our foreign trade began its slide in mid-1983 and was a negative $65 billion for the first quarter of 1985 alone.

One dilemma caused by this problem is that the U.S. government needs the strong dollar and trade deficit to finance federal borrowing. Unfortunately, at the same time, it is destroying some U.S. industries and therewith depressing economic activity.

Another serious problem is the *federal deficit*, which has grown from $75 billion in 1980 to $200 billion in fiscal 1985. The government's need to service this debt is drawing capital away from domestic investments in industry.

Another important trend is the rapid shift to a *deregulated* economy. A fundamental change such as this often results in technological upheaval. Both the financial services and the telecommunications industries are being deregulated, and the worldwide revolution in financial services is converging with what amounts to a revolution in information technology. In financial markets, the old rules determining who can do what with whose money are disappearing.

*Inflation*, as reflected in both wholesale and consumer price levels, is in a state of "disinflation." That is, the rate of inflation remains low, while the prices of certain goods and services are actually declining. Many analysts expect inflation to return later in the decade, but other observers see a continuing decline in inflation as prices for oil and other commodities continue to decline.

For fear of triggering a new burst of inflation, the Fed will cautiously accommodate economic growth for the next several years. The evidence suggests that growth abroad will proceed at modest rates in coming months. In most foreign countries, as in the United States, the pace of expansion probably will be moderate. However, even moderate growth will help keep the U.S. economy on an upward path. Eco-

**FIGURE 13-1**
**The Growth of the Gross National Product**

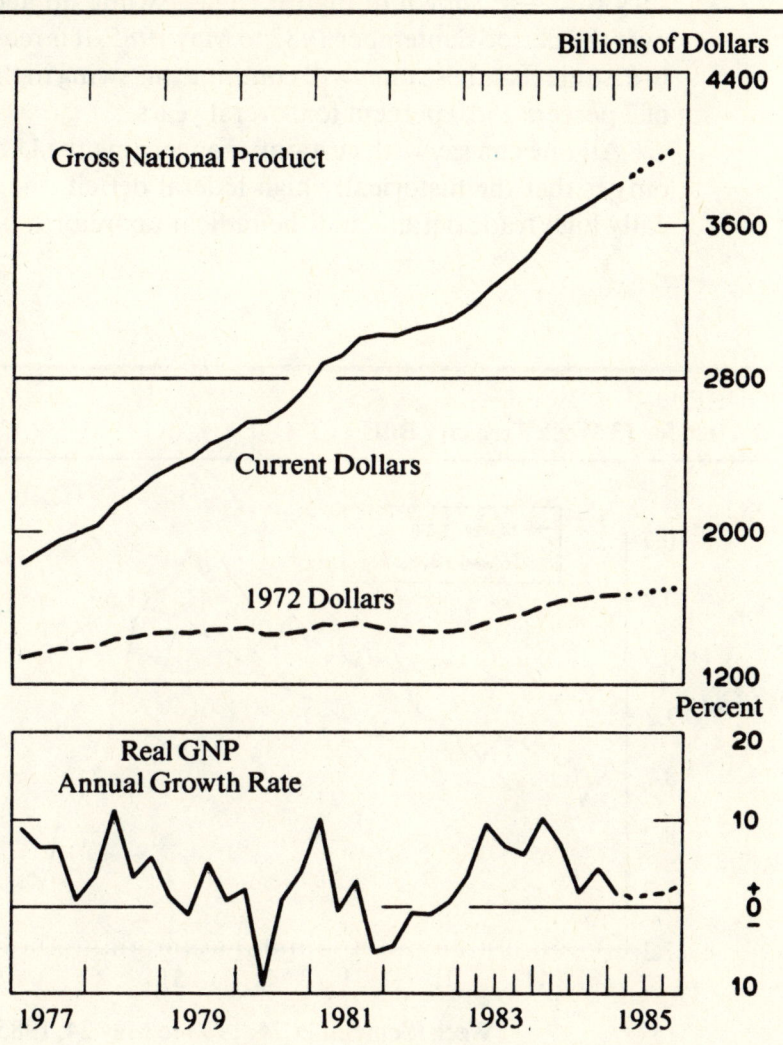

nomic growth can be expected to continue in the United States at a modest rate (as shown in Figure 13-1), with modest improvement in corporate profits.

Interest rates as measured by short-term 13-week Treasury Bills—as shown in Figure 13-2—swung up and down over the period September 1983 to May 1985. It is reasonable to assume that these rates will continue this swing in the range of 7 percent to 10 percent for several years.

All one can say with certainty concerning the U.S. economy is that the historically high federal deficit, the historically high trade deficit, and the radical tax-reform proposal

FIGURE 13-2
**The Yield for 13 Week Treasury Bills**

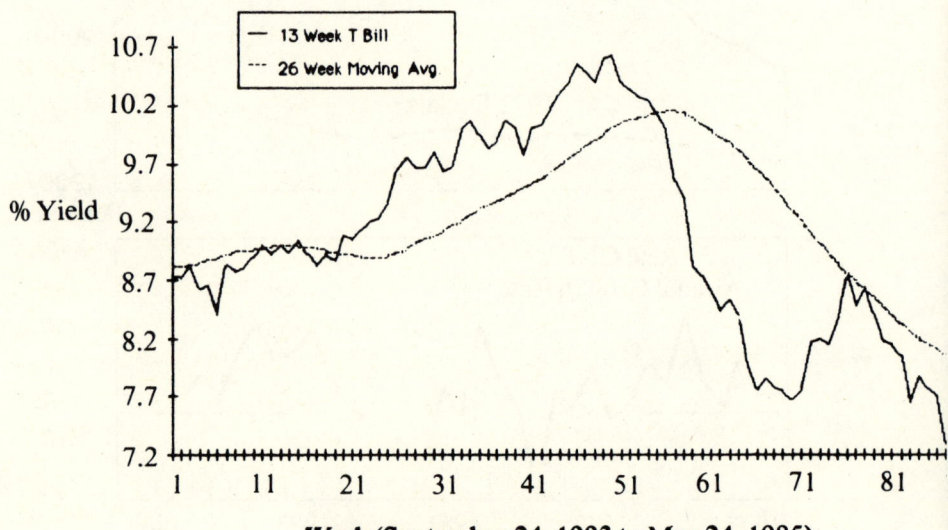

of 1985-1986 have led us into uncharted waters and have made economic prediction even more difficult than usual. Interest rates, inflation, trade and federal deficits, the service industry boom, manufacturing decline, deregulation, corporate profits and GNP performance all present novel challenges for the U.S. economy.

## THE STOCK AND BOND MARKETS

The stock and bond markets directly reflect economic activity. Bonds and stocks, two financial vehicles that turned in lackluster performances for their owners in 1983-84, made a striking comeback in the first half of 1985. The S&P 500 index is shown in Figure 13-3 for the period September 24, 1983 to May 10, 1985. Note that the S&P index declined until July 27, 1984 when it began a climb in a series of two large moves.

Despite recurring spasms of fear that the U.S. economy will skid into recession, it keeps trudging along. It will climb for the next year or two, though the pace will be remarkably languid. By the end of 1986 the recovery will be 49 months old—just a month short of the second-longest peacetime expansion on record.

Despite new highs in the stock market there has been no real outpouring of investor enthusiasm. One reason for this is that a large part of the strength in major indices has come from sectors that usually do not develop much excitement—utilities, insurance, banks and food have been among the best gainers over the period August 1984 to August 1985. Meanwhile, old growth favorites such as computers, electronics and other technology-oriented industries have been among the market's weakest groups during the same period.

Another reason for this lack of enthusiasm among investors stems from the belief of some analysts that the sluggish performance of recent months is an indication that the

FIGURE 13-3
**The S&P 500 Index and the 26 Week Moving Average**

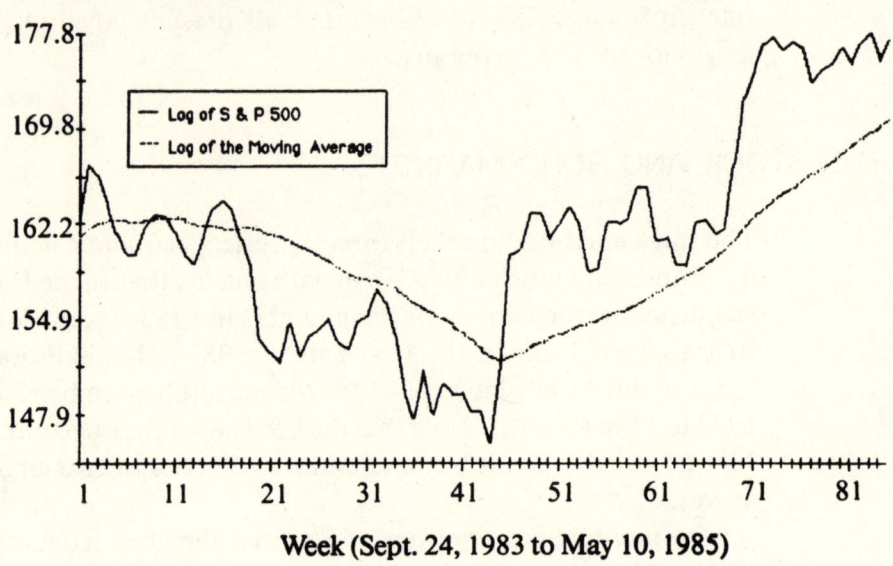

Week (Sept. 24, 1983 to May 10, 1985)

long recovery from the recession of 1981–1982 has run its course and that a new recession is likely to develop in 1986 or 1987.

For the years 1982–1985, defensive stocks and shorter term bonds have performed admirably, as reflected in the good performance of growth and income funds as well as income funds. Lower risk funds with *betas* of less than 0.80 have performed, on a risk adjusted basis, significantly better than more speculative, aggressive funds. As the economy faces the challenges of the next five years, these defensive funds may continue to out perform their aggressive cousins.

Stocks and bonds will continue to provide the best market return for the late 1980s. If you held stocks and bonds during the one-year period ending June 1, 1985, you would have earned 28.7 percent, while bonds returned 42.9 percent as shown in Table 13–1. Over the five year period ending June 1, 1985 stocks returned 15.2 percent annually.

The return on stocks held in international mutual funds have been lackluster over the past several years due to the strength of the U.S. dollar. Foreign stock returns in recent years (capital gains plus dividends) have outpaced U.S. returns in local currency terms, with the dollar's climb wiping out gains for Americans investing abroad. Since the beginning of 1985, however, the pattern has reversed as the dollar declines in value.

Funds that invest overseas stand to reap handsome foreign-exchange gains when the proceeds of their investments are converted back into dollars. Moreover, several foreign stock exchanges have recently posted record highs. This combination of foreign-exchange gains and appreciation can mean a welcome double bonus for savvy investors.

**TABLE 13–1**
**Return on Selected Assets**

|  | One Year % Return Ending 6/1/85 | One Year % Return Ending 6/1/84 | Annual % Return for 5-Year Period Ending 6/1/85 |
|---|---|---|---|
| Bonds | 42.9 | −7.2 | 13.2 |
| Stocks (S&P 500) | 28.7 | −1.2 | 15.2 |
| Gold | −20.3 | −4.0 | −11.0 |
| Houses | 2.5 | 5.5 | 4.3 |
| Consumer Price Index | 3.7 | 4.6 | 5.7 |

## MARKET CYCLES

The stock and bond markets have three distinct periods of activity:

(1) a period of rapid rise in the indices;
(2) a period of sharp decline; and
(3) a period of indecisive movement when the indices move with no trend and can be discerned to move sideways.

In each cycle, the market moves up rapidly about 10% of the time and down rapidly another 10 percent of the time. In the remaining 80 percent of the time, it moves sideways. However, returns on funds can be made 100 percent of the time. It is important therefore, that we learn how to operate in the non-stimulating, often frustrating sideways environments. This is extremely difficult, because it runs counter to our nature. We lose interest quickly when the excitement wanes. It takes willpower to overcome this endemic lethargy, expertise to identify the independently strong sectors of the market and discipline to buy funds without the stimulus of an exciting market. The key is to be in the market, select the right funds, and take a long-term view.

## STRATEGIES FOR MUTUAL FUND INVESTORS

As mutual fund investors, we should always be looking for funds that provide consistent, good risk-adjusted returns over periods of uncertainty. Regardless of economic uncertainty, we should seek mutual funds that provide conservatism, good judgment and consistency in fund objectives, and combine these with our own patience, discipline, and common sense. We should not be guided by temporary emotional upheavals in the market.

Further, we should recognize that few fund managers

excel forever, and as performance declines we should turn to new funds, selected on the basis of past performance and potential future risk-adjusted performance.

As the United States and foreign stock and bond markets pass through their business cycles, opportunities will continually arise to purchase well managed funds at relatively low prices, which you must be willing to hold for a significant number of years (greater than five).

Do your buying after the stock market has undergone a major sell-off, this way you will buy at low prices. Such opportunities now occur about once or twice a year. On the other hand, it may be the time to avoid buying new mutual funds when all the media, government and stock brokers are agreeing that a bull market is racing onward. Look for buying opportunities when positive sentiment is directed elsewhere, when investors are worried, and when the market indices have stabilized at moderate levels.

Alternatively, you can select good funds and use dollar cost averaging. Most of us have some savings to invest monthly or quarterly and can just follow the discipline of periodically purchasing fund shares with fixed amounts on a regular basis.

If inflation remains under control and deficit problems are ameliorated, then the stock market will be the place to buy valuable assets. In 1968, the Dow Jones Industrial average first approached 1,000. In the 17 years since then, it has risen, unimpressively, by about 35 percent. During this same time, adjusted earnings for companies making up the Dow increased from $57.89 per share to $130.06, or by 125 percent. Dividends have grown from $31.34 to $58.30, an 86 percent increase. Book value has risen 73 percent, with the replacement cost of assets representing a significant multiple over book value. Values are even more impressive when inflation is taken into account.

In 1968, the DJIA sold at 17 times earnings, and the dividend yield was only 3.1 percent. In 1985, the price-to-earnings multiple is half the 1968 level, with the dividend yield close to 5 percent. As I suggested in Chapter 1, while the market may be efficient, to the extent that information is quickly disseminated, individual investors are not. Portions of the market inevitably respond inefficiently, which results in undeveloped opportunities for the alert investor to seize upon. During market lows it is possible to buy assets at their long-term values. Many such opportunities appear in the trough of any four-year market cycle. To take advantage of these swings, look for funds that actively seek out value in the stock market. Two such funds are Mutual Shares and Strong Investment.

Optimally, you should select and manage a portfolio of five to ten mutual funds. Within this portfolio will be growth and income funds, growth funds, and some aggressive funds. The aggressive funds will be used for market timing while the lower *beta* funds will be held for the long-term. With the addition of two or three funds specializing in industrial sectors, gold or precious metals, or international markets, you can achieve a completely diversified portfolio with relatively limited capital.

You should seek *total return*: yield plus share appreciation, not just one or the other. For example, Vanguard's High Yield Fund, a bond fund, had a respectable 1984 yield of 14.4 percent, but a total return of only 7.9 percent. This was due to a decline in the fund's net asset value. Several funds have recently adopted the total return philosophy and name. One example is the Evergreen Total Return Fund, an equity fund, which has a relatively high 6.4 percent yield, and also participates in growth-stock rallies. Over the five years ending in March 1985, it showed a compound annual return of 25 percent, and has never had a down year.

In sideways or slow growth stock markets, we are wise to hold funds with *betas* less than 1.00. However, in periods of great and rapid rise in the market indices, it is wise to have more significant holdings in higher risk, more aggressive funds. Because rapidly rising periods are infrequent and short, it is necessary to use market timing signals to anticipate these periods so as to move into aggressive funds.

If you decide on using market timing for your portfolio, you will need to generate buy/sell signals. The advisory letters, charting services and technical indicators that you maintain are, of course, crucial. An efficient market timing strategy will limit the number of round trips to one every year, retaining (if at all possible) long-term capital gains tax status. To achieve this, you can use a 26 week moving average of a mutual fund index to provide your timing signals. As an example, consider the Lipper Growth Index plotted in Figure 13–4 for the period September 24, 1983 to May 24, 1985.

FIGURE 13–4
**The Lipper Growth Index**

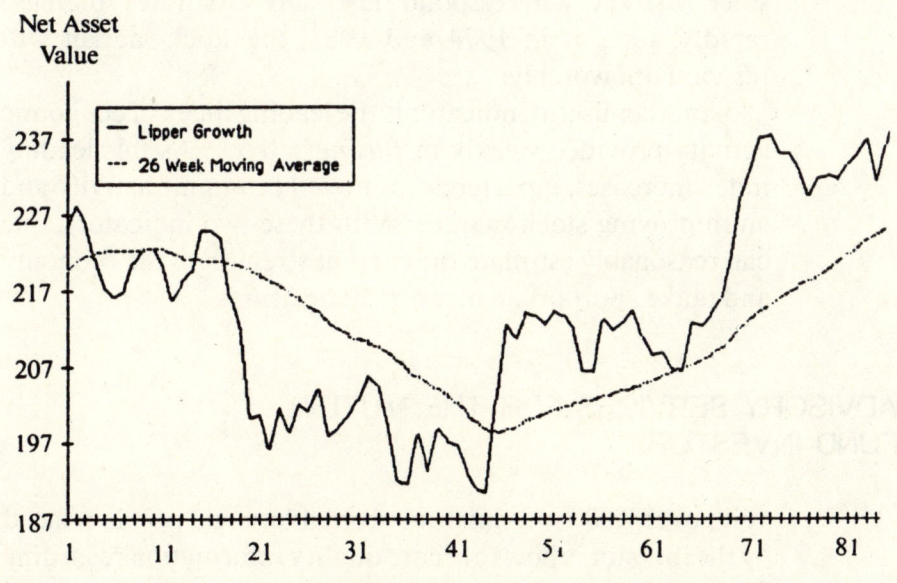

Week (Sept. 24, 1983 to May 24, 1985)

Using the 26 week moving average, one would have sold on January 28, 1984 and bought again on August 3, 1984. This would have enabled the timer to avoid the drop in the market during that period.

If you cannot spare the time, effort and psychological energy to develop market timing information, you probably should consider a buy and hold strategy relying on the more consistent less volatile fund performers. For example, if you had purchased the Pioneer II Fund on January 1, 1974 and held to May 31, 1985 your investment would have grown 20.1 percent annually (including a 7.75 percent sales charge). Other consistent growth funds during the ten-year period 1975 through 1984 are American Capital Pace (26 percent annually) and Nicholas Fund (24 percent annually).

Economic indicators provide the best signals for determining where we are in the business cycle. The easiest indicators to track are the interest rates of 13 week Treasury Bills. As indicated by Figure 13-5, as interest rates decline, the stock market will respond favorably. As rates increase rapidly, such as in 1974 and 1981, the stock market will respond unfavorably.

Another useful indicator is the leading index of economic activity provided weekly in *Business Week*. As this leading index increases, it portends improved economic activity and an improving stock market. With these two indicators, one can reasonably estimate the current strength of the economy and make appropriate investment decisions.

## ADVISORY SERVICES FOR THE MUTUAL FUND INVESTOR

With over 1,000 mutual funds available, a real problem faced by the investor is how to secure quality information regarding fund performance and objectives. Many newsletters, advisory services, financial planners, magazines and other media

**FIGURE 13-5**
**The S&P 500 Index and the 13 Week Treasury Bill Rate for 1968-1985**

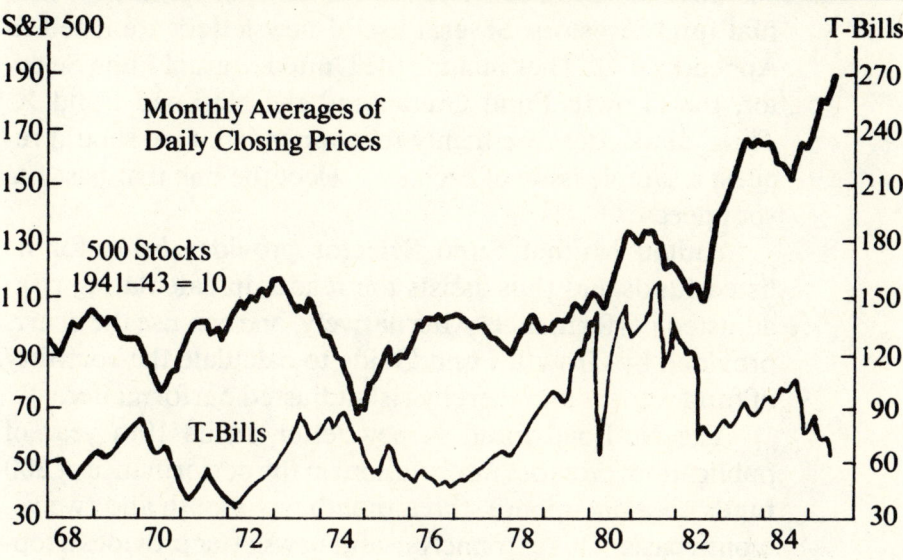

provide advice regarding mutual funds. Several magazines such as *Fact, Money, Forbes* and *Financial World* include regular columns concerning mutual funds in each issue. (Addresses of these magazines are provided in Appendix D-1.) *Fact* magazine and *Money* magazine provide monthly lists of the top performing funds for selected periods of time. *Forbes* magazine provides an annual directory of mutual funds with their risk-adjusted performance. This annual *Forbes* directory, appearing each August, is supplemented by articles on specific funds in each bi-weekly issue of the magazine.

Information regarding mutual funds, including net asset values and other indices of performance, is provided in financial newspapers such as *Barron's, The Wall Street Journal,* and *Investor's Daily* as well as many local papers.

Advisory newsletters provide a range of services to mutual fund investors. Several useful newsletters are listed in Appendix C-2. They include the United Mutual Fund Selector, the Growth Fund Guide, and the No-Load Fund X. These newsletters are highly recommended. One should request a sample issue of each and select the one that best fits your needs.

United Mutual Fund Selector provides *betas* for its listed funds and thus assists the reader in calculating risk-adjusted performance. Alternatively, one can use the charts provided by Growth Fund Guide to calculate the volatility of fund returns and thereby risk-adjusted performance.

The No-Load Fund X newsletter, in its 10th year of publication, provides information on the performance of 300 funds on a one-month, three-month, six-month and twelve-month basis. This extremely useful newsletter provides a top-five ranking of funds based on their one, three, six, and twelve month performance levels. The letter also recommends a method of continuously upgrading no-load fund portfolios to keep investors in the top performing funds at all times. This strategy has produced remarkable long-term results. Subscribers can check their funds' rankings each month, and upgrade when one falls below a predetermined ranking. It emphasizes current performance and rotates purchases to funds that have current momentum.

The serious mutual fund investor requires good information on mutual funds if the appropriate funds are to be selected. Also, one requires up-to-date and relevant information regarding the state of the economy and the performance of investment related indicators. The New Mutual Fund Advisor letter is available to those who wish to follow up on the strategies outlined in this book. (The address for the New Mutual Fund Advisor letter is given in Appendix

C–4.) With a working knowledge of market conditions, accurate assessments of risk-adjusted fund performance, and timely information on selected indicators for timing the market, the serious investor will be in a position to reap the rewards of the next decade's investment opportunities.

# Appendix A
# Glossary

**ACCOUNT:**
A mutual fund investor's business arrangement or record of investment transactions with the fund. It records initial share purchases, distributions, reinvestments, redemptions, changes in net asset values.

**ADVISOR:**
The organization employed by a mutual fund to manage the fund's assets.

**AGGRESSIVE GROWTH FUND:**
A mutual fund that seeks maximum capital appreciation through the use of investment techniques involving greater than ordinary risk, such as investing borrowed money to provide leverage, short selling, hedging, and trading options and warrants.

**AUTOMATIC REINVESTMENT:**
The option available to mutual fund shareholders whereby income dividends and capital gains distributions paid by the fund are left in the fund to buy additional shares.

**BETA:**
: A coefficient that measures a fund's volatility relative to the volatility of the total market. Market volatility usually is represented by the volatility of the S&P 500, which has a *beta* coefficient of 1.00. High *beta* funds typically have price fluctuations greater than low *beta* funds and are riskier.

**BOND FUND:**
: A mutual fund that invests in medium-to-high grade corporate bonds, convertible bonds or combinations of bonds and preferred stocks. Its main investment objective is security of principal with as much income as possible.

**CAPITAL GAINS DISTRIBUTIONS:**
: Payments to mutual fund shareholders of gains realized on the sale of securities held in the fund's portfolio. These amounts usually are paid once a year.

**CLOSED-END INVESTMENT COMPANY:**
: An investment company that issues a fixed number of shares, which it does not redeem.

**COMMON STOCK FUND:**
: A mutual fund whose portfolio consists primarily of common stocks. Such a company may at times take defensive positions in cash, bonds and other senior securities.

**CURRENT YIELD:**
: The payments to investors expressed as a percentage of current asset price. The payments usually are in the form of dividend or interest distributions.

**CUSTODIAN:**
: The organization (usually a bank or trust company) that holds in safekeeping the securities and other assets owned by a mutual fund.

**DISTRIBUTIONS:**
: The payments to shareholders of a mutual fund's interest, dividend or capital-gains income. Shareholders may take distributions in cash or in additional shares of the fund.

**DIVERSIFICATION:**
    The method of spreading investments among many different securities to reduce certain risks inherent in investing.

**DOLLAR COST AVERAGING:**
    Investing equal amounts of money in a mutual fund at regular intervals.

**EXCHANGE PRIVILEGE:**
    Enables a mutual fund shareholder to transfer investments from one fund to another (usually within the same mutual fund family). Such exchanges may or may not be accompanied by a transaction charge.

**EX-DIVIDEND:**
    The date on which declared distributions are deducted from total net assets.

**EXPENSE RATIO:**
    The proportion that a mutual fund's annual expenses bear to the fund's average net assets for the year.

**GOLD FUND:**
    A mutual fund that invests primarily in shares of gold stocks.

**GROWTH FUND:**
    A mutual fund for which the primary investment objective is long-term appreciation of invested capital. It invests principally in common stocks with growth potential.

**GROWTH AND INCOME FUND:**
    A mutual fund that seeks both capital growth and current income. The assets of these funds may be balanced between equity and fixed-income securities or may consist of common stocks with high dividend yields.

**INCOME FUND:**
    A mutual fund for which the primary objective is current income rather than growth of capital. Investments usually are in bonds and stocks that pay high levels of interest and dividends.

**INDEX FUND:**
: A mutual fund with an investment objective to match the investment performance of a large group of publicly-traded common stocks, such as those represented by Standard & Poor's 500 Composite Stock Price Index.

**INCOME DISTRIBUTIONS:**
: Payments to mutual fund shareholders of dividends, interest and short-term capital gains earned on investments.

**INVESTMENT COMPANY:**
: A corporation, trust or partnership in which investors who share common investment goals pool their money to obtain professional management and diversification of their investments. Mutual funds are the most popular type of investment company.

**LOAD:**
: Sales charges or commissions assessed by a mutual fund.

**MANAGEMENT FEE:**
: The amount paid by a mutual fund to the investment advisor for its services. The average annual fee industrywide is about one-half of one percent of the fund's assets.

**MARKET TIMING:**
: The active shifting of assets into or out of a mutual fund to maximize investment returns.

**MONEY MARKET FUND:**
: A mutual fund that invests in short-term "money market" securities, such as certificates of deposit, short-term government securities, bankers' acceptances, and so forth.

**MOVING AVERAGE:**
: A statistical device to smooth out data series to reveal trends.

**MUNICIPAL BOND FUND:**
: A mutual fund that invests in a broad range of tax-exempt bonds issued by states, cities and other local governments.

Interest obtained from these bonds is passed through to shareowners free of federal tax.

**MUTUAL FUND:**
A professionally managed investment company that pools the common financial interests of many investors (shareholders). Shares generally are offered on a continuous basis, which the fund stands ready to buy back (redeem) from shareholders on demand at the then current share price (per-share net asset value).

**NET INVESTMENT INCOME:**
Dividends and interest earned by a fund on the securities it owns, minus the fund's expenses.

**NET ASSET VALUE:**
The current market worth of all assets held by a mutual fund, including securities plus cash and any accrued dividend or interest income, less liabilities.

**NET ASSET VALUE PER SHARE:**
A fund's net asset value divided by the total number of shares outstanding.

**NO-LOAD FUND:**
A mutual fund that offers its shares to investors at the net asset value, without deducting a sales charge.

**OPEN-END INVESTMENT COMPANY:**
An investment company that continuously offers new shares to investors. Mutual funds are the most common form of open-end investment company.

**PORTFOLIO:**
The group name for the securities owned by a fund.

**PROSPECTUS:**
The official document that formally describes a mutual fund's operations and policies and offers its shares for sale to the public. It contains information required by the Securities

and Exchange Commission on such subjects as the fund's investment objectives and policies, services offered, investment restrictions, officers and directors, and fees and expenses.

**RETURN:**
See TOTAL RETURN.

**RISK:**
The possibility of loss of future income.

**SALES CHARGE:**
An amount assessed by a fund to purchasers of shares. The charge is added to the net asset value per share in determining the offering price.

**SPECIALTY FUND:**
A mutual fund that specializes in the securities of certain industries or regions.

**TOTAL RETURN:**
The income realized by an investor from a mutual fund investment expressed as a percent of the amount invested. It is used to express a fund's investment performance over a stated period of time and can be compared to the total returns provided by other investments.

**TRANSFER AGENT:**
The organization employed by a mutual fund to prepare and maintain records relating to the accounts of shareholders.

**TURNOVER RATIO:**
A measure of a mutual fund's annual purchase and sale activity of the securities it holds in its portfolio. It is calculated by dividing the lesser of the fund's annual purchases or sales (exclusive of purchases or sales of securities with maturities of less than one year) by the monthly average value of the securities owned by the fund during the year.

**YIELD:**
See TOTAL RETURN.

# Appendix B
# References

Amling, F., *Investments*, Prentice-Hall, Englewood Cliffs, New Jersey, 1984.

Andersen, C. E., *Andersen on Mutual Funds*, Scott, Foresman and Co., Glenview, Illinois, 1984.

Donoghue, W. E., *No-Load Mutual Fund Guide*, Harper and Row, New York, 1983.

Dreman, D., *The New Contrarian Investment Strategy*, Random House, New York, 1982.

Hulbert, M., and Wittenberg, J. B., *The Hulbert Financial Digest Annual Review of Investment Newsletters*, Reston Publishing Co., Reston, Virginia, 1985.

Lerner, E. M., and Koff, R. M., *Increasing Your Wealth in Good Times and Bad*, Probus Publishing, Chicago, Illinois, 1984.

Malkiel, B. G., *A Random Walk Down Wall Street*, Norton and Co., New York, 1981.

Perritt, G. W., and Shannon, L. K., *The Individual Guide to No-Load Mutual Funds*, American Association of Individual Investors, Chicago, 1985.

Pope, A., *Successful Investing in No-Load Funds*, Wiley and Sons, New York, 1983.

Rugg, D. D., and Hale, N. B., *The Dow-Jones Irwin Guide to Mutual Funds*, Dow-Jones Irwin, Homewood, Illinois, 1983.

Sharpe, W. F., Asset Allocation Tools, *The Scientific Press*, Palo Alto, California, 1985.

Sharpe, W. F., *Investments*, Prentice-Hall, Englewood Cliffs, New Jersey, 1985.

Slater, K., "For Investors in Stock Funds, Newsletters Offer Advice on Timing the Market's Turns", *The Wall Street Journal,* March 12, 1984, p. 18.

Smith, T. L., *Investors Can Beat Inflation*, Liberty Publishing Co., Cockeysville, Maryland, 1981.

Stoken, D. A., *Strategic Investment Timing*, MacMillan Publishing Co., New York, 1984.

Wallace, G. D., "The Case Against Banks as Money Managers", *Business Week,* December 12, 1983, pp. 33–35.

# Appendix C–1
# Magazines and Newspapers

*Barrons*
200 Burnett Road
Chicopee, MA 01021
(800) 345-8505
(Weekly newspaper, $77/year)

*Fact* Magazine
305 E. 46th Street
New York, NY 10017
(212) 319-6868
(Monthly, $24/year)

*Financial World* Magazine
1450 Broadway
New York, NY 10018
(212) 869-1616
(Semi-monthly, $42/year)

*Forbes* Magazine
60 Fifth Avenue
New York, NY 10011
(Bi-weekly, $39/year)

*Investor's Daily*
Box 25970
Los Angeles, CA 90025
(800) 223-2154
(5 Days/week newspaper, $84/year)

*Money* Magazine
1271 Avenue of the Americas
New York, NY 10020
(212) 589-1212
(Monthly, $22/year)

*The Wall Street Journal*
200 Burnett Road
Chicopee, MA 01021
(800) 841-8000
(Newspaper, 5 days/week, $107/year)

# Appendix C–2
# Mutual Fund Advisory Letters and Information Sources

*Computer Directions Advisors*
11501 Georgia Avenue
Silver Spring, MD 20902
(301) 942-1700

>CDA publishes a monthly and quarterly report covering the performance of 400 mutual funds, including statistics on risk adjusted returns. The monthly and quarterly subscriptions are $385 and $275, respectively.

*DAL Investment Co.*
235 Montgomery Street
San Francisco, CA 94104

>Publishes the *No-Load Fund X* monthly newsletter ($95), which monitors over 340 no-load and low-load funds highlighting top performers in six fund categories. Makes trading suggestions.

*Forbes* Magazine
60 Fifth Avenue
New York, NY 10011

>Provides a full mutual fund performance ranking and risk analysis in the 2nd issue in August each year.

*Growth Fund Research*
Box 6600
Rapid City, SD 57709

>Publishes the monthly *Growth Fund Guide* ($85/year) which provides extensive data and charts for 30 to 40 funds.

*Institute for Econometric Research*
3471 N. Federal Highway
Ft. Lauderdale, FL 33306
(800) 327-6720

>Publishes a monthly *Mutual Fund Forecaster* ($100/year) that provides profit projections and risk ratings for load and no-load funds.

*Investment Company Institute*
1600 M Street N. W.
Washington, DC 20036

>Publishes the *Mutual Fund Fact Book*, an annual report of the Institute ($2) that provides historical and technical data on mutual funds.

*Investor Information Services*
205 Wacker Drive
Chicago, IL 60606

>Publishes the monthly *Mutual Fund Letter* ($60/year) which provides performance data regarding selected funds. Offers buy/sell recommendations.

*Johnson's Charts*
246 Homewood Avenue
Buffalo, NY 14217
(716) 876-4669

    Provides twenty, fifteen and ten-year charts for 325 mutual funds. ($215/year.) The annual edition of the charts is $215.

*Larry Luce*
1412 Spruce Street
Berkeley, CA 94709
(415) 841-6359

    Publishes *Mutual Fund Monitor*, a monthly ($40/year) that includes analysis and recommendations of no-load funds.

*Lipper Analytical Services, Inc.*
74 Trinity Place
New York, NY 10006
(212) 269-4080

    Publishes a quarterly performance review of mutual funds.

*The No-Load Fund Investor, Inc.*
P.O. Box 283
Hastings on Hudson, NY 10706
(914) 478-2381

    Publishes the Handbook for No-Load Investors ($32) and the *No-Load Investor* monthly newsletter ($49).

*No-Load Mutual Fund Association*
11 Penn Plaza
New York, NY 10001

    Publishes a directory ($5) which has a listing of 300 no-load funds with addresses and fund objectives.

*Schabacker Investment*
8943 Shady Grove Court
Gaithersburg, MD 20877
(301) 840-0301

> Publishes the *No-Load, Low-Load Mutual Fund Directory* (free) that groups funds together according to investment objective—long-term growth, capital gains, tax-exempt income and so on. Each fund's address, phone number and purchase requirements are listed.

*Wiesenberger Investment Companies Service*
**Warren, Gorham and Lamont**
1633 Broadway
New York, NY 10019

> Publishes an annual ($295) and a quarterly of performance data for over 1,000 funds.

*United Business Service*
210 Newbury Street
Boston, MA 02116

> Publishes the *United Mutual Fund Selector* (semi-monthly—$98) which contains statistical information on over 400 mutual funds and comments on developments in the industry. Also offers fund recommendations. Covers both load and no-load funds.

# Appendix C-3
# Computer Services and Programs

*Fundgraf*
Price: $100 (demo disk—$10)

Parsons Software
118 Woodshire Drive
Parkersburg, WV. 26101

Fundgraf is a computer program that graphs up to 260 weeks of a fund's progress on linear or semi-log plots. The program runs on either the IBM PC or compatibles using MS-DOS. A graphics board and 128K memory are required. A user may add data and account for dividends. One may superimpose up to four funds on a graph for comparison. The program also provides buy and sell signals based on moving averages and strength ratings for each fund based on performance over four selected periods.

# Appendix C-4
# Mutual Fund Selection, Timing and Advisor Services

*DAL Investment Co.*
Bert Berry
235 Montgomery Street
San Francisco, CA 94104
(415) 986-7979

DAL Investment Co. is a private investment advisory firm registered with the Securities and Exchange Commission and the State of California since 1969. DAL uses an upgrading system that stays with the top performing no-load funds only *while* they are excelling, and then moves to others. An annual fee is 1 percent or less of assets. (Minimum $400,000 initial investment.)

*Fundline*
David Menashe
P.O. Box 663
Woodland Hills, CA 91365
(818) 346-5637

A newsletter that provides trading strategies based on performance charts and technical indicators for 40 funds. A telephone hotline recording is included in the $87 subscription for the semi-monthly letter. The charts provide easy to follow moving averages for buy-sell decisions.

*Gordon E. Harper Investment Management*
800 Oak Grove Avenue, Suite 203
Menlo Park, CA 94025
(415) 329-1560

An SEC registered investment advisor specializing in selecting and managing portfolios of mutual funds for clients.

*Hubert Cafritz*
Box 8565
Silver Spring, MD 20907
(301) 588-1957

A newsletter that provides a model portfolio and technical indicators for timing selection. The letter provides three, six and nine month performance data for approximately 60 funds. A performance ranking based on the three periods is used to select funds. The system buys any fund that appears in the top three rankings and sells those that drop below rank 26.

*Mutual Fund Specialist*
Box 1025
Ean Claire, WI 54701
(Monthly letter, $65/year)

A newsletter that attempts to time the market by relying primarily on technical indicators. It also provides a ranking system for over 500 mutual funds.

*New Mutual Fund Advisor*
Richard C. Dorf, editor
Box 1975
Davis, CA 95617
(10 issues, $45/year)
(916) 756-6222

A newsletter that provides continuing information regarding funds that fit the investment strategies discussed in this book with emphasis on risk-adjusted performance, timing, and long-term investing.

*No-Load Mutual Fund Selections and Timing Co.*
2001 Bryan Tower
Dallas, TX 75201
(214) 754-0111
(Monthly letter, $88/year)

A newsletter that monitors 300 no-load funds ranking them for relative performance and listing the top performing funds. Uses technical indicators to provide major market timing signals as well as short-term timing points. Firm also manages investments on a fee basis.

*Switch Fund Advisory*
8943 Shady Grove Court
Gaithersbury, MD 20877
(301) 840-0301
(Monthly letter, $125/year)

A newsletter that provides extensive data on mutual fund performance and provides a telephone hotline for timing advice.

*Telephone Switch Fund Advisory*
Box 2538
Huntington Beach, CA 92647
(714) 840-4747
(Monthly, $117/year)

The largest newsletter and telephone hotline timing service. It attempts to time the market directly by using a trading plan based on the Dow Jones Industrial and Transportation averages and on a proprietary mutual fund composite index. The letter monitors three separate areas: domestic equity, international and gold funds. Provides separate buy/sell signals in each area.

*Timer Digest*
Box 30247
Ft. Lauderdale, FL 33303
(305) 764-8499
(Monthly digest, $150/year)

> A newsletter that monitors over 30 timing services and provides rankings. Also provides timing signals. Offers twice weekly telephone hotline.

*Wellington Financial Corp.*
Honolulu, HA
(800) 367-7048
(Monthly letter, $96/year)

> A newsletter that charts up to 40 funds and provides easy to follow timing signals for each as well as for a composite fund index. The charts use moving averages to provide buy-sell signals.

# Appendix D
# Addresses of Selected Funds

American Capital
P.O. Box 3247
Houston, TX 77001
(713) 522-1111

Boston Company
One Boston Place
Boston, MA 02108
(800) 343-6324

Dreyfus
767 Fifth Avenue
New York, NY 10153
(800) 223-5525

Evergreen Funds
550 Mamaroneck Avenue
Harrison, NY 10528
(800) 635-0003

Fidelity Group
82 Devonshire Street
Boston, MA 02109
(800) 225-6190

Kemper
120 So. La Salle Street
Chicago, IL 60603
(800) 621-1048

Lehman Funds
55 Water Street
New York, NY 10041
(800) 221-5350

Massachusetts Financial
200 Berkeley Street
Boston, MA 02116
(617) 423-3500

Nicholas Funds
312 E. Wisconsin Avenue
Milwaukee, WI 53202
(414) 272-6133

Scudder Funds
175 Federal Street
Boston, MA 02110
(800) 225-2470

Stein Roe and Farnham
P.O. Box 1143
Chicago, IL 60690
(800) 621-0320

T. Rowe Price
100 E. Pratt Street
Baltimore, MD 21202
(800) 638-5660

Templeton
P.O. Box 3942
St. Petersburg, FL 33731
(800) 237-0738
(813) 823-8712

Twentieth Century
P.O. Box 200
Kansas City, MO 64141
(816) 531-5575

Vanguard Group
Box 876
Valley Forge, PA 19482
(800) 523-7025
(800) 662-SHIP

# Index

Account definition, 229
Adjusted return index, 88, 91
   risk premium and, 1979-83; figure, 90
Adjustment factor, 159, 161
Adjusted share value, equation for, 161
Administrative costs, 34
Advisor, 14, 229
Advisory services, 224-227
Age:
   diversification in retirement, 196
   fund selection related to life cycle, 43
   investor risk related to; figure, 44
   portfolio based on personal factors, 97
   risk in investments and, 95
Aggregate fund cash ratio, 144
Aggressive growth funds, 121, 181
   definition, 229
   greatest return; highest risk, 44
   objectives, 42, 48
Alpha:
   market line, 80
   modern portfolio theory, 72-73
   risks, 5-6, 59
Annual return:
   calculating; equation, 29
   equation for calculating, 159
Annual report, choosing a fund, 25
Annual statements, 159
Asset allocation, 103, 105
Assets:
   breakdown; fund totals (1983); table, 45
   mutual fund families; amount, 33
   number of funds; table, 16
   total assets; equation determining, 32
Automatic reinvestment, 39, 229

Balance sheet, 14
Balanced fund, 51

Beta:
   definition, 230
   dollar cost averaging with, 148
   expected return, 3-fund portfolio, 100
   expected return vs., figure, 83
   individual coefficients, 7
   market line; equation, 80
   market timing, 116
   modern portfolio theory, 72-73
   optional 3-fund portfolio; returns, 102
   portfolio; calculation, 95
   portfolio; 3 funds (0.80); table, 96
   risk, 5-6
   total performance, 1978-83, by fund category; table, 45
   weighted portfolio beta; equation, 99
Bond funds, 52
   average returns (1979-85); table, 54
   calculating the total return, 76, 79
   definition, 230
   interest rates; change in prices, 52-53
   investment categories, 53
Bull markets, 48, 49
Buy-and-hold:
   efficient market theory, 5
   funds for; table, 155
   timing services vs., 151-156
Business cycle:
   indicators, 122
   market timing, 118-122
*Business Week* Leading Indicator, 139

Capital gains:
   calculating; four methods, 177-180
   distributions, 230
   effective tax rate; percentages, 175
   long-term, 170, 181
   realized or unrealized, 169
   tax methods for redemptions, 180

Capital losses, 170, 176
Cash:
  needs, 98
  percentage held, 143
Cash flow, as indicator, 144-146
Cash position, determination of, 144
Classifications of funds, 41-69
Closed-end investment, 12, 230
Collateralized mortgage obligations, 62
Commodity fund, 61
Common stock:
  returns, 2
  of small firms, 50
Common stock fund, 230
Community property, 207, 208
Composite Fund Index, 130
Constellation Growth Fund, 48, 49, 50, 89, 129, 131, 155
Contrarian approach, 122
Convertible securities, 61-62
Conveyance, 208
Co-ownership, 206, 208
Copley Tax Managed Fund, 64, 182-183
Corporate AAA bond rates, 133
Corporate bond funds, 52
Corporate profits, 140
Cost averaging, 146-151
  advantages, disadvantages, 147
  basic idea of, 146
Cost of ownership, 20-23, 34
Current yield, definition, 230
Custodian, definition, 230
Custodian bank, 32

Death, co-ownership of funds, 208
Debt, 14
Deficit, Federal, 214
Deregulation, 214
Discount, 19
Discount brokers, 39-40
Disinflation, 214
Distributions:
  adjusting share values to, 160, 162
  definition, 230
  expense, 34-35
  options, 33
  taxable, 169
  three forms of, 169
Diversification, 20, 59, 222, 231
  alpha risk reduction, 6-7
  modern portfolio theory, 72
  mutual funds and, 7
  portfolio, 93, 94
  retirement plans, 196
  risk reduction; figure, 8
Dividends, reinvestment, 20, 39

Dollar:
  strength of, 67, 68, 219
  value, as indicator, 136
  value; trade weighted; 1970-85, 138
Dollar cost averaging, 147-148, 231
  with high *beta* fund, 148
Dow Jones Industrial Averages, 113, 136, 137, 221
Dreyfus funds, 33, 249

EAFE market index, 68
Eaton Vance Tax Managed Trust, 182-183
Economic cycles, 118
  four phases, 121
  interest rates and; figure, 119
Efficient market:
  market dynamics and, 4
  outperforming the market unlikely, 113, 115
  price equals investment value, 3
Energy and Utility Fund, 58
Evergreen Total Return fund, 51, 155, 222, 249
Exchange privilege, 231
Ex-distribution date, 170, 176
Ex-dividend, 231
Expense ratio, 231
Explorer fund, 50, 109, 155

*Fact*, 225, 237
Fannie Maes, 62
Federal Reserve, 213
Fees:
  disguising the load charge, 19
  as function of fund size, 22; figure, 23
  layered; fund-of-funds, 110
  management fees, 232
  monitoring, 33-37
  total investment expenses; table, 35
Fidelity Equity Income fund, 51, 52, 149, 155
Fidelity funds, 59, 63, 249
Fidelity Investments, 33
Fidelity Magellan, 108
Fidelity Utilities, 58
Financial Programs, 59
First in, first out (FIFO), 178
Flexibility, 21-22, 199
Forecasting, 113, 115
Foreign trade deficit, 213
Form B prospectus, 25
44 Wall Street Fund, 89, 145, 153, 155
Franklin Gold Fund, 67
Franklin U. S. Government Securities Fund, 63

# INDEX

Freddie Macs, 62
Fund of funds, 109
Futures fund, 61

G. T. Pacific, 68
Gateway Option, 61
Gifts to minors, 210-211
Ginnie Maes, 62-63
Gold, inflation, and gold prices, 65
Gold funds, 64-67, 231
Government securities funds, 63
Greenwich Montrend, 152
Gross national product,growth of, 215
Growth and income fund, 231
    objectives, 50-51
Growth fund(s), 149, 231
    objectives, 41, 46
    return expected from, 48
Growth Fund Guide, 140, 226, 240
Growth Fund Research, 240

Hartwell Leverage, 48, 49, 50, 89, 155
Hidden charges, 34
Holding period(s), 98, 102

Income, needs and age of investor, 44
    portfolio, 11
Income distributions, 232
Income funds, 41, 42, 52, 231
Income tax,Federal, rates, figure, 171
Index funds, 60, 108-109, 232
Indicators:
    business and economics, 133-143
    business cycles, 118
    *Business Week* Leading Indicator, 139
    composite index, 142
    economic, 224
    efficient market theory, 116
    market bottoms, 144
    monetary, for 1983-85; figure, 137
Individual Retirement Accounts (IRA), 188-192
    managing your funds, 191
    transfers, 189
    withdrawal plans, 201-202
Inflation:
    bond and income funds, 53
    Federal Reserve and, 213
    gold prices and, 65
    retirement planning, 196-197, 200
Institute for Econometric Research, 240
Interest rates:
    bond holdings; risk, 52
    daily chart, 136
    economic cycle; figure, 119
    expectations, 216
    measures of, 133
    money expansion and, 133
    real rate of interest, 136, 138
    stock market reacts to, 224
Internal Revenue Service:
    IRA or Keogh withdrawals, 202
    mutual fund distributions, 179
International mutual funds, 67-69, 219
    value increase expected, 68
International stock markets, 69
Investment(s):
    objectives; choosing a fund, 26, 28-29
    outperforming the market, 4-5
    planning, 187-197
    strategies, 213-227
Investment company:
    definition, 232
    objectives, 11-12, 13
    regulations, 12
Investment Company Act of 1940, 15
Investment management company, 14
Investor Information Services, 240
Investor's Daily Fund Index, 124, 226, 238
Irrevocable trusts, 210

Joint tenancy, 206, 208

Kemper funds, 57, 63, 249
Keogh retirement plan, 192-193,201-202

Last in, first out (LIFO), 178
Life expectancy, 187
Linder Fund, 106, 108
Lipper Growth Fund Index, 152, 223
Liquidity, 21, 55
Living trusts, 209-210
Load, definition, 232
Load funds, 16, 18, 20
Long-term capital gains, 170, 181
Long term holding period, 98
Low-load funds, 19
Lowry Management Corporation, 117

Management, monitoring, 33-37
Margin account, 40
Market line, 80, 86, 87
Market timing:
    beta values, 116
    buy low, sell high, 111
    commercial timing systems, 129
    cost averaging methods, 146-151
    definition, 111, 232
    funds for; table, 155
    investment strategy, 223
    methodologies, 115

moving averages; buy/sell, 126
Massachusetts Investor Trust, 15
Modern portfolio theory (MPT), 72-73
Money, 133
Money market funds, 43, 55-58, 108-109, 121, 149
   definition, 232
   growth, 15
   risk negligible in, 57
Monitoring fund performance, 157-168
Mortgage funds, 62-63
Moving averages, 123-132
   buy and sell signals; table, 127
   definition, 123, 232
   exponential, 156, 123-125
   sources of data; table, 132
   straight/simple; calculation, 123
   timing system; two rules, 126
   Treasury bill rates; figure, 135
   using two averages, 128
Municipal bond funds, 52
   definition, 232
   taxes, 53-54
Mutual fund(s):
   annual sales (1975-84); figure, 17, 18
   benefits and costs of owning, 20-23
   classifications and characteristics, 41-69
   as corporations, 14
   definition, 1, 233
   growth of the industry, 1-2, 15-16
   history; growth, 15-16
   legal title to, 206-208
   registration of shares, 39
   types, 12
   types and objectives; table, 43
Mutual fund families, 22
   fund services, 33
   switching, high/low betas, 116
Mutual Fund Specialist, 246
Mutual Shares Fund, 60, 86, 89, 91, 106 153, 155, 222

Net asset value, 233
   calculating, 29
   moving averages; 12 weeks, 125
Net asset value per share, 233
   determining, 32
Net investment income, definition, 233
New Horizons Fund, 88, 89
   fees; from prospectus; figure, 36
   financial information, 29, 30
New York Stock Exchange, 15, 84, 85, 143
Newsletter timing services, 152
Nicholas Fund, 37, 38, 46, 49, 76, 77, 155, 196, 224, 250

No-load fund, 233
   purchasing, 37
   versus loads, 16, 18

Open accounts, 39
Open-end investment companies:
   definition, 12, 233
Optimism, 122
Option funds, 60
Option income funds, 61

Paperwork, 21
Past performance of funds, 105-106
Pennsylvania Mutual, 108, 155
Pensions, 187
Performance:
   bank trusts; S&P 500, mutual funds, 23
   calculating; example, 29
   calculations, 71-91
   charting, 163-166
   comparison; figure, 31
   fund size and, 106-108
   future potential, 105
   monitoring, 157-168
   perfect timing (with and without), 114
   record of sample fund (1984), 158
   stability in, 37
   total return, with perfect timing, 113
   total returns, 1978-83, by category, 45
   tracking portfolios, 167-168
   up and down markets; fund types, 49
Portfolio, 233
   acceptable returns, unacceptable risks, 5
   advantages of building, 93
   beta of 0.80; table, 96
   determining best possible return, 99
   diversification; 3 funds; table, 96
   meeting personal objectives, 95-98
   minimum/optimum number of securities; risk, 72
   optimal six-fund portfolio; table, 104
   personal factors, age, risk; table, 97
   for retirement plans, 195-196
   selection, 93-110
   strategy, phases of economic cycle, 121
   successful management of, 11
   time horizon, 98
   tracking performance of, 167-168
   two-fund, an alternative, 108-109
Prices, business cycles and; figure, 120
   consensus of expectations, 115
   fluctuations; technical indicators, 133
   random movement of, 3
Probate, 207

# INDEX

Professional management, 20
Property, laws re spouses, 205
Prospectus:
  choosing a fund, 25
  cover page; sample, 27
  definition, 233
  financial information in; figure, 30
  items to note in, 26
Purchasing a fund, 37, 39, 170, 176

Random walk, 3
Rate of return:
  inflation adjusted, 200-201
  low correlation, two funds; figure, 94
Real estate mortgage securities, 62
Real rate of interest, 136, 138
Recession, 217, 218
Record-keeping, 157
Redemption of shares:
  fee, 34
  identifiable cost, 178
  taxes, 176-177
Registration of shares, 39
Reinvestment of dividends, 20, 39
Republic National Bank of N.Y., 109
Retirement plans, 187-197
  fund selection related to life cycle, 43
  portfolio for, 195-196
  withdrawal factors; table, 197
Return(s):
  actual, and risk adjusted, for six funds; table, 104
  annual return vs *Beta*, 1979-83, 87
  before and after taxes, 172, 173
  calculating, for period of n years, 74
  down period (1983-84) vs up period (1982-83); figure, 154
  equation for calculating, 159
  expected; *beta*, 3-fund portfolio, 100
  five assets (June, 1985); table, 219
  five-year period; table, 82
  fund return vs. market return, 81
  holding periods, various; table, 102
  load vs. no-load funds; net return, 19-20
  Lowry market timing, S&P 500, 117
  performance, six funds; table, 103
  risk correlated with, 6
  size of firms invested in and, 107
  three-fund portfolio; weighted, 102
Risk, 234
  age of investor and; figure, 44
  calculating, 79-85
  holding period related to, 98
  investments, related to age, 44, 95
  measures of, 5-6, 72

reduction by diversification; figure, 8
return correlated with, 6
tolerance, 97-98
Risk premium:
  and adjusted return index, figure, 90
  calculation; equation, 86
Rollovers, 189-190

S&P 500, 31, 46, 49, 61, 88, 103, 117, 120, 217, 218, 219, 225
Sales charge:
  definition, 234
  reinvested dividends, 20
  Schwab rates, 40
Schabacker Investment, 242
Schwab, Charles, and Co., 39-40
Scudder Funds, 250
Sector funds, 59
Selection of funds, 25-40
  factors; table, 28
  fees/expenses to be considered, 37
  selection possibilities, 7, 9
Seligman fund, 165
Share values:
  adjusting; fund distributions, 160
  adjusting past share values, for distributions, 161; table, 162
Shearson Lehman Treasury Bond Index, 137
Sideways markets, 50, 220
Simplified Employee Pension Plan (SEP):
  401 and 403 plans, 193-195
  matching by employer, 194
  value, 5-25 years; table, 195
  related to fund performance, 106-108
Small firms, 50, 107
Social Security, 187, 188
Specialized common stock funds, 58-60
Specialty fund, 234
Standard deviation:
  equation for calculating, 79
  risk; returns, 5
Star Fund, 109
Statements, 157, 159
Stock market:
  behavior rules, 136
  cycles; three distinct periods, 220
  market behavior, 2-3
Strong Investors, 153, 222
Strong Total Return Fund, 106
Success, efficient market theory, 3-4
Survivorship, right of, 207
Switch Fund Advisory, 152, 247
Switching:
  limit: one or two a year, 118

moving averages, use of, 128
mutual fund families, 33
tax considerations, 181

T. Rowe Price funds, 33, 57, 88, 250
T. Rowe Price Growth Fund, 46, 51, 86, 89
T. Rowe Price New Income Bond Fund, 53
Tax(es):
  after-tax return; equation, 174
  average cost method, 179
  before and after-tax returns, 172-173
  capital gains; redemptions; table, 180
  different, for distributions, 170
  effective tax rate; equation, 174
  effective tax rate/percentage capital gains; figure, 175
  form 1099-DIV, 170
  liability kept low, 180-182
  municipal bond funds, 53-54
  "passed through" to shareholders, 14-15
  redemption of shares, 176-177
  reform act of 1986, 185-186
  timing strategy, 181
  turnover rates, funds with high, 182
  unnecessary, avoiding, 180-182
  *See also* Capital gains; Income tax.
Taxable equivalent yield, equation, 184
Tax-free bond funds, 183-184
Tax-free money funds, 55
Tax-loss, selling stocks at year-end, 181
Tax-managed funds, 64, 182-183
Telephone Switch Newsletter, 152
Templeton Growth Fund, 163-165, 250
Tenants-in-common, 207, 208
Testamentary trusts, 209
Thompson, McKinnon, 61
Timing methods:
  formula method, 149-151
  formula plan; figure, 150
  technical analysis, 133
Timing services vs. buy and hold strategy, 151-156
Title:
  evidence of ownership, 206
Total return:
  calculating, for bond fund, 76, 79
  definition, 234
  equations for measuring, 73-79
  as goal, 222
  with perfect market timing, 113
Total return funds, 51
Transaction costs, 21
Transfer agent, 32, 234

Treasury bills, 133, 134, 135
  rates, 1968-85; figure, 225
  yield; figure, 216
Trusts, 209-210
Turnover ratio:
  definition, 234
  high, funds to be avoided, 182
20th Century funds, 63, 250
20th Century Select, 47, 48, 49, 89
20th Century Ultra, 155

Uniform Gift to Minors Act, 39, 210-211
Unit investment trust, 12
United Business Service, 242
United Mutual Fund Selector, 226
United Services Gold Shares, 64-67
United States, economic conditions, 213
U. S. Department of Commerce composite index of key indicators, 142
Up and down markets, performance; type; name; table, 49
Up-front sales charge, 19-20

Vanguard Group, 33, 57, 59, 63, 109, 250
Vanguard High Yield Fund, 53, 222
Vanguard Index fund, 60
Volatility:
  *beta* coefficient, 6
  calculating relative V; equation, 85
  highest risks, 43
  measure of risk, 83, 85
  over-insurance against, 105

Weingarten Equity, 155
Windsor Fund, 49, 76, 89, 91, 107, 153, 155
  cover page of prospectus, 27
  performance; figure, 31
Withdrawal plans, 199-203
  cost averaging/fixed payment, 203
  flexibility, 199
  IRAs and Keogh plans, 201-202
  redemptions as needed, 201
  years that payments can be made, 200

Yield:
  current, 230